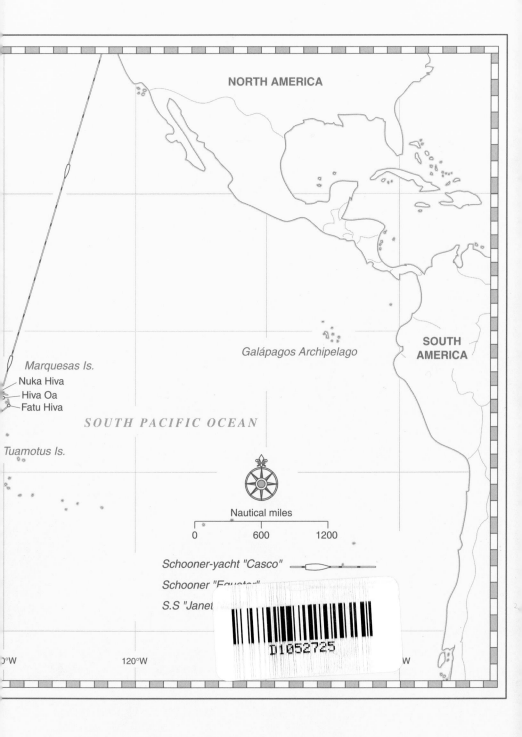

TREASURED
ISLANDS

TREASURED ISLANDS

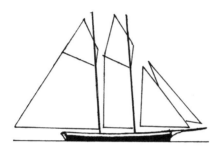

Cruising the South Seas
with
Robert Louis Stevenson

LOWELL D. HOLMES

SHERIDAN HOUSE

First published 2001 by
Sheridan House Inc.
145 Palisade Street
Dobbs Ferry, NY 10522
www.sheridanhouse.com

Library of Congress Cataloging-in-Publication Data

Holmes, Lowell Don,
    Treasured islands : cruising the South Seas with Robert Louis Stevenson /
Lowell D. Holmes.
       p. cm.
    Includes bibliographical references.
    ISBN 1-57409-130-1 (alk. paper)
    1. Stevenson, Robert Louis, 1850–1894—Journeys—Oceania. 2. Holmes, Lowell
Don, 1925—Journeys—Oceania. 3. Authors, Scottish—19th century—Biography.
4. Scots—Oceania—History—19th century. 5. Oceania—Description and travel.
I. Title.

PR5495 .H65 2001
828'.803—dc21
[B]   2001049357

Edited by Janine Simon
Designed by Jeremiah B. Lighter

Printed in the United States of America

ISBN   1-57409-130-1

Far over seas an island is
Whereon when day is done
A grove of tossing palms
Are printed on the sun.

And all about the reefy shore
Blue breakers flash and fall
There shall I go, me thinks'
When I am done with all.

*   *   *

Fair Isle at Sea—thy lovely name
Soft in my ear like music came
That sea I loved, and once or twice
I touched at isles of Paradise.

ROBERT LOUIS STEVENSON

ACKNOWLEDGMENTS

The research and writing of this book has been assisted by numerous individuals and institutions. Raymond Aker who did the reconstructive drawings of Stevenson's three charter vessels also read the text and made numerous valuable suggestions based on his many years as a ship's officer in the South Pacific. His drawings of the CASCO, EQUATOR and JANET NICOLL I believe definitely set the stage for the drama of the Stevenson family's adventure in the South Seas. By sheer coincidence I first found his reconstructive art work several years ago in a maritime magazine I came across in the library of the schooner ZODIAC on which I spent a week in the Pacific northwest. It was this article more than anything that motivated me to write about the Stevensons, although I had visited the author's villa in Samoa and even climbed the mountain to photograph his grave many years before.

Tom Trant, Patrick Adams and fellow anthropologist Philip DeVita, sailors all, made valuable contributions as readers of the manuscript. Their critiques were perceptive and often challenging, but their encouragement never failed.

I am also indebted to Dr. Curtis Drevets, a respiratory specialist in Wichita, Kansas. I had long questioned the belief that Robert Louis Stevenson's debilitating illness was tuberculosis, as most Stevenson biographers had maintained. Dr. Drevets' analysis of Stevenson's medical history for me provided a plausible alternative.

It is extremely valuable when writing about the people of the South Seas to have a wife who is also a Pacific anthropologist and an excellent writer. Ellen's valuable suggestions concerning the text and her unbelievable ability as an editor made the production of this book a great deal more pleasurable.

The staff of the Ablah Library at Wichita State University, particularly Betty L. Smith and Ted E. Naylor in the inter-library loan office, deserve special commendation for their persistent efforts to acquire difficult-to-find research materials. John D. Duncan, author of *The Sea Chain*, was also of great assistance in my fact gathering.

Elaine Greig, curator of the Writer's Museum in Edinburgh, Scotland, was most accommodating in providing me with visual material. The staff of the San Francisco Maritime National Historical Park library also provided me with photographs and documents which greatly aided my research. I also appreciate assistance with photographs from the Museum of Wellington City and Sea, Wellington, New Zealand; Beinecke Rare Book and Manuscript Library, Yale University; and Puget Sound Maritime Historical Society, Seattle. The original artist's drawing of the Stevensons' arrival on the Apia waterfront was done for me by my former student Loy Neff. I am also grateful to Joe Jares for his photograph of the CASCO's anchorage in Anaho Bay in the Marquesas.

Last, but not least, I would like to recognize Edmond Reynolds, the director of the Silverado Museum in St. Helena, California for his friendship and his permission for me to use the painting of the schooner CASCO by Charles Robert Patterson for the cover of my book.

CONTENTS

INTRODUCTION

This is an account of a man's desperate search for health, and his fulfillment of a lifelong ambition of crossing broad oceans in tall ships to gain an understanding of the world beyond the frontiers of what in the nineteenth century was considered civilized society. It is the story of the famous Stevenson family—Louis, Fanny, Maggie and Lloyd—and the ships that took them to high adventure in Polynesia, Micronesia and Melanesia between the years 1888 and 1890. The principal protagonist is Robert Louis Stevenson, a brilliant but sickly writer, just 38 years old as this narrative begins, but already famous for such novels as *Treasure Island, Kidnapped, Prince Otto, Dr. Jekyll and Mr. Hyde,* and for a charming volume of children's poetry, *A Child's Garden of Verses.* It is a story of his quest in the warm and salubrious climates of the South Seas for the restoration of a body which had lived with constant pain since childhood. It is also the story of a mind challenged and broadened through close association with indigenous men and women whom most white men of his time valued only for their lands and labor or as converts to their religion.

Stevenson was one of the world's first cultural relativists. He saw Pacific islanders as social and intellectual equals, and as noble representatives of cultures whose ways were as rational and appropriate to their needs as any in Victorian Europe or America. Their arts, their religions, their ways of getting a living, and their social and political systems were cultural treasures which were rapidly being taken from them in the name of profit, progress and Christianity.

As important to this story as the Stevenson party itself were the three vessels, the CASCO, the EQUATOR, and the JANET NICOLL which transported them to high adventure. They all had personalities of their own and were sometimes loved and sometimes hated for their unique strengths and weaknesses. The ship captains, the deck crews, the super cargoes and the resourceful cooks represent a cast of characters as colorful and memorable as can be found in any adventure novel or Hollywood windjammer spectacle. This is a story of discovery, of exotic islands and strange cultures, and of the ways of the sea—sometimes kind and sometimes cruel. It is a tale of personal growth and learning, of hardship and sacrifice on cruises to islands whose names are hardly known in the Western world and it is a story which involves humor, mystery, danger, political intrigue, religious conflict and scientific discovery.

Readers might wonder what would motivate someone to spend several years researching and writing a book like *Treasured Islands: Cruising the South Seas with Robert Louis Stevenson.* In my case it involves a unique set of circumstances. It all started in the late 1940s with my falling in love at first sight with a 32-foot ketch named IDLE HOUR lying anchored in Seattle's Lake Union. As I was growing up, I spent nearly every summer in Seattle, where I was accompanied by my mother, to visit her side of the family. I had done some sailing in a little converted rowboat up and down Lake Union, admiring the tall sailing ships which were anchored there after discharging their cargoes of Alaskan lumber.

My aunt knew about my crush on the IDLE HOUR and suggested that I read *Seven Seas on a Shoestring*, the account of a circumnavigation in that boat by Dwight Long, a University of Washington student. I checked out the book at the library and after reading it in a couple of days I was hooked. My high school grades suffered the next couple of years, as I read every round-the-world sailing adventure I could get my hands on. It was too bad my high school in Minneapolis didn't offer a course in geography, for I had become familiar with every island in Polynesia, Micronesia, Melanesia and Indonesia, and every ocean, sea and strait from the Tasman Sea to Narragansett Bay. Furthermore, I knew about island peoples and their cultures throughout the Pacific and what adventures could be had in scores of ports and anchorages around the world. But mostly I was intrigued by the South Seas and by the sailing ships that could carry you there.

When World War II came along I joined the Coast Guard hoping for duty with the Offshore Sailing Patrol, but wound up first on a relief lightship and then on a destroyer escort, that took me not to Tahiti, but to the Aleutians, Siberia, Northern China and finally Japan.

After the war I enrolled at Northwestern University and majored in English literature, intending ultimately to teach literature and composition in high school or perhaps college. However, in my junior year I somehow got signed up for a course in Cultural Anthropology and found to my great delight that it was all about people in foreign lands with exotic cultures just like the ones I had read about in the cruise stories which had dominated my interest during high school.

I received my degree in English Literature but decided to enter graduate school in Anthropology and ultimately did research for my Ph.D dissertation in the same village in Samoa where Margaret Mead had done her research on adolescent girls 28 years earlier. It was at this time that I first learned of Robert Louis Stevenson's years spent in Samoa. After receiving my degree and being employed as a professor of Anthropology at Wichita State University I made four more research trips to Samoa and frequently visited the Stevenson home at Vailima, and on one occasion climbed Mount Vaea to visit his grave.

While my childhood had been enriched by Stevenson's charming poetry volume, *A Child's Garden of Verses*, I had never read much of his work in college, as my professors tended to consider him a writer of juvenile fiction and not quite on a par with such people as Henry James, Thomas Hardy, Rudyard Kipling, Charles Dickens or D. H. Lawrence.

My visits to Stevenson's home have inspired me to read a considerable amount of his work, particularly *In the South Seas*, *Ebb Tide*, *Footnote to History* and *Beach of Falesa*. From these volumes I came to realize that his attitude toward Samoans and island peoples in general was atypical of other European writers and even most nineteenth century anthropologists, who labeled South Sea islanders "savages" or at least "primitives" and "heathens," generally inferior to civilized folks.

As I read the accounts of Stevenson's cruises through the islands, as found in his journal and those of his mother and his wife, I was able to identify more and more with the man, for I too have spent time on inter-island trading ships in the Samoan islands, the Cooks and the Marquesas. On Nuku Hiva our ship anchored, as did the CASCO, in Anaho Bay and tied up in Taiohae where the family went to visit Queen Vaekehu. And that inter-island trader took on copra at Atuona on the island of Hiva Oa where Stevenson and Brother Michel visited the ceremonial center (*meae*). I have visited atolls in the Cooks and the Tuamotus and have shot the reef in whaleboats through heavy breakers. I have made ceremonial visits (*malaga*) in Samoa, have spent hours sitting cross-legged at deliberations of Samoan chiefs, have been presented the *kava* cup on occasions of high ceremony, and have come to know the island king of Tonga.

Like Stevenson I have loved the sea all my life, and sail a sea-going cruising boat of my own. My wife and I have been on several charters in Puget Sound, Penobscot Bay, and in the Caribbean—working sail and standing helm watches on sailing schooners much like the CASCO and the EQUATOR.

Considerable time and research went into the production of this chronicle. The facts were gathered from Louis's correspondence with scores of friends and relatives and from the letters written by Fanny Stevenson and Aunt Maggie (Stevenson's mother). Journals kept by Fanny, Maggie and Louis and books written after the death of Stevenson by Fanny, her daughter Belle and son Lloyd help fill out the record. Then there are books of reminiscences by people who met the Stevensons on their way through the South Seas. Few could forget the dynamic, warm personality of Louis or the sometimes petty and domineering behavior of Fanny, but all appear to have felt proud to have known them.

One of the most interesting accounts is that documenting the EQUATOR voyage which was written by a young crewmember, Thomson Murray MacCallum, who shared cooking duties with Stevenson's chef, Ah Fu. Interestingly enough he had also spent some time on the JANET NICOLL as a stowaway out of Auckland at the age of 17. After being landed on the beach at Apia, Samoa, "Samoa Mac," as he was called, worked as a carpenter's helper, a blacksmith, an island trader and copra buyer, and ultimately, a cook in the crew of the schooner EQUATOR. His observations of the behavior and activities of the Stevenson clan add greatly to this seagoing saga of Tusitala in the South Seas.

The information concerning the CASCO, the EQUATOR and the JANET NICOLL was gathered through extensive library research and photo acquisition from maritime archives throughout the world. Blueprints, plans or specifications could not be found, and perhaps never existed, since even in the late 1800s vessels were often built according to carved hull models or by builders who trusted their eye to produce a proper hull more than a ship-wright's mathematical calculations.

Reconstructions of the hull design, rigging and below deck accommodations of the schooner CASCO and the topsail schooner/steamer JANET NICOLL which appear in this volume have been derived from photographs which have been analyzed by Master Mariner and reconstructor of historic ships Raymond Aker, and are believed to be extremely reliable. The weathered hull of the EQUATOR, which has undergone major modifications over the years, lies under a protective roof in Everett, Washington. It has been saved with the intention of restoring it as an indoor museum ship.

One of the more important facets of the research on the Stevenson South Sea adventure is believed to be an investigation of the nature of Stevenson's malady, which he quaintly referred to as "Bluidy Jack," and cited as the motivating factor for the trip. In the epilogue will be found a discussion of the medical case history of Louis's 44-year life span and an etiology of Stevenson's poor health which has been suggested by Dr. Curtis Drevets, a respiratory specialist from Wichita, Kansas. His analysis of the data not only casts doubt on the possibility of Stevenson having tuberculosis but suggests he may have suffered from another bronchial disease which would not only account for many of the symptoms which plagued him throughout his short life, but also could explain the cause and nature of his early death.

TREASURED
ISLANDS

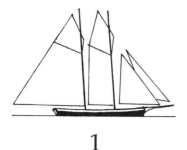

1

The CASCO—A Schooner to Paradise

T HE FIRST RAYS of the newborn sun silhouetted the Oakland hills and highlighted the spars of a beautiful little 93-foot sailing schooner that bobbed at anchor just off the breakwater of San Francisco's North Beach area. It was an amazingly clear summer morning for San Francisco, with no fog and just a light breeze that little more than ruffled the surface of the bay. While most of San Francisco's residents on nearby Telegraph Hill slept, there was little rest aboard the schooner, whose carved name boards fore and aft identified her as the CASCO.

The CASCO was preparing for sea, and while her charter passengers were saying goodbye to a host of friends who had come aboard with baskets of flowers and fruits, the schooner's small crew was dealing with more pressing matters. The captain, Bert Otis, scarcely acknowledged the presence of the well-wishers as he moved about the vessel's deck issuing orders to check the lashings on the ship's tenders, to clear the deck of unstowed gear, to remove the binnacle cover from the helmsman's compass, to prepare to break out the colors—the American flag, the Union Jack and the San Francisco Yacht Club pennant—and to prepare to weigh anchor. The tug PELICAN which would tow them out through the Golden Gate had already been sighted leaving Oakland. As the tug drew near, Captain Otis gruffly announced, "All visitors ashore," and began urging people to move toward the boarding ladder that led down to the small craft tied up alongside. A deckhand was sent forward and caught the heaving line as its weighted monkey fist sailed over from the tug. The towing hawser was then dragged aboard and made fast to the bitt on the CASCO's forward deck. As the last of the visitors cast off their launches, a shout from the bow of the CASCO of "anchor aweigh" signaled that an historic cruise was about to get underway.

The helmsman stepped to the beautifully varnished wheel in the center of the cockpit, the towing hawser became rigid, and the CASCO, like an obedient puppy on a leash, swung into line behind the not-to-be-denied tug PELICAN. They headed northwest toward Alcatraz Island, but then when they reached the center of the channel they turned due west toward the Golden Gate and the ominous open sea. On the port side was the Presidio and Fort Point with its massive brick ramparts with Civil War vintage batteries pointed seaward. To starboard, the profile of Mount Tamalpais, vaguely resembling that of a sleeping Indian maiden, could be seen above the rugged terrain of the Marin Peninsula.

The departure of the CASCO had been well publicized, since its passengers were celebrities, and as they traveled down the bay, ferries, and even a train on a siding along the shoreline, saluted the trim little yacht with three blasts from their steam whistles. As the tug and its tow passed a government cutter, a CASCO crewmember dipped "Old Glory" three times and waved to the sailors who threw back a hand salute. A number of yachts had sailed down from the San Francisco Yacht Club in Belvedere to escort the CASCO out of the bay, and many flew the signal flags ROGER, BAKER, AFFIRM (Goodbye) to which the CASCO responded with the flags OPTION, VICTOR, GEORGE (Thank you). A group of Italian and Portuguese fishermen, on their way to their fishing grounds off Pigeon Point and Monterey, waved and shouted a cheerful farewell from the decks of their exotic feluccas. As the CASCO was being towed up and out of the bay, a very slender, pale and long-haired young man, sitting with his family in one corner of the ship's cockpit, was occupied with a pad of paper and a pen. As he wrote he occasionally looked back at the receding skyline of San Francisco. His face reflected a complex mood—one with a mixture of joy and sadness. He was writing a poem and it read:

> *Farewell, and when forth*
> *I through the Golden Gates to Golden Isles*
> *Steer without smiling, through the sea of smiles,*
> *Isle upon isle, in the seas of the south,*
> *Isle upon island, sea upon sea,*
> *Why should I sail, why should the breeze?*

I have been young, and I have counted friends.
A hopeless sail I spread, too late, too late.
Why should I from isle to isle
Sail, a hopeless sailor?

The author of the poem was Robert Louis Stevenson. Three years earlier he had written another poem much less melancholy:

I should like to rise and go
Where the golden apples grow;
Where below another sky
Parrot islands anchored lie.

Sensing that Louis was harboring mixed feelings, his mother moved closer to him and whispered, "Lou, isn't it wonderful that we are going to see all these strange out-of-the-way places. When I was just a little girl in school I remember wishing for just such a holiday. I even learned a little poem which has now come back to me. It went

Full many are the beauteous isles,
Unseen by human eye,
That, sleeping 'mid the oceans smiles,
In sunny silence lie.

Stevenson smiled, put his arm around her shoulders, gave her a little hug and thought to himself, "This lady is going to be the best sailor of us all."

Once through the famous golden portal to the sea, the tug PELICAN reduced speed, turned to port, and signaled the CASCO to release the tow line. The line was taken in and the stubby little tugboat headed home with its funnel trailing black coal smoke and its engine beating a noisy tattoo. The wind freshened and the seas increased, and the CASCO looked tiny and terribly vulnerable in this wilderness of waters. Now the die was cast and the event recorded in the *San Francisco Chronicle* under the heading of "Marine Intelligence": *Sailed Thursday, June 28, Schooner CASCO, Captain Otis, destination Tahiti, via Marquesas.*

The crew made sail—setting foresail, main, forestaysail, jib and outer jib—and the CASCO suddenly came to life, heeling to port and burying her rail in the massive swells and tumbling seas as she sped south-southwest like a graceful magical creature born of the wind and the waves. Again and again, her plunging bow sent showers of spray flying back along the deck. Barely visible ahead was the bleak and craggy southeast Farallon some 30 miles offshore, and astern were the Seal Rocks and one last view of a symbol of civilization—the castlelike towers and spires of Cliff House just south of Point Lobos. On the windswept deck of the CASCO just three people observed this scene, a forward lookout, the helmsman and Robert Louis Stevenson, a man who had once remarked he would gladly exchange all his literary notoriety for a 70-ton schooner. Now he had one under charter, and a lifelong dream of adventure was becoming a reality. The power of the sea frightened him but also made him feel alive, vigorous, at peace with himself and the world—feelings he had rarely experienced in his short and troubled life.

Although Stevenson came from a long line of lighthouse engineers and had often written about sailing ships and sailing men, his history of poor health had greatly limited any personal experience on the water. He and a college friend, Walter Simpson, had sailed the Hebrides Islands off Scotland in the 10-ton schooner HERON in July and August of 1874, and in 1876 they had explored the river and canal system in northeast France in a canoe, an experience which resulted in Stevenson's first book, *An Inland Voyage*. But now, as he sat in the cockpit of the CASCO, he realized that he was actually on a real sailing adventure to the exotic South Seas, something he had dreamed of ever since he was a child when he read R. M. Ballantyne's *Coral Island*. This obsession had been further encouraged by reading Charles Warren Stoddard's *South Sea Idylls*, and meeting the author in San Francisco some eight years ago.

As Louis gazed up at the billowing sails and the straining spars he couldn't help but feel a bit of apprehension. After all, the CASCO was not really a seagoing packet but rather a rich man's pleasure yacht, and he wondered if this vessel, designed primarily for sport racing on San Francisco Bay, wasn't over-rigged and over-sparred. He would have to discuss this with Captain Otis.

Somewhat less enthusiastic about the romance of tumbling seas and flying spray than Stevenson, the rest of the passengers and most of the crew had long since sought shelter below decks. Concerned with his family's welfare, Louis slid open the hatch at the forward end of the cockpit, backed down the companionway ladder, and peered into the after cabin. While the passengers were a bit apprehensive and some were even ill—as might be expected of any group of landlubbers on their first day at sea in a 93-foot sailing yacht—this collection of voyagers was hardly commonplace. In the handsomely appointed after cabin the rest of the Stevenson party—his wife Fanny, his stepson Lloyd, his mother Maggie and the family maid, Valentine—were coping with their new environment and fears as well as could be expected. Fanny and Lloyd were already in their bunks suffering from seasickness. Louis noticed that the door to Captain Otis's cabin was closed and he wondered if their skipper had also fallen victim to the tyranny of the waves and weather. Valentine was pale and fading fast, but Maggie, the most elderly of the group, was cheery, inquiring about breakfast and appearing irritatingly immune to *mal de mer*. But when Maggie learned that the meal would consist of red herrings and mutton chops, even she decided to wait for lunch.

Heading the Stevenson clan was, of course, Robert Louis who at the age of 38 was already a very successful and eminent poet, essayist and novelist, primarily as a result of his published novels, *Treasure Island, Kidnapped, Prince Otto,* and *Dr. Jekyll and Mr. Hyde.* His *Child's Garden of Verses* had only been published two years but had already found a permanent place on the shelves of most nurseries in Europe and America.

Just before sailing, Louis had weakened and generously agreed to an interview with a young reporter from the *San Francisco Chronicle,* although the author was counting the days until he could escape the nuisance of his notoriety. The young man had approached him with utmost courtesy and respect and opened the interview by asking him how he would like to be addressed—Mr. Stevenson or Robert. Whereupon the author replied, "Well, young man, I prefer Mr. Stevenson to Robert, as no one calls me that. However, the members of my family call me Louis although my mother occasionally prefers Lou. But many of my friends just use RLS, and I kind of like that myself." The young reporter, somewhat overwhelmed by all this, merely said, "That's very interesting, Mr. Stevenson." In the article he produced, he outlined the plans and purpose of the forthcoming voyage and then proceeded to describe the author's appearance and demeanor. He depicted the Edinburgh-born Scotsman as

> a medium-sized gentleman . . . with a pale face, gray or light-brown eyes and brown hair. He has a horse-shoe shaped moustache of not very heavy texture. . . . Stevenson possesses the faculty of making a stranger feel at ease almost at once. He invariably smiles when speaking, his eyes sparkling and his whole face beaming with intelligence and good nature.

A few days earlier another reporter had penned one of the few descriptions to which the author took real offense. It described him as having "a tall, willowy figure surmounted by a classic head from which issued a hacking cough."

Most people tended to be impressed by his wide-set, brilliant eyes, maintaining they illuminated his face and radiated charm or, on rare occasions, anger. When Captain Otis first met Stevenson at the home of CASCO's owner, Dr. Merritt, he thought the writer looked much younger than his 38 years. But what he remembered most was Stevenson's fragile body—5 feet 10 inches in height and weighing but 98 pounds—his shoulder-length hair, and the deathlike whiteness of his face which caused the captain to doubt whether the man could possibly return from the proposed island cruise alive. Many people remembered Stevenson's chain-smoking habits, which seemed imprudent given his respiratory problems which had plagued him since childhood. He smoked only Willis Three Castles tobacco, which he rolled into cigarettes by hand. His habit was described by a friend as "cigarettes without intermission except when coughing or kissing."

Stevenson's wife Fanny, born Frances Matilda Van de Grift in Indianapolis, Indiana, on March 10, 1840, was ten years Louis's senior. She was small in stature and bone structure, dark (with "swarthy Gypsy beauty" and jet-black hair), energetic, artistic, unconventional, and more than a bit neurotic and domineering—even dictatorial when it came to enforcing measures protective of Stevenson's health. A fellow artist in Europe, Birge Harrison, portrayed Fanny as "both physically and mentally the very antithesis of the gay, hilarious, open-hearted Stevenson, and for that reason perhaps the woman in all the world best fitted to be his comrade and helpmate." Stevenson referred to her as his "stormy petrel" and one wonders if he was emphasizing the "stormy" aspect or the fact that petrels appear to walk on water. Most of all Fanny was totally devoted to Louis, willing to accept any lifestyle, any hardship to ensure his health and happiness. Perhaps one of the world's worst sailors, Fanny lived almost daily with seasickness during the Pacific cruises, which she judged to be absolutely necessary for Stevenson's physical survival.

Samuel Lloyd Osbourne, Fanny Stevenson's son, better known as Lloyd, was born in Oakland, California. At the beginning of this South Sea adventure he was 20 years old. Encouraged by his mother to think of himself as the center of the universe, he tended to be somewhat snobbish, vain and haughty-looking, acting and talking much like an Englishman. He has been described by some biographers as having "a heart of ice." He was tall and slender, fairly handsome, with a shock of blonde curly hair, and wore extremely thick glasses. He was intelligent, witty and well-mannered but with a somewhat unimpressive academic career. He had entered the University of Edinburgh to study engineering but soon dropped out, claiming his eyesight was too poor. After returning from a tour of the West Indies, financed by Stevenson, which was supposed to cure his vision problems, Lloyd announced that he had decided to become a novelist and not return to school. Stevenson was supportive and took him under his wing, suggesting that they might even co-author something in the future. Just prior to the departure of the CASCO, Lloyd appeared aboard properly fitted out for the schooner cruise with a sailor's golden ear ring in his newly pierced left ear lobe.

Margaret Isabella Balfour Stevenson, affectionately known as "Maggie" or "Aunt Maggie," was 59 years old but looked considerably younger. She was of medium height, slender, graceful and dignified, with a pleasant and sympathetic nature. She was a rather attractive woman with an oval face, a fair complexion and a slightly aquiline nose. She was the daughter of a Presbyterian minister. Like her son, she had a history of pulmonary problems, resulting in her visiting spas in Germany, southern France and England when Louis was small. Widowed in 1887, she dressed very conservatively, usually in black, and was seldom seen in public without her organdy widow's cap with streamers down the back and white gloves. Maggie had been very straight-laced most of her life, although she became somewhat more liberal after her husband, Thomas, a lighthouse engineer, died of a cerebral hemorrhage in 1887 and she went to live with Louis and Fanny in America. While Maggie insisted on Sunday services on the CASCO and grace before meals, she would join them for champagne toasts; she appeared somewhat less prejudiced in regard to those she called "Popeys" (Catholic missionaries and their converts in Polynesia), and as time went by, she became remarkably accepting of native cultural differences, even their "heathen" belief systems.

Because Maggie was so intrepid aboard ship she was referred to as a "regular sea bird" by the rest of the clan who felt they had to watch her or she might get washed overboard or want to climb the rigging. However, they never thought of protecting her from hammocks. When crossing the Atlantic on the S.S. LUDGATE HILL in September 1887, a hammock was slung for her in her cabin. Instantly Lloyd, his sister Belle and some friends piled into it, with Maggie leaping in last. Under the weight, the rope broke, dumping everyone onto the deck. Lloyd got up pale and dizzy while Maggie sustained a bad jar to her spine and laid where she landed for some time before cheerfully getting to her feet. While aboard the CASCO there were times when Maggie was the only one aboard who was not seasick, and that included the crew.

The Stevensons' maid, Valentine Roch, was born in Switzerland into a large French family and had come to work for Louis and Fanny in 1883 while they were living in Hyères in the south of France. Although Valentine had had no previous experience as a maid, she proved to be bright, energetic and loyal in addition to being young, pretty and blonde—characteristics undoubtedly noticed by Louis and Fanny in different ways. Louis, who was extremely fond of Valentine, nicknamed her "Joe" because of her extroverted personality and high spirits. Fanny, on the other hand, found it difficult to coexist with such an attractive house servant, and treated her shabbily until an occasion when Louis suddenly took ill and nearly died of influenza, and the two women closely cooperated in nursing him back to health.

As Stevenson sat in the rear of the after cabin empathizing with his yet-to-be-conditioned sea-going family, he carefully and meticulously reviewed the events of the last twelve years which were a prelude to what was happening today.

Was it a selfish move on his part to insist on this voyage into who knew what dangers just to improve his own health and well being? From the looks of most of his clan so far, their health appeared almost as threatened as his own. But hopefully they would soon recover, and he was not certain that for him there was any other avenue to life than the enterprise in which they were now engaged. His gaze carefully moved from individual to individual—some in their berths and others sitting on the couches, holding on to keep from being thrown to the deck as the ship rolled and pitched.

Here was his family, brave, loyal and attentive to his needs, who for his sake alone were leaving civilization behind and trusting their lives to fate, to a little sailing schooner and to its youthful captain in an unselfish attempt to realize Louis's seemingly impossible dream, that they could find a benevolent world where he could live without fever, without hemorrhages, and without the constant threat of death. Yes here, in this somewhat foul-smelling ship's quarters was his cast of characters, as unique and colorful as any his creative mind might conceive. And as his thoughts moved from his beloved cast of characters to the events leading up to the present, Louis wanted to remember and savor every event, every decision, every happy moment and even every incident of conflict. How sharp and clear it all was to him now. He must not forget so much as one precious incident no matter how joyous or painful the memory might be. The last twelve years were, after all, the first act in his new drama of life and death.

Louis met Fanny Osbourne in Grez-sur-Loing, an artist colony in France where Fanny fled with her children, Belle and Lloyd, after the death of her youngest child Hervey from tuberculosis in Paris in 1875. Her husband, Samuel Osbourne, whom she married at age 17, had proven to be charming, but restless, shiftless, and unfaithful, continually pursuing get-rich-quick schemes which took him away from his family in East Oakland for extended periods of time. Rather than divorce her husband, Fanny settled for separation and took her children to France where she wanted to study art.

Shortly after her youngest child's death, she met Robert Louis Stevenson's cousin Bob Stevenson, who according to a letter from Fanny to her sister, "is the best artist here, a charming musician, speaks all languages, does all sorts of feats of strength and has no ambition." Bob was more interested in Fanny's 18-year-old daughter Belle than in her mother, and he promoted his cousin Louis to Fanny as "a gentleman she could trust and depend on." Louis had already encountered Fanny in the dining room of the Hotel Chevillon when he claimed that he fell in love with her at first sight and vaulted in through an open window to introduce himself. After a formal introduction by Bob, Louis and Fanny became great friends, although she was nonplused by his somewhat eccentric behavior and violent mood swings. Fanny developed great admiration and affection for this struggling author, however, and thought him "the wittiest man I have ever met." Louis responded to her feelings, and when Fanny returned to Paris in the fall of 1876, he followed her there. In 1878, Fanny and her children spent several weeks in London where she frequently saw Stevenson before returning to Oakland.

Shortly after Fanny returned to California, Sam Osbourne moved his reunited family to Monterey, where he was working as a court reporter for the Bureau of Mines, and there was a brief period of reconciliation. Fanny had no sooner arrived in Monterey than their daughter Belle eloped, unfortunately with Joe Strong, a young artist whose character and lifestyle greatly resembled that of her father. It soon became apparent to Fanny that her marriage to the colorful, physically attractive, but promiscuous Sam Osbourne could not be salvaged, and she was seriously contemplating filing for a divorce. Meanwhile, Louis had managed to put together enough money to travel "second cabin" class across the Atlantic, and by day-coach across the United States. After arriving in Monterey he spent several months living in an old adobe inn working on manuscripts of the travel books *The Amateur Emigrant* and *Across the Plains*, while Fanny agonized over whether or not to initiate divorce proceedings. She did finally make up her mind and received her divorce from Sam on May 19, 1880, whereupon she and Louis were married in San Francisco, very much against the wishes of Louis's parents.

However, both his mother and father became reconciled to the union, with Thomas Stevenson coming to admire Fanny for her "good judgment and intellectual attainments," and Maggie in time making it known that she believed Fanny was the best thing that ever happened to Louis.

After their marriage the couple honeymooned in a deserted cottage on the site of an abandoned gold and silver mine on the south-eastern slope of Mount Saint Helena high above Napa Valley. Here Stevenson would pen *The Silverado Squatters*, an account of their joys, hardships and characters they met.

Louis, Fanny and her son returned to Scotland in late August, but spent the winter in Davos, Switzerland for reasons of Louis's health, which was rapidly deteriorating. His pulmonary problems, which had begun to involve frequent hemorrhaging, and were referred to by him as "Bluidy Jack," often necessitated his spending considerable time in bed with doctor's orders not even to speak. In spite of his numerous physical setbacks, the period spent in the British Isles and various locales on the continent between 1880 and 1886 were extremely productive years in which he published *Treasure Island, A Child's Garden of Verses, Kidnapped*, and *Dr. Jekyll and Mr. Hyde.*

Following the death of his father in May 1887, the Stevenson clan, which now consisted of Louis, Fanny, her son Lloyd, Stevenson's mother, Maggie, and their maid Valentine Roch, decided to return to the United States where Louis would seek to benefit from the therapy which might be provided by a Dr. E. L. Trudeau in his famous sanitarium at Saranac Lake in the Adirondack mountains of northern New York State. Here they rented a small cottage and began an existence which Fanny maintained was "very like camp life." One room was reserved as a study for Louis, while the rest of the family huddled together making the best of what were crowded, primitive accommodations, while the temperature outside often dipped below minus 30°F.

Fanny spent very little time at Saranac Lake. Because of the less than adequate living conditions and the unpleasant weather, she did considerable traveling, visiting friends and relatives in New York City, Philadelphia, Montreal and Danville, Indiana. While she ordinarily hovered over Louis like a mother hen, his health at Saranac Lake had improved greatly, his writing was going well—except when the ink in his inkwell froze—and Lloyd, Louis's new writing apprentice, Maggie and the maid Valentine seemed to be handling Louis's physical needs quite adequately.

During that long and bitterly cold winter at Saranac Lake, Stevenson became more and more certain that what he needed for further improvements in his health was a cruise to the South Seas, something he had dreamed of for many years.

As early as June 1875 Louis began seriously entertaining the possibility of a South Sea sailing adventure. William Seed, Governor of New Zealand, was a guest in Louis's parents' home at 17 Heriot Street in Edinburgh, and when the elder Stevenson made a comment concerning Louis's ubiquitous pulmonary illness, Seed suggested that his son should settle in Samoa for his health. After dinner Seed talked with Louis at length about the South Seas and its benign climate. And some five years later Stevenson met Charles Warren Stoddard, the author of *South Sea Idylls* and heard still more about the therapeutic climate of the South Pacific. Even as a child RLS had been intrigued by the South Seas after reading R. M. Ballantyne's *Coral Island*, and as a teenager he had managed to arrange spending an evening with the author. From that time on the Pacific island world held a magical attraction for him, and he knew that someday he must go there.

The Stevenson family's interest in a South Sea island voyage was greatly encouraged when Sam McClure, owner of the New York World newspaper syndicate contacted Louis with an offer of $10,000 a year to do a weekly column. When he heard of Stevenson's South Sea interests he suggested that the author charter a yacht and publish a series of columns describing his voyage. To encourage him further he sent RLS a copy of Findley's *Directory of the Pacific,* and it soon became the family's favorite pastime on bitterly cold evenings to read aloud the descriptions of islands and island people and to imagine balmy days and hair-raising adventures in strange exotic island ports of call. Although Louis had inherited a considerable amount of money from his father, McClure's encouragement, backed by his offer of financial support, pretty much settled the question of whether or not a Pacific island voyage was feasible.

When Fanny left Saranac Lake on a trip to visit her sister

Nellie Sanchez in Monterey, Louis told her to look for a yacht which they could charter to test once and for all whether or not a Pacific Ocean voyage could possibly be the elixir of life that so many people had claimed. Upon arriving in Oakland Fanny set to work exploring possibilities of a schooner charter. She hardly knew where to start, although she did remember reading in the newspaper back in 1880 that an Oakland doctor named Samuel Merritt had sailed on a pleasure cruise to Hawaii and Tahiti with seven friends, four of them women, on a schooner yacht named CASCO. At the time Fanny had been particularly interested in the trip, because her Oakland home was located on the San Antonio Estuary, and this is where the CASCO was berthed. While not a great fancier of boats, she recalled how lovely the little schooner was with its spotless bleached decks, its shiny black topsides and its sails furled neatly on the booms.

When approached by Fanny, Dr. Merritt appeared lukewarm to the idea of the charter, but he promised her that he would consider it. The more he thought about it the more he was intrigued with the idea of chartering his schooner to a man of Stevenson's literary reputation and popularity. Although it would interfere with his usual participation in the San Francisco Yacht Club racing schedule, he did after all have a smaller boat, a 28-foot sharpie named DAISY, which he could use to compete while the CASCO was off earning money, and Merritt had never been a man to turn down a chance to make a good profit. What was a major concern, however, was whom he could select to serve as captain, for he reserved the right to select the ship's skipper. There was one man, Albert Otis, his nephew from Maine, who was well qualified to command the vessel, but he had not been to sea in over three years after having been a first mate on a vessel in which the captain had been killed in an accident.

Although the charter arrangement was far from being worked out, Fanny rushed to a telegraph office after leaving Dr. Merritt and sent the following wire to Louis:

CAN SECURE SPLENDID SEA-GOING SCHOONER YACHT CASCO FOR SEVEN HUNDRED AND FIFTY A MONTH WITH MOST COMFORTABLE ACCOMMODATION FOR SIX AFT AND SIX FORWARD. CAN BE READY FOR SEA IN TEN DAYS. REPLY IMMEDIATELY

And reply he did: BLESSED GIRL, TAKE THE YACHT AND EXPECT US IN TEN DAYS.

Shortly after his meeting with Fanny, Merritt invited Otis to dinner and asked him to accept a commission as captain for the charter. The young seaman was unfortunately not thrilled when Merritt informed him that the charter party was headed by the world famous author of *Treasure Island*, which incidentally was a book Otis had read but he had not been impressed with the author's knowledge of the sea and seamanship. Otis, who had often wished he could return to the South Pacific on a ship much like the CASCO, discovered that the commission document Merritt offered him gave him full control of the vessel and the right to approve or reject any ports of call. Feeling the offer was too good to turn down, and having no other source of income at the moment, Otis accepted the commission.

After Fanny and Merritt had finally worked out all the financial aspects through extremely hard bargaining, Merritt said rather gruffly, " And now, little lady, I hope you are satisfied." Fanny shot back with an impish smile, "Yes, big man, and I hope you are."

"Just one more thing, Mrs. Stevenson. Captain Otis and I will have to meet with your husband and other members of your party so that we have some idea of the kind of people to whom I am entrusting my beloved schooner for seven months."

The charter price was to be $500 a month, which was not what Fanny had reported to Louis in her telegram setting this whole enterprise in motion. The $750 figure in the telegram may have been an estimate which would include wages for the crew, provisions, insurance, and a contingency fund to cover possible repairs and other unforeseen expenses that might be incurred during the trip.

Dr. Merritt had heard that one of the passengers would be a 59-year-old woman and he particularly wanted to check on the nature of her health before giving final approval. When they finally met, Merritt's first words were, "You're a healthy looking woman." Maggie smiled and replied sweetly "Thank you, Doctor," but she thought to herself "And you, Sir, are a very stout man." Merritt, who tipped the scales at 340 pounds, had in fact, had the CASCO built with the belief that sailboat racing would result in weight loss and improved health for him. Earlier he had confided to Fanny that he had already dropped approximately 60 pounds sailing, but hoped "it doesn't have the same effect on Mr. Stevenson as there would be nothing left of him."

Both Merritt and Otis had been equally skeptical of the advisability of undertaking a charter with what they had heard was an eccentric, bohemian, long-haired, emaciated writer of novels and poetry, but after meeting with Stevenson, Merritt is known to have commented to Otis, "Why, Captain, Mr. Stevenson seems quite as sensible a man as you or I."

When all the legal and financial details had finally been worked out and the CASCO was truly theirs, the women began the arduous task of provisioning the vessel for seven months for eleven people. Louis remained in the Hotel Occidental nursing a cold while Fanny, taking the advice of South Sea expert Charles Warren Stoddard, ordered kegs of dried beef, great quantities of flour, sugar, rice and beans, buckets of butter, lard and syrup, dozens of hams and sides of bacon, and crates of dried and canned fruits, several cases of wine and liquor, and of course, a substantial supply of Louis and Fanny's cigarette-making supplies. A huge quantity of reading materials plus hundreds of gifts for South Sea islanders filled the storage areas, and in the lockers of the after cabin were stowed the Stevensons' cruising wardrobe and such vital items as Louis's flageolet and sheet music, three revolvers, Lloyd's new camera, his musical instruments (guitar, fiddle and banjo) and his typewriter—the badge of a would-be novel writer. The women had acquired a tropical-style wardrobe of flowered *muumuus* and *holakus*, at the urging of Fanny's daughter, Belle, who was temporarily back in the Bay area after several months in Honolulu where her husband was painting island scenery and where they had managed to be adopted in royal social circles. These dresses had been custom-made by Yee Lee, a Chinatown tailor. Everyone had acquired large brimmed straw hats, and Louis had purchased a yachting cap and several suits of striped pajamas, the typical day-to-day wear of South Sea traders. Of course, he also had packed his velvet jackets which had been a kind of sartorial trademark most of his life.

While the provisioning was proceeding Fanny encountered Paulie Osbourne, who had married Sam after his divorce from Fanny. Tearfully Paulie confided to Fanny, "You were right about that man and I was wrong." Sam had continued in his womanizing and irresponsible ways. And within a year of their marriage he had disappeared—never to be heard from again. His wife was having a desperate time financially on their vineyard at Glen Ellen in Sonoma County, and Louis and Fanny provided considerable financial support to the unfortunate woman until she was able to work out her personal and financial problems. Sam's children, Lloyd and Belle, would not believe that their father had abandoned Paulie, but preferred to suspect that he had been waylaid, robbed and killed.

During the excitement of preparing for the great South Sea island adventure the family had almost forgotten the ultimate purpose of the voyage. But not Louis, who was still hoping for a miracle to be found somewhere over the horizon to the south-southwest. In a letter to his old friend and university classmate Charles Baxter, penned prior to departure, Louis wrote, "If I cannot get my health back (more or less),'tis madness; but of course, there is hope, and I will play big. . . . If this business fails to set me up, well £2,000 is gone, and I know I can't get better."

And to his American artist friend Will Low, Stevenson announced, "I loved the Pacific in the days when I was at Monterey, and perhaps now it will love me a little. . . . In a better climate on the Pacific, surely a better life awaits me."

By the second day out of port the ship's routine had been well established with wheel watches set two hours on and six hours off and with all hands also being responsible for ship maintenance and sail handling whenever required, day or night. Not counting Captain Otis, the CASCO had a five-man crew of the skipper's own choosing. There was no first mate and only four seamen to steer, handle sails and maintain the ship. There was a Russian with the unlikely name Charles Olsen, two Swedes with the equally unlikely names of Fred Schröder and John Lassen, and a Finn, Charles Wallin. Perhaps the most unusual individual in the whole ship's company was the steward/cook who was Chinese but insisted he was Japanese and signed the ship's articles as Antone Cousina. Valentine, the Stevenson maid, was unofficially listed on the roster as "cabin boy." Two men who applied for positions in the crew were turned down when one was discovered to be a newspaper reporter, undoubtedly seeking an exclusive feature story, and the other was a Seventh Day Adventist, who perhaps felt he had a calling as a missionary in the heathen islands of the South Pacific. The five-man crew re-cruited by Captain Otis was often sarcastically described by him as a "bunch of sea lawyers," meaning that they had a tendency to question orders and demand their rights, but after a few stern threats from the skipper they did begin to work together as a team. The biggest problem with the ship's company was that none of them but the captain knew anything about celestial nav-igation, a situation which could have been extremely serious if anything should happen to Otis.

From the very beginning of the voyage Stevenson was somewhat wary of the skipper who would be in charge of their destiny for the next seven months. Louis realized that Otis had originally refused Dr. Merritt's offer of sailing master for the voyage on the ground that he didn't like rich folks and that Stevenson would probably bore him to death with intellectual talk. Otis was also opposed to the idea of having three women aboard, one an "old lady."

Furthermore, the author had heard ominous rumors at the yacht club and along the waterfront about Bert Otis's involve-ment in an "accident" at sea involving the death of Bert's uncle, Captain Henry Otis, who was master of the 1,915 ton square-rig-ger, CHARLES E. MOODY. On the ship's second long voyage from San Francisco to Liverpool in 1884, Bert Otis was serving as first mate at the age of 24. His uncle's wife Emma (16 years younger than her 55-year-old husband) was aboard, as was her usual pat-tern on extended voyages. On October 20 the ship encountered very heavy weather off the coast of Chile and Captain Henry Otis sent someone to his cabin to bring him a muffler. In trying to put it on it was reported that he released his hold on the rail and at just that moment the ship took a sea aboard which struck him, causing him to bash his head against the rail. He was car-ried unconscious to his cabin where he died a few minutes later. Since Bert Otis ultimately married Emma Otis, his uncle's 42-year-old widow, in East Oakland in October 1887, and she died less than a month after the marriage of what a medical doctor di-agnosed as Brights Disease, considerable suspicion was cast on the 24-year-old Bert by Emma's relatives. Emma's brother, Fred Duncan, for example, himself a ship captain, maintained that old Captain Henry Otis was too good a seaman not to have hooked his arm through the rigging while putting on his scarf. Never having liked Bert Otis much anyway, Fred questioned whether the man hadn't murdered his captain to acquire his wife and her share of the ship valued at $40,000, of which her husband had been part owner. As it turned out, Bert Otis did inherit one fifth of the value of the ship when it was sold in 1898. At Emma's death eleven years earlier, he had inherited only $50 worth of personal property.

While Stevenson had no basis for determining the validity of the rumors concerning Bert Otis's possible guilt, he found him an extremely short-tempered taskmaster with his crew and somewhat rude in dealing with the passengers, especially the women. On one occasion he observed that Otis was so angry with a crewmember that Stevenson thought the captain might have killed the man if he had not been present on deck at three in the morning. Something of the nature of Captain Otis's behavior can be seen from what Stevenson wrote in his journal and later incorporated into the novel *The Wrecker*, which is highly autobiographical. By Stevenson's own admission the ship captain Nares is Otis. In the novel the main character Loudon Dodd describes Nares as follows:

"At first I was too much horrified by what I considered his barbarities, too much puzzled by his shifting humours, and too frequently annoyed by his small vanities, to regard him otherwise than as the cross of my existence. It was only by degrees, in his rare hours of pleasantness, when he forgot (and made me forget) the weaknesses to which he was so prone, that he won me to a kind of unconsenting fondness."

Earlier in the novel Dodd's partner, Jim Pinkerton, also discusses Nares' reputation and capabilities. He asserts:

"He's a typical American seaman—brave as a lion, full of resource, and stands high with his owners. He's a man with a record." "Of brutality at sea," interjected Dodd.

The daily routine aboard the CASCO was as follows: at 6 a.m. the crew, as well as any early rising passengers—usually only Louis and his mother—had morning coffee. Breakfast was served at 8 a.m., and a typical morning meal consisted of mackerel, corn meal mush, coffee, hot rolls and jam. The "forecastle," or crew menu, was more filling and less fancy. After breakfast the Stevenson clan moved to the cockpit while Valentine, the designated "cabin boy," made up the after cabin bunks so that the area could serve as a drawing-room throughout the rest of the day.

Once the after cabin was shipshape and Bristol-fashion, the Stevensons, including Valentine, would repair to the cockpit for a morning of reading aloud from the second volume of Gibbon's *Decline and Fall of the Roman Empire,* or Thomas Hardy's *The Woodlander,* or writing. There were at least three journals being kept, and Louis was committed to a series of magazine articles about his South Sea voyage which would partially defray the cost of the adventure. When not writing RSL also spent considerable time playing his flageolet. The consensus of opinion (which included his own) was that he played it very badly. In spite of that, he got a great deal of pleasure out of his efforts. He had brought a considerable quantity of classical music with him, and he spent long hours attempting to perform passages from the works of Chopin, Bach and Mozart. He even tried his hand at creating his own compositions.

A major interest for Stevenson throughout the entire voyage was the bird and animal population of their new maritime environment. Porpoises were a special attraction, and in his journal he described them as "gambolling under the ship's nose like dogs before a carriage" or perhaps more like gymnasts nimbly racing, leaping and rolling for the sheer delight of it.

Pilot birds and boatswain birds were also objects of interest, and the subject of many questions directed to Captain Otis or to whomever might be on wheel watch. The pilot birds, better known as stormy petrels, followed the CASCO for several days waiting for the ship's garbage buckets to be emptied over the side. And strangely enough they appeared to walk on the crest of waves while feeding on tiny fish, shrimp or plankton. Their foamy white footprints on the water were said to have given rise to their name which derives from the word Peter, the name of Christ's disciple who also walked on the water. Stevenson described their coloring as that of "brown lace."

The boatswain (or bo's'n) birds, which were actually red-tailed tropic-birds, joined them south of the equator when the petrels were no longer in evidence. In spite of their splash of color, Louis portrayed them as "white against the blue of the sky and sea." Captain Otis maintained that their name came from the long white central tail feathers tipped with red which some said resembled the marlin-spike, so frequently used by ship's bo's'ns. Stevenson said he appreciated the information, but personally could not see the resemblance between the feathers and the tool. Later that day, after Captain Otis had retired to his cabin, the helmsman, John Lassen, quietly communicated that some seamen believed that the name bo's'n bird came from the fact that the high shrill notes of the bird's call greatly resembled those produced by a boatswain's pipe. And as they watched the ever-present convoy of birds they were often startled by flying fish coming aboard, hitting the mainsail, and falling into the cockpit where the Stevensons quickly returned them to the sea. Maggie was intrigued by the little aquatic flyers, thinking they looked happy at play and wishing she could join them.

Lunch was served on the CASCO promptly at noon, and often consisted of a tin of corned beef, succotash and a tin of fruit. The afternoon was spent in the cockpit much like the morning, then dinner was served at 5 o'clock in the forward cabin and included Captain Otis. This meal was a bit more formal, with pea soup, salt beef ("which stays on the fire and cooks all afternoon for cabin dinner"), a tin of green beans, fruit fritters and a bottle of Bordeaux.

The evening's entertainment started with observation of the sunset, heralded as "the great spectacle of the day." After watching the great fiery ball plunge into the sea and savoring the spectrum of color as it faded from the western sky, Maggie would announce it was time for whist. Aunt Maggie initially chose Captain Otis to be her partner. Somewhat less than thrilled with this selection, he none the less led the way to the after cabin and broke out the cards. Much to his surprise the "little old lady" proved herself to be an excellent whist player, and within a few days Maggie and Otis were eight rubbers ahead and more than holding their own with all challengers.

The Stevensons usually played just two rubbers of whist after dinner and then they returned once more to the deck for an evening of watching what they referred to as "the sparkling heavens" and the ascent of the new moon which all agreed looked much larger than they had ever seen it before. Astern was the big dipper pointing to Polaris, the Star of the North. In a few days they would cross the equator and then there would be the fun of searching for the Southern Cross, that constellation of stars which served as a signpost marking the portal to the famed paradise of the South Seas. As they turned their attention from the heavens to the ship's bow waves and wake they found yet another visual delight, the sparkling, tumbling jewels of phosphorescence leaving a greenish-silver trail in the midnight blue of the sea.

When Lloyd and the women would turn in for the night Louis would often go to the dining saloon with his traveler's writing chest and write for another hour or two. The writing chest was something all Victorian travelers carried in their luggage so they could keep a travel diary and write postcards home. It was a small mahogany chest with a hinged cover which could be latched shut and it contained a wood stylus, several nibs, a glass writing pen and a bottle of ink. He was still experimenting with a newly purchased writing invention, a fountain pen, the brain storm of an American named Waterman in 1884. Like the typewriter the Stevensons had in their luggage, Louis was open to any inventions which furthered his production. However, he refused to learn to use the typewriter himself, claiming that its noise distracted him. Lloyd, on the other hand, proved to be a quick learner and typed all of Stevenson's manuscripts.

Actually it was in the cockpit that the Stevensons spent most of their time, and RLS often slept there on warm evenings. Maggie referred to it as "our open air drawing-room" and stated that there they always had the helmsman for company. Otis took a dim view of this fraternization, however, and clearly communicated this to the passengers. But Fanny was not one to take orders from anyone, and she persisted in an on-going deluge of questions to whomever was on the wheel about the weather, the ship, the marine life or the crewmembers' personal history. On one such occasion Captain Otis came out of his cabin, climbed the companionway ladder, and as he emerged from the hatch looked sternly at Fanny and said sarcastically, "Please don't talk to him today, Mrs. Stevenson. Today I want him to steer."

Perhaps the disregard of the captain's instructions which proved most serious had to do with the passengers' insistence on leaving the deadlights (porthole covers) open for greater ventilation, although strict orders were given to keep them tightly dogged. This could have sent the CASCO to the bottom later in the voyage when the ship suffered a knockdown as the result of a sudden violent squall and tons of water flooded in through the open ports.

Aunt Maggie often irritated the captain as well when she insisted on saying grace before each meal and was even more exasperating in her attempts to discuss Louis's literary achievements with the captain. When she asked him if he had read all of Louis's novels, he replied rudely that he had read only *Treasure Island*, but had found Stevenson's knowledge of seamanship so inferior in that book that, although he had looked at others, he decided not to waste his time. Maggie was quite upset by his response, but just then Louis stepped into the cockpit and said,

"Captain, you have raised yourself in my estimation by your frank statement to my mother that you had only read one of my books through and that you did not care for the others; if you had told her that you had read them all and liked them, as most people tell me whether or not, I will be as frank and tell you that I would have thought you lied."

Otis also found it somewhat disconcerting that Aunt Maggie made it an almost daily habit of taking her exercise by way of walking laps around the deck. The deck space between the coach roof and the very low bulwarks was narrow, and on rough days she could be seen lurching down the deck grabbing shrouds and halyards to steady herself. One day when Fanny and Captain Otis were on deck observing this precarious activity she asked Otis what he would do if her mother-in-law should fall overboard. The captain, who seldom disguised his irritation at some of the foibles of his passengers, dryly remarked "I'd put it in the log." And in response to a request by Fanny later in the day, Valentine tossed one of the saloon cushions up the companionway ladder. The cushion nearly went over the side; Louis turned to Otis with a sly smile and asked "Would you have put that in the log if it had gone over?" "Yes," answered the captain, "if you thought it worthwhile to send Valentine after it."

Stevenson, who fancied himself as knowing a bit about the sea and sailing ships, was not only concerned about the fact that they had only one celestial navigator aboard, but he had his doubts about the seaworthiness of their schooner as well. Knowing that the CASCO had been built primarily for racing in San Francisco Bay and limited coastal cruising, Louis communicated to the skipper his belief that the ship was "over-rigged and over-sparred." Otis was quick to straighten him out, revealing that there had been rigging changes before departure and that CASCO was now sporting her cruising rig, and was perfectly safe for ocean cruising. He made special mention of her capacity to be triple reefed in bad weather, her sea-kindly hull design, and her potential speed. Pointing out to Louis that she had covered 256 nautical miles on her first day out of San Francisco, he bragged that she could walk away from bad weather or anything afloat. This boast, however, was never repeated after July 5, their sixth day out of port, when a full-rigged English ship bound for Cape Horn overtook them and quickly sailed out of sight.

Otis also reminded the writer that the owner, Dr. Samuel Merritt, and a small crew under the command of Captain Colcord had taken the CASCO to Hawaii and Tahiti in 1880 with seven guests, five of whom were women. Otis assured Stevenson that on that voyage the CASCO had performed quite adequately and without serious incident. Otis insisted that except perhaps for the fisherman's staysail the CASCO was quite appropriately canvased for ocean travel. And he was right, for during the seven month duration of the cruise, water was taken into the cockpit but once.

Sunday July 1-fourth day out of port

The first Sunday of the cruise was marked by religious services in the cockpit attended by the Stevenson family and the crew at 4 o'clock. They were conducted by Louis at the request of his mother, much to the annoyance of Bert Otis who took a dim view of hymn singing old ladies and their dutiful psalm reading sons. The day was cloudy and squally and the worshipers were occasionally baptized by flying spray.

Saturday July 7-ten days out of port

The day was marked by a rapidly falling barometer that Otis speculated was the result of an approaching cyclonic storm. Attempting to bypass the center of the storm, the captain altered his course to the west, hoping against hope that he had estimated the course of the storm center correctly. Fortunately he had, but the next 30 hours were none the less marked by strong winds and heavy seas, and Otis, the only member of the ship's company sufficiently experienced to handle the ship in storm conditions such as these, spent most of that time at the wheel with little relief and with almost no time off for sleep.

During this stressful period the only person aboard who suffered any injury was Aunt Maggie, who, while sitting in the captain's chair in the dining saloon, was sent spinning and struck her head on the sofa when the CASCO was buffeted by a rogue wave. More embarrassed than injured, Maggie announced that her "hard Scottish head" was not hurt in the least. Nevertheless Louis banished the chair from the saloon for the duration of the passage.

Another ship in the general area had not been as fortunate as the CASCO. The bark TROPIC BIRD, which departed San Francisco two days after the CASCO, had not altered her course and had unfortunately sailed directly into the center of the storm, consequently suffering considerable damage—several crewmembers were injured and it lost an entire suit of sails.

July 13-14

After the storm, the CASCO had several days of good weather when the ship covered 200 nautical miles or more in 24-hour periods, but then calms, head seas, and easterly currents cut the CASCO's daily run to a mere 35 nautical miles. The yacht was now in the doldrums. Sails slatted and flapped, blocks groaned and booms swung aimlessly back and forth, freed from the pressure of the wind. The seas were glassy, with only great swells gently lifting and lowering the vessel. Breaking seas no longer partially obscured the horizon which now looked very far away, and the CASCO passengers felt very Lilliputian in a vast encircling watery world. The sails could not be depended upon to block out the sun and cast a cooling shadow on the cockpit. The thermometer registered 89° in the cabin, and it was hotter on deck. RLS gave up his stateroom, finding it cooler to sleep in the after saloon where the women's berths were located. His cabin was then quickly converted into a dressing room as well as a room for salt-water tub baths which all enjoyed each morning.

The women shed their Victorian frocks and even their shoes and donned their *muumuus* and *holakus*. They were very comfortable, but Maggie thought herself "a queer looking customer" in her Polynesian garb. After adopting her South Sea-style wardrobe, Fanny never wore any other type of clothing again. With her close-cropped hair and her chain smoking, she set a shocking example of the liberated woman. Maggie spent afternoons knitting Louis wool socks which, of course, he would never wear. Wide brim hats were brought out for protection for pale faces, and woolen clothing was packed away for the duration of the cruise. Captain Otis relaxed in the cockpit, whipping the ends of lines and repairing sails, and Maggie was intrigued by his use of the sail palm which she called "his thimble."

That night Louis excitedly announced that they had indeed reached the tropic South Seas as he pointed to a portion of the Southern Cross which appeared low on the horizon.

In one of their many discussions in the CASCO's cockpit Captain Otis made the statement to Louis that he must be terribly fond of the sea to have indebted himself to the tune of more than $3,500 for a charter sea voyage in a small pleasure yacht. Louis smiled and replied,

> Captain, I really think the sea is a terrible place and no one but yourself is probably more aware of its perils. Actually I regard this voyage as the highest form of gambling, and yet I love the sea as much as I hate gambling. You see, for the last ten years my health has been declining and when I decided to set forth on this voyage I believed that I was about to come to the final act of my life. I really had only a nurse or an undertaker to look forward to. I believed that a long cruise in warm sea waters would either cure me or hasten my death and if the latter occurred I wanted to be far enough from land so that I would be buried at sea. It is one of the reasons that I chose the Marquesas, 3,000 miles away, as an initial port of call. I wanted to begin with an extended voyage to settle my fate once and for all.
>
> And Captain, I think we must have been of like minds, since I know that you brought aboard everything necessary to accommodate me in the event of my demise—a canvas bag, a plank, lead weights and an extra Union Jack. And although I already told you I hate gambling I'm now betting that your ship and the South Seas are going to make a new man of me.

"Well, Mr. Stevenson, do you think the warm Pacific ocean air is working the way you hoped?" Louis reached down and picked up his journal which lay on the cockpit cushions and opened it to a page headed July 15.

"This is what I wrote earlier today. I will probably use this passage in a novel someday, but just between you and me, it is highly autobiographical." He read,

> Day after day, the air has the indescribable liveliness and sweetness, soft and nimble and cool as the cheek of health. Day after day, the sun flames, night after night the moon beckons, or the stars parade their lustrous regiment. I am aware of a spiritual change, or perhaps, rather a molecular reconstitution. My bones are sweeter to me. I have come to my own climate, and look back with pity on those damp and wintry zones, mis-called the temperate.

At that point Fanny, who had overheard the tail end of Otis and Louis's conversation while walking on deck, sat down in the cockpit, turned to Otis and said, "Yes, Captain, the other day when we had lost our wind and were making very little headway I watched Louis leaning over the bow dangling a fishing line and I thought to myself, 'I never thought I'd see him looking so well. His eyes were bright with relaxation and fun'." Fanny's demeanor and tone of voice clearly indicated that she also believed that the voyage had so far been well worth the price.

July 16

It had been a long and turbulent day marked by numerous squalls. The crew had been called out a half dozen times to shorten sail and then to shake out the reefs as the squalls passed over. It was late evening now and Louis sat alone in the saloon writing in his journal. The women and Lloyd had long since taken to their bunks, and it was quiet except for the creaking of the spars and the sound of rushing water surging past the hull. Stevenson closed his journal, laid down his pen, and climbed the companionway ladder leading to the cockpit. Time for one last cigarette before going to bed.

As he stepped through the hatchway into the cockpit, helmsman Charlie Wallin, the Finnish seaman, barely identifiable in the red glow of the binnacle lamp, said a courteous "Good evening, Mr. Stevenson. Come up for a smoke and a peek at the weather, did you?"

Louis laughed and commented that now that they were south of the equator the southwest trades were supposed to put them in what was usually called "the fine weather latitudes." As he spoke he looked up at the heavens and watched clouds darken the moon and then scurry past. Pointing toward the scud just ahead of the ship Stevenson repeated a traditional inquiry which he had heard the captain make repeatedly. "Is there any wind in them?"

"A cupful at least" came back the equally traditional answer. And then Wallin added, "But the moon is out now and we have little to fear."

"What's the moon got to do with it?"

"Well, Mr. Stevenson, don't you know that the moon is the sailor's friend. While she's up there she will 'eat the squalls' as they come by her as sure as you're born."

"I think you've got something there, Charlie," Louis responded. "I think I have noticed something like that myself. Clouds seem to scatter when the moon touches them, and the ship seems to be in a kind of protective magical circle when the moonlight floods down. Indeed there seems to be no dark and ominous shadows and no strong gusts of wind."

"I believe it, Mr. Stevenson." Then he added, "Let me tell you a little story about what happened when I was on a sugar brig in the Caribbean several years ago. We had a darky mate that went below and woke up the skipper to tell him a bad squall was comin' and the skipper told him to go to hell unless he had somethin' important to tell him. A little bit later the mate came back again and told the old man 'I swear, this squall is really a bad 'un Cap'n.' Then the skipper asked him, 'Is the moon up?' and when the mate said it was, the old man said 'Oh, she'll scoff it up. Now git out of here and leave me alone.' But not long afterwards the mate pounded on the old man's door again. 'Is that you again?' the skipper yelled. 'What the hell do you want now?' 'I don't want nothin, sah. I just wanted to tell ya that the moon done scoff up our fo'top's'l.'

Chuckling, Stevenson started to go below and said, "Well, Charlie, I guess there is always an exception to the rule."

July 27

The closest threat to calamity on the CASCO occurred just one day before the Marquesas were sighted. It involved, according to

Captain Otis, a "freak squall unlike anything he had ever seen." He later described the event:

> The squall, which was black as a cat, first passed the yacht to leeward; when well off the quarter, it suddenly turned and came down upon us, like the dropping of a cloak. All whips were let go, and the wheel was put hard down; but before the CASCO could be brought into the wind, she was struck and knocked down until the wind spilled out of her sails, and the edge of the house was under water, with the sea pouring over the cockpit like a torrent.

After the excitement of the day Captain Otis was spending a few moments in the evening relaxing in the cockpit before turning in for the day. He was about to go below when he was joined by Stevenson who always seemed to be the last of the passengers to hit the sack.

"Well, Mr. Stevenson, are you excited about our Marquesas arrival tomorrow? According to my star sights this evening, the strength of the wind and the nature of the sea, I would expect to raise Nuku Hiva between 5:00 and 6:00 a.m. Think you are up to such early hours?"

"I wouldn't miss it for the world, Captain. When you have waited all your life for your first Pacific island landfall, sleep seems very unimportant."

As was his habit throughout the voyage, Louis was indeed up bright and early, even before Captain Otis appeared on deck. It was a pleasant morning with a moderate sea and a good steady wind. Stevenson had taken a position out on the bowsprit where nothing could interfere with his view. In the half-light of the morning he scanned the horizon ahead, but for some time he was unable to make out anything but a great pile of clouds which seemed to merge with the greenish gray of the ocean. Other seamen joined Stevenson on the bowsprit, all squinting and straining to see what all normal sailors prize after a month at sea. Close to 5:30 a.m. Louis called out "Land, Land," as the apex of the cloud mass ahead dissolved, revealing the lofty peaks of Nuku Hiva, that magical isle where in 1842 Herman Melville and his shipmate Toby deserted ship and lived among the cannibals of Taipi valley for four adventurous weeks. To port, just barely visible on this misty morning was the island of

Ua Huka, smaller than Nuku Hiva but with steep mountainous slopes rising to 2,805 feet. To the south just beyond Nuku Hiva could be seen the extraordinary needles of Ua Pou, the 4,000-foot pinnacles of rock which Stevenson likened to steeples of "some ornate and monstrous church."

As the CASCO approached its destination it was as though a veil of moisture-laden clouds had suddenly been pulled aside to reveal the soaring heights of Nuku Hiva, with volcanic crags rising 3,000-4,000 feet in the center of the island. Along the north coast was a precipitous face of gray-black basalt with waterfalls plunging into the sea. To the east lay the Bay of Anaho, where the CASCO would anchor, bordered to port by a long narrow peninsula and to starboard by a 1,000-foot mountain. The bay, which was recessed a good mile and a half, would provide a relatively sheltered anchorage but could be uncomfortable when the wind came from the north and would send great swells surging through the bay. The low peninsula to the east would do little to protect the ship from easterly storms or high winds.

The CASCO moved slowly and deliberately into the bay with a seaman stationed at the crosstree surveying the bottom as they entered. The passage into the bay was fully a half-mile wide and the water was deep and dark blue in color. The chartreuse water, indicating coral reefs, appeared to hug the shore closely. Captain Otis had been advised to anchor in a spot to be identified by the gushing of a blow hole, and when they passed Point Mesange they spotted it, turned to starboard and dropped anchor on a sand bottom in eight fathoms of water just three hundred yards off the village of Anaho. The sails were furled, the awning rigged, the compass binnacle covered, and the ship's tender was lowered and tied up alongside. The CASCO had safely brought the Stevensons to their much anticipated first South Sea island. The first to comment was Maggie. With her usual exuberance and cheerful tone of voice she exclaimed, "The harbor is one of the loveliest spots imaginable, and the climate is delightful."

Louis descended the companionway ladder, entered his cabin, and finding his journal, described the morning activities:

> It was half-past five before we could distinguish our expected islands from the clouds on the horizon. The interval was passed on deck in silence of expectation, the customary thrill of

landfall heightened by the strangeness of the shores that we were approaching. Slowly they took shape in the attenuating darkness. The first experience can never be repeated. The first love, the first sunrise, the first South Sea Island, are memories apart and touched a virginity of sense.

Stevenson turned the page of his journal and wrote across the top of the next :

July 28, 1888. The Marquesas— our South Sea island adventure begins.

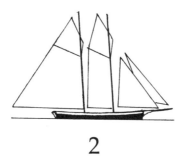

2
The Marquesas—The Land of Men

AFTER THE CREW had secured the CASCO, Stevenson sat for some time on the ship's coach roof surveying the breathtaking vista that was his first Pacific island anchorage. His eyes followed the encircling shoreline fringed with palms, their fronds rustling in the tradewinds. With the massiveness of the mountain slopes rising behind them, the palms looked dwarfed and insignificant. To the southeast was a soaring mountain ridge a thousand feet high and rising above it were lofty basaltic finger peaks three times that high. Louis calculated that the colors along the ridge "ran through fifty modulations in a scale of pearl and rose and olive." And all of it was crowned by iridescent clouds. To the east was the rich green of a tropical forest that covered a low pass leading to Haataivea Bay, and to the south, three or four miles inland, was the lush vegetation of a valley known as Taipivai, that infamous "cannibal land" where Herman Melville found refuge from the oppression of a whaling captain less that 50 years earlier.

What struck RLS most was the silence of the scene, broken only periodically by the lonely sound of swells breaking on the shore and the bleating of sheep on the hillside above Anaho village. The smell of the island was overpowering—like nothing he had ever experienced, not even in his beloved Scottish highlands. It was a mixture of the savor of fertile black earth, of the floral incense of exotic blossoms, of the acrid scent of morning wood fires used for baking breadfruit in the village, and all this tempered by the clean smell of tradewinds fresh from the sea. And then there was that wonderful aroma of freshly-brewed coffee drifting up from the galley below.

With all this beauty and tranquillity, Louis found it hard to imagine that such a paradise could have the notorious reputation of the "man-eating islands." He had chosen these islands as his initial port of call because their inhabitants had the reputation of being "less civilized" than most South Sea islanders. Contrary to expectations, however, everything about these islands looked extremely peaceful and benign.

In the handful of huts which were the village of Anaho and along the beach he could see no human activity. Only on the hillside above the village could a small boy be seen driving a great herd of sheep. But as he watched, the scene began to change. There was now some activity on the beach. A canoe was launched and it headed for the CASCO with two men aboard. When it arrived alongside, what appeared to be a European hailed the ship with,

"Captain, may we have permission to come aboard?"

Captain Otis, who was now at the ship's gangway, shouted back his permission, and soon the visitors were on deck introducing themselves and shaking hands with everyone. One was a German cotton planter and trader named Regler, dressed in a typical cotton pajama suit, and the other was a handsome, noble-looking chief—Taipi Kikino—six feet four in height, slender and muscular, with broad shoulders. He was dressed in a spotless white linen coat and trousers, but the most striking feature about him was his beautifully tattooed face. His countenance was embellished with an intriguing display consisting of a horizontal bluish-black stripe across the eyes plus adjacent horseshoe forms, concentric arcs and single spirals.

Not far behind these initial greeters was a whole fleet of canoes loaded with Marquesans of both sexes who did not bother to ask permission to come aboard but swarmed over the rails and immediately began admiring the many features of the beautiful little yacht. Somewhat frightened at first by the number and inquisitiveness of the islanders who came aboard, and with the idea always in the back of their minds that these people were but a step removed from warlike cannibals, the Stevensons soon learned that they had nothing to fear. In fact, in his first letter from the Marquesas to his lifelong friend Sidney Colvin, Louis revealed that although he had chosen to come to these islands because they were renowned for having a most "beastly population," he had found them "more civilized than we are."

This opinion was to some extent a reaction on the part of

RLS to his embarrassment for having initially committed a series of violations of Marquesan etiquette. While respectful of Marquesan lifeways, Stevenson had, in his cultural naiveté, insulted the people by standing in their presence when they were seated, thereby having his head higher than theirs. Equally offensive to the islanders was Louis's practice of continuing to write in his journal while guests were present. They also thought it strange that this white man failed to join them in clapping hands at the start of their welcoming *kava* drinking ceremony. But perhaps the most damaging of his cross-cultural blunders was that his gifts to the people apparently were not presented formally enough. On one occasion the gifts were left untouched on the beach for this very reason. Then there was the time when Louis insulted a man by offering to pay for a drinking coconut to quench his thirst, because he did not understand that drinking nuts were always offered to guests as a token of good will and not as a commodity to be purchased.

Once past the confusion and irritations of dealing with a totally exotic culture, RLS began to admire the Marquesans for their dignity and reserve. Even one famous old chief, Ko'oamua, who had the reputation of being "one who ate his enemies (usually a hand or a severed arm) as he walked home from killing them" was pronounced "a perfect gentleman and exceedingly amiable."

As they came aboard, the Marquesans were courteous and cordial, offering *"kaoha"* (the equivalent of the Hawaiian *"aloha"*), laughing and shaking hands all around. The women wore long flowered *holakus*, but their feet were bare and tattooed with elaborate patterns, and as they walked with graceful strides they exposed their tattooed ankles, the designs giving the appearance of open-work silk stockings. This very much impressed Maggie and Fanny who joked about their pale white legs which contrasted so markedly with those of the Marquesan women. But Maggie did manage to attract a good deal of attention herself with her lace gloves, which one chief called "British tattooing." He borrowed them, repeatedly putting them on and holding up his hands so he could admire them.

Perhaps the most startling event associated with the display of the Marquesan body art occurred when one of the chiefs, somewhat intoxicated by convivial rum from the after cabin, was asked by the Stevensons if he would show them his tattoos. He immediately removed his scanty tapa cloth wraparound and stood before them stark naked with a look of great pride on his face. Neither Fanny nor Maggie appeared embarrassed and pronounced the display "a most beautiful sight."

Regler, who with Chief Taipi Kikino, was the first to come aboard in Anaho Bay when the CASCO arrived, was the only white man in the village, and his offer of help in acquiring fresh food for the ship's passengers and crew was greatly appreciated. He and Captain Otis departed in his outrigger canoe and returned with a welcome bounty of milk, chickens, fruit and pork.

Shortly after Regler returned to the village the CASCO was visited by several canoes laden with fruits of all kinds, pieces of tapa cloth, and what the Stevensons considered "poorly made baskets." Since the ship was already well-supplied with island produce, and because the curios were of inferior quality and priced too high, Louis and his family were showing little interest. After a great deal of bargaining, the author bought only a few bananas, but as a gesture of good will, he invited the merchants aboard and had the steward serve them biscuits and chocolate. Having thoroughly enjoyed their treats, one of the island salesmen managed to communicate to his hosts that "it is a very beautiful ship to have so little money aboard."

In his journal Stevenson described his role as official greeter and tour director, citing some of the island visitors' impressions of this magnificent sailing ship. "I was the showman of the CASCO," he wrote,

> She, her fine lines, tall spars, and snowy decks, the crimson fittings of the saloon, and the white, the gilt, and the repeating mirrors of the tiny cabin, brought us a hundred visitors. The men fathomed her dimensions with their arms, as their fathers fathomed out the ships of Cook; the women declared the cabin more lovely than a church; bouncing Junos (i.e., women of rank) were never weary of sitting in the chairs and contemplating in the glass their own bland images; and I have seen one lady strip up her dress, and with cries of wonder and delight, rub herself bare-breeched upon the velvet cushions.

The Stevensons accepted their exotic visitors as few Victorian Europeans would. Each of the family members had his or her own special qualities which allowed them to relate easily to these Polynesian people.

Louis, of course, more than most men of his times, had a capacity for accepting people who were different, regardless of whether it involved differences in race, culture or status. In San Francisco's Chinatown he was repelled by Caucasian attitudes toward resident Chinese, particularly when they were forced to share cable cars. He had never been in a situation where he observed such prejudice based on color, and since he personally respected the Chinese for their ancient culture, he considered the attitudes of his fellow Caucasians to be stupid and ill-mannered.

Fanny, who, during her previous marriage to Samuel Osbourne, had lived a pioneer existence in such Wild West mining towns as Virginia City, and whose dusky appearance often caused people to suspect her of being a Gypsy or part Mexican, could be described as warm-hearted and accepting of the racially and culturally different.

Lloyd, in his youthful pursuit of adventure, accepted the interaction with these native peoples as one more exciting episode in his ever-unfolding life scenario. Maggie, with her missionary enthusiasm, considered these new-found folks yet another variety of God's children to be accepted and loved in spite of their differences. She even commented to Louis that "their conduct to each other and to strangers, so far as kindness and courtesy is concerned, is much more Christ-like than that of many professing Christians."

In the late 1800s, such liberal attitudes were most uncharacteristic of Europeans. Even the anthropologists of that day could not bring themselves to consider island peoples such as the Marquesans as equals or even as entirely human. The famous American anthropological scholar Lewis Henry Morgan, a top theorist of his day and author of *Ancient Society*, in 1877 defined Polynesians as representatives of a state of cultural development which he labeled "Middle Savagery." Such peoples were described as being "underdeveloped, inexperienced and held down . . . by low animal appetites and passions." According to Morgan, "they existed in a low state of development, left in isolated sections of the earth as monuments of the past."

On their second day in port the Stevensons were honored by a visit from the notorious Ko'oamua, the chief with the reputation of once having been the island's foremost cannibal. When this honored elder—now wealthy, peace-loving, and the owner of a fine European house wherein he often entertained the governor—came aboard, he looked every inch a cannibal. His only garment was a strip of tapa barkcloth around his waist and from the top of his head to the soles of his feet he was a wonderful exhibit of the tattooer's art. After greeting the family cordially and presenting a gift of island fruits, he managed to communicate his desire to see everything this elegant sailing ship contained. He closely examined Captain Otis's rifle (which he admired), Lloyd's fiddle (which didn't impress him much), and he marveled at the carved woodwork and the polished mirrors in the saloon below. But most of all he was fascinated with Louis's typewriter, and once he saw how it worked he requested that Lloyd show him how to type out his genealogy, which he claimed would give him a permanent record of his ancestry that he could mount on his wall. Stevenson was soon to learn that this elderly chieftain who appeared so much the savage was a very important figure in the local government, serving as a consultant on everything from legal disputes to agricultural and trade issues. Even the missionaries respected his opinions. And he hadn't been known to eat anyone for at least a decade.

At their very first contact with the people the Stevenson family acquired special names, as names are extremely important to Marquesans, and one of their foremost customs of respect is trading names with people they admire. This would occur at another Marquesan port of call on the island of Hiva Oa.

RLS was at first referred to as *Ko'oua*, "the old man," a title of respect in this culture where status increases with age, but later his name was changed to "*Ona*," meaning wealthy owner of the CASCO. Fanny was merely called *Vahine* "wife;" Maggie was honored with the title "*Pakahio*," "old woman," and Lloyd was dubbed *Mata kalahi*, "the young man with glass eyes (spectacles)."

During the stay at Anaho there were numerous visits ashore—for shelling, hiking, and most fun of all, meeting their Marquesan neighbors who almost always asked them to stay for a meal. The menu was often much the same—roast breadfruit dipped in coconut cream, raw fish caught daily in the bay, lobsters, crabs and shrimps, and pork from the small pigs that ran freely in the village and lived with the families like pet dogs. Prior to the meal, however, there was invariably a welcoming *kava* ceremony. Here the dried roots of the Piper methysticum plant were pulverized through mastication and steeped in a large wooden bowl to produce a khaki-colored potion, the drinking of which was sacred to the ancient Polynesian gods and believed vital to the maintenance of the social order. The drink, which was mildly narcotic and tasted much like old wood, was always given first to guests as a sign of respect. Since some islanders sometimes overindulged in the drink, it was high on the missionary and government lists as a custom to be stamped out.

At one of these Marquesan meals the Stevensons were served *ka'aku*, a very tasty pudding made of baked breadfruit and coconut cream. Everyone shared a communal bowl and ate with their fingers and were then offered what Fanny described as a "finger bowl" to cleanse their hands. Fanny was so impressed with the confection that the very next day she collected a large mixing bowl and a beater and headed in for the beach to try her hand at making it.

Her first stop was Mr. Regler's store to acquire the proper ingredients, and while he had coconuts, he had no breadfruit. Whereupon a Marquesan farmer in the store selling Regler his cotton rushed home and brought two back. He was somewhat insulted by offers of payment, feeling that food is to be given, not sold, but seemed delighted to be able to supply even more breadfruit than Fanny required. He was also pleased when invited to the *ka'aku* feast which would follow.

While the breadfruit was baking in an open fire in back of the store, green coconut meat was grated to a fine pulp, mixed with the clear water from the young nut, and then squeezed through a piece of cheesecloth. When the breadfruit was completely baked, the rind was removed and the pulp was crushed in the manner of mashed potatoes. Finally the coconut cream was poured over it in Fanny's mixing bowl. After sampling the finished product, Regler declared it "excellent," passed out spoons to all in the store and then sat back to watch the enjoyment of the Polynesian treat. As the last bit of *ka'aku* disappeared, Fanny announced to everyone that she now had her first recipe for what would be her South Sea Island cookbook.

A few days after the CASCO's arrival in Anaho Bay Louis and

Captain Otis were ashore for some after-lunch exploring; and Maggie and Fanny were spending the afternoon at their favorite bathing place, searching for shell treasures and enjoying the soothing warm water as it washed across the beach and bubbled about their feet. About 4:30 the CASCO's tender arrived to pick them up, and as they headed for the schooner Maggie commented that the CASCO appeared to have altered its position, but then her attention was diverted to the shore where Mr. Regler was signaling that they should call at the village before going back to the ship. When they reached the village they found a young, pleasant-looking man in white shirt and trousers wearing a black alpaca coat and a black tie. He introduced himself as Chief Kapiau of Atuatua, a village in the bay to the east of Anaho. He asked if he might pay a visit to the yacht, but when permission was granted, he asked if they might first go across the bay where he could pick up a gift he wanted to present to them. When they reached that destination they found the chief's wife and three brothers-in-law in charge of the gift, which was a live pig and 14 coconuts.

With everything aboard the tender they headed back toward the ship, but suddenly to everyone's alarm, they could see that the vessel was dragging anchor and drifting seaward. It also was drifting toward the most rocky section of the shoreline. Apparently no one on board was aware of the danger, for there was not a soul on deck. The crew of the tender shipped their oars and set a sail in an attempt to reach the ship before it went on the rocks. When the tender was within hailing distance one of the boat crew shouted "Ahoy CASCO! You're drifting ashore!" Within minutes they were alongside, where Captain Otis, very pale and agitated, began shouting orders. The crew aboard the CASCO hoisted a sail while the boat crew secured a line to the schooner and rowed with all their strength to move the ship into deep water. The women and Lloyd were ordered to take the visitors below and keep them occupied and out of the way. It was a terrifying experience being below deck where they could only hear running and shouting on deck but where they had no knowledge of the effectiveness of the activity being carried on over their heads. Then the order came down, "Lloyd, bring the chief and the other men up on deck. We need their help." Lloyd and the four Marquesans were on deck in a matter of seconds and were put to work lending a hand at the windlass in order to raise the anchor which had apparently fouled. CASCO had two anchors down, the large fisherman's anchor and a smaller kedge anchor, which were set so the two anchor rodes formed a 60° angle. Ordinarily this would have provided extra security, but a sudden unexpected shift in the wind caused the ship to swing, making the anchor lines foul and break their anchors loose from their hold on the bottom.

In what seemed an eternity, but in reality consumed but a few moments, the ship was able to move away from the threatening shoreline with the help of the tender's oarsmen and the ship's emergency sail. The anchors were reset and CASCO was now out of danger.

Otis came forward and thanked the local benefactors who leaned against the rail breathing heavily and perspiring but clearly enjoying the fact that they had helped save this beautiful sailing ship. Otis immediately called for the steward to bring wine, ship's biscuit and plugs of tobacco for the young men, and he personally presented each of them a shiny new American half dollar.

That evening a much chagrined Captain Otis confessed to Louis, Fanny and Lloyd that he had returned from ashore and had been below eating an early supper when the calamity occurred, and while eating he had been admiring the view through a porthole of a peculiar peak he had not noticed before, but he had not been aware that the ship was dragging toward the shore until hailed from the tender.

Although the runaway schooner incident reminded the Stevensons that they were indeed involved in some high adventure not without danger, the most disturbing incident in this port of call from Fanny's perspective took place two days later in connection with a shelling expedition along the Anaho Bay shoreline.

On this particular occasion both Louis and Fanny were exploring the beach, intrigued by the vast variety of shapes and colors of the millions of cones, cowries, cat's eyes, cockles, mother-of-pearl shells, and pieces of coral. After perhaps an hour's search in the shallow water of the beach the two of them sat down on the sand to rest and were immediately approached by a Marquesan who stepped out from the line of coconut trees that fringed the shore. Louis promptly motioned for him to join them and when he did, offered him a cigarette which Stevenson lit and passed to the man to share, as was the Polynesian custom. The man accepted the cigarette, took a puff or two and returned it to Louis for his turn. As the writer accepted the cigarette he noticed that the hand returning it was the disfigured extremity of a leper. To his wife's horror Stevenson calmly took the cigarette, put it to his lips and finished smoking it.

After the leper left, Fanny regaled Louis for his foolhardy behavior, and asked him why in heaven's name had he behaved so irresponsibly. RLS merely said, "I couldn't mortify the man. And if you think I *liked* it. That was another reason; because I didn't want to."

This was not to be their only encounter with this dreaded disease which many claimed was brought to the islands by Chinese coolie laborers in the 1860s. A few days later a messenger came by the CASCO one morning in a whaleboat requesting that the Stevensons come and see if they might have some idea what strange ailment had beset a young white girl living in a nearby village. Braving a high wind and a choppy sea, Louis and Fanny set out immediately in the CASCO's tender. They had packed a lunch which they ate on the beach when they landed and then proceeded to the house where they were told the sick child lived.

As they approached the house the child's mother came out to greet them and invited them to have lunch with her, stating, "I have a most excellent cook; here he is now." The cook she so proudly introduced was an elderly Chinese who was obviously in an advanced stage of leprosy. When the man left the room Louis asked the woman if she were not afraid of contagion. And she answered, "I don't believe in contagion." "Well, Madam," replied Stevenson, "I am sorry to inform you that I am certain that your daughter is suffering from leprosy and I can only advise you to take her to Santa Maria Bay where there is a doctor who can advise you what can be done for her."

As the Stevensons returned to the beach where the CASCO's tender awaited, they were very depressed and said very little to one another except "Aren't you glad we ate before we arrived."

That evening, however, while Louis and Fanny sat on deck enjoying a cool breeze coming in from the sea, Louis began talking about Father Damien, a priest he had read about, who had dedicated his life to the care of lepers on the island of Molokai in Hawaii. "I understand that Damien has an advanced case of leprosy himself, and when we reach Hawaii I want to meet this man. I hope I am not too late. I must see Molokai. I must somehow manage to see Molokai."

The weather at Anaho was nearly perfect, and Louis had almost completely forgotten what it meant to be ill. His appetite was robust, and his color was remarkable for a man who had spent much of his life indoors nursing a cough or a cold. In a letter to a friend he wrote, "I am browner than the berry. Only my trunk and the aristocratic spot on which I sit retain the vile whiteness of the north." Above all he was living a life he had always dreamed of; one where he could live and write and explore the world without pain and fear.

Each night the entire Stevenson clan, and occasionally even Captain Otis, would relax on deck, enjoying the gentle breeze from the sea which made crinkly patches of catspaws on the water. And then there was that fragrant scent of the island—of the flowering trees and the island greenery—accompanied by the gentle whisper of the tradewinds passing through the palms along the shore and muffling the lonely sound of water breaking on the strand. After the sunset colors faded from the sky above the soaring mountains around the bay, the reflection of lanterns being lit in the village sparkled on the black-enamel surface of the bay. On evenings such as this Stevenson could not help but be reminded of his beloved Scottish highlands.

His diary for August 3, under the heading of *Tropical Night Thoughts* reads as follows,

> I could have fancied I had slipped ten thousand miles away and was anchored in a Highland loch that when the day come, it would show pine and heather, and green fern, and roofs of turf sending up the smoke of peats; and the alien speech that should next greet my ears must be Gaelic, not Kanaka. The Highland and Islands somewhat more than a century back were in much the same convulsive and transitionary state as the Marquesas today. In the one, the cherished habit of tattooing; in the other, a cherished costume, proscribed; in both, the men disarmed, the chiefs dishonoured, new fashions introduced, and chiefly that new pernicious fashion of regarding money as the be-all and end-all of existence.

Nearly as good an anthropological researcher as he was a man of literature, Stevenson took advantage of every opportunity to observe native life, sample the local cuisine, collect myths and legends, and ask questions of specialists about arts and crafts, historical traditions, religion, and social and political structure. Louis was especially well-known as a good listener, believing he had something to learn from everybody. In the Marquesas he found the people to be responsive, courteous, generous with their time, sensitive, and above all, excellent mentors on matters that he desperately wanted to understand.

Stevenson found the Marquesans physically very attractive, perhaps the handsomest race in the Pacific, and certainly one of the most noble. The men averaged nearly six feet in height, with slender but muscular bodies, huge arms and barrel-like chests, and in spite of their size he found they had the ability to move swiftly and gracefully. Moreover, he described them as having kind, fine-featured faces.

The women were considerably shorter in height but slender and well-formed. Stevenson perhaps revealed an ethnocentric bias, however, when he described them as quite pretty and more European looking than most Pacific islanders.

As the author researched their traditional cultural lifeways by questioning elders concerning how things were in the good old days, he learned that before the coming of the white man Marquesans had no concept of private land. Villagers owned land communally and everyone worked it under the direction of their chiefs. When the chiefs were deposed by the French, there was no leadership and no will to compete with the white man, who quickly acquired the land and attempted to institute his work ethic. The *tuhuna nui*, or mastercraftsmen, who traditionally had produced tapa cloth, stone carvings, canoes and chiefs' houses, operated under a guild system that involved them working with their apprentices and journeymen. Now the *tuhuna nui* were gone, and the people either had no interest or saw no advantage in accepting the white man's system, which might bring them property and wealth but no self-esteem or pride of accomplishment.

Louis's investigations into aboriginal culture unearthed facts concerning the gender system which Fanny and Maggie both found somewhat troubling. Traditionally this island culture attributed some degree of sanctity to all males, but ordinary women (that is to say those not directly connected with a chief's family) were regarded as secular. Nuku Hiva, he found, had been a major site of male spiritual authority, but throughout all of the Marquesan islands men were less inhibited by ritual prohibitions than women. Women were subject to numerous *tapu*, which only at the time of the Stevenson visit were being relaxed or totally done away with.

Traditionally, women could not sit on the *paepae* (i.e., stone foundation) in front of a house, nor could they approach it by the masonry stairway. They were forbidden to eat pork, and could not cook with a fire kindled by a man. They were not allowed to walk on man-made roads or use a bridge men had built. They could not approach a boat, let alone ride in one. The use of a canoe by a woman was punishable by death in Melville's time. However, a woman holding a chief's title was exempt from the depressive litany of prohibitions. Even at the time of Stevenson's visit, he would record in his journal that, "*Tapu* encircled women on all hands. Many things were forbidden to men; to women we may say few were permitted." But without question the *tapu* system had been much more oppressive in the past—when Melville was in residence.

As RLS learned more and more about the traditional ways of these island people he began to believe that their reputation for being obsessively cannibalistic was a fallacy resulting from the ignorance and ethnocentrism of Western observers and the opportunism of writers such as Herman Melville, who found accounts of living among "man-eating savages" a highly marketable commodity. In the limited library of historical literature on the South Seas which Louis had brought with him he also found contradictory evidence regarding the practice. For example, the U.S. naval officer David Porter in 1812–13 maintained that the Marquesans' "gentle and dignified personality was not compatible with cannibalism," while Melville (1842) accepted the fact that they were cannibals, but "in other respects humane and virtuous."

Although there were reports of soldiers, sailors and beachcombers in the 1840s being killed and eaten, this was discounted by others who claimed that it was common knowledge that

"Marquesans did not eat white men, because they found them too salty."

Most historians and anthropologists agreed that Marquesan cannibalism was associated with warfare, human sacrifice and other aspects of religion. It was generally believed that human flesh was not consumed as food, but that the eating was always for revenge or as a symbol of contempt for the enemy. Violators of a *tapu* were often condemned to death by the tribal *tau'a*, or priest, and taken to the *me'ae* (ceremonial center) where they would be killed and eaten, often by the *tau'a*.

Tau'a were extremely powerful religious leaders who were basically sorcerers and soothsayers, interpreting the will of the gods concerning human sacrifice or going to war. They are described as unkempt men of prophecy, who were characteristically subject to violent possessions by deities or spirits. When one of these men died it was believed that several victims (often captives from another tribe) were required as sacrifices. After being put to death, their bodies were dismembered and placed in an oven in preparation for ceremonial eating by other priests.

The Marquesan reputation for cannibalism served the white man well. It reduced the incidence of desertion from whaling ships that called at the islands for food and water, it tended to increase financial support from home for missionaries who would civilize these "savages," and it made greedy and often ruthless colonial administrations in the islands look good in comparison with their "murdering, man-eating vassals." Stevenson, who tended to take a liberal view of Marquesan peccadilloes, wondered why these people had been specially singled out for their flesh-eating habits when such practices had also been carried on in Tahiti, Hawaii, Samoa and New Zealand.

Stevenson's journal contained an interesting account of meeting his first missionary in Nuku Hiva, Père Simeon. He wrote,

> I had feared to meet a missionary, feared to find the narrowness and self-sufficiency that deface their publications, that too often disgrace their behavior. There was no fear of it here; Père Simeon admired these natives as I do myself, admired them with spiritual envy; the superior of his congregation had said to him on his departure: "You are going among a people more

civilised than we." What then was Père Simeon doing here? The question rose in my mind. . . . Truly they were a people, on the whole, of a mind far [more like] Christ's than any of the races of Europe. . . . A kindness, a generosity, a readiness to give and to forgive, without parallel.

Shortly after meeting Père Simeon, Louis was invited to come to the village of Hatiheu and see the "university of the north islands" which was a school for boys, ages 9 to 15, taught by Catholic Brothers and Priests. Hatiheu was located in the next bay west of Anaho, and the two bays were separated by the "knife edge of a single hill" which could be traversed by a trail through heavy bush-covered land. It was an hour's undertaking at best, but Stevenson wisely chose to make the trip by whaleboat with an islander crew. Hatiheu Bay was less sheltered than Anaho Bay, and consequently the sandy beach was pounded by heavy surf which spewed spray and mist all along the village shoreline with its flowering trees and colorful shrubbery. Two or three dozen houses and the boys' school buildings were located along a beach road, and on the west end of the village three basaltic spires towered a thousand feet in the air. On the peak furthest to the left a speck of white could be seen at the very summit. It was a Madonna figure which had been sculpted by a Brother named Michel Blanc 16 years earlier. Brother Michel had also designed and built the village church which was made of stone with twin towers and a front entrance enhanced with carvings of angels, cherubs and gargoyles. Louis's day in Hatiheu consisted not only of visiting the school and meeting artist-architect Brother Michel, but being personally escorted by him on a tour of the ancient ceremonial grounds which lay approximately a mile behind the village. They toured the ancient *tohua* Hikokua (ceremonial grounds) with its dance floor, stone terraces, platforms, and tikis, but also the Kamuihei *me'ae* (sacred place) with its huge petroglyph-decorated boulders shaded by huge banyan trees. It had been a wonderful, exciting day, and several years later when asked what his favorite village was in the Marquesas, the author responded, "By all means, Hatiheu."

While Stevenson was not a religious man, he did find the missionaries, originally encouraged by French authorities to "soften up the savages," the least of the European villains. Throughout his residence in Polynesia Stevenson made many friends among both Catholic and Protestant missionaries, believing them to be the only white men honestly trying to improve the life of the people. Although he opposed many missionary goals, such as the banning of native dress habits, traditional ceremonials, dancing and tattooing, he also saw them as protectors rather than exploiters of Polynesians. It had been the politicians, the traders, the labor recruiters, the beachcombers and the whaling crews who had exploited the people for economic gain and sexual pleasure. Island colonization had brought smallpox, leprosy, syphilis, alcoholism, opium addiction, and disillusionment with the French administration, resulting in psychological depression, a decline in the will to live, and a dramatic reduction in the population from 100,000 to less than 9,000 in a 65-year period in the nineteenth century.

One of the reasons for calling first at the Marquesas was the curiosity created in Louis when his friend Charles Warren Stoddard loaned him Herman Melville's book *Typee* some ten years earlier. Anxious to see the valley of the Taipi where Melville lived among the Taipi tribe for several weeks, Louis immediately set out on an expedition to see for himself the locale of the "cannibals" so dramatically described by Melville. Stevenson found little in the way of Taipi villages, in fact, almost no one seemed to inhabit the region at all. "Civilization" had been too much for them. RLS was much depressed over what he observed to be Marquesan depopulation and believed it the result of "the coming of the whites, the change of habits, and the introduction of new maladies (syphilis) and vices (opium)."

In regard to the impact of Western culture, Stevenson revealed himself as somewhat of a theoretical anthropologist when he formulated a general law that for him seemed to explain what had happened to the paradise that was Polynesia since the coming of the white man. He maintained that "where there have been fewest changes, important or unimportant, salutary or hurtful, there the race survives. Where there have been most, important or unimportant, salutary or hurtful, there it perishes;" and he believed that the rate of change was as important as the amount of change.

Louis had carefully studied Herman Melville's account of living among the Taipi natives on the island of Nuku Hiva; and prior to CASCO's departure from San Francisco he also discovered through library research that a number of competent observers had described life on the islands between 1812 and 1832 with details covering the social system, religious beliefs, warfare and cannibalism. The majority of these observers were sea captains, military men, or missionaries who had spent many months and even years in the Marquesas. So armed, he felt himself better able to relate to the experiences described by Melville.

Upon arrival in the islands it was not long before Stevenson became aware of Melville's inadequacies as an observer of the native culture by his incapacity to record the language properly. Commenting on the American author's "grotesque misspelling of *Hapar*," the valley and the tribe which should have been spelled *Hapaa*, and his spelling *Typee* for *Taipi*, Stevenson sarcastically wrote

> At [Melville's] christening some influential fairy must have been neglected. "He shall be able to see." "He shall be able to tell," "He shall be able to charm," said the friendly godmother. "But he shall not be able to hear."

This comment is known to have irritated a number of literary critics who felt that Melville had superior knowledge of the South Seas, having lived among the islanders and participated in their way of life, while Stevenson was merely a tourist passing through. But the more Stevenson compared the Melville book with his own research and observations of Marquesan culture and history, the more he found errors which went beyond mere errors in name recording. First of all, he noted that the title of Melville's book was *Typee: A Peep at Polynesian Life during a Four Months' Residence in a Valley of the Marquesas*, but in reading elsewhere about the young man's adventure he noted that Captain Valentine Pease's affidavit of Melville's desertion from the whaler ACUSHNET of Fairhaven was dated July 9, 1842, and his escape from the *Taipis* took place in the middle of August 1842, when he was taken aboard the whaler LUCY ANN. In other words, the "four month's residence" in the valley of the Marquesas, specified in the title of Melville's book, was actually only slightly longer than five weeks, hardly enough time to account for the volume of relatively accurate ceremonial details described by the author, who incidentally had almost no knowledge of the language. As Louis traveled further in the Pacific, he met others who also questioned the validity of Melville's account. Some believed that much of the cultural data had been lifted from the 1829 edition of missionary William Ellis's *Polynesian Researches*. Others suspected that Captain David Porter's *A Voyage to the South Seas in the Years 1812–1814*, or C. S. Stewart's *Visit to the South Seas* (1832) had been heavily drawn upon also.

Regardless of who collected the ethnographic facts, however, most students of Polynesian culture recognize *Typee* as a fairly accurate picture of Marquesan life except where Melville distorts the facts to increase his book's salability. His relationship with the Marquesan girl Fayaway is an example. He describes how he and the girl were sailing in an outrigger canoe on a lake in Taipi Valley when she removing her tapa-cloth wraparound, using it as a sail, with her nude body functioning as the mast. Undoubtedly such a lurid episode enhanced the book's sales among red-blooded young men of that day, but it runs contrary to credible fact. To begin with, there has never been a lake in Taipi Valley, and in 1842 it was *tapu* for young women to even ride in an outrigger canoe, although Melville maintains she had special dispensation from the chief to accompany him on this afternoon frolic. *Tapu*, especially one involving a death penalty for violation by women, were not that easily set aside at that time in Marquesan history.

While Stevenson became highly skeptical of the validity of the Melville classic, it did raise a number of provocative questions in Louis's mind. For example, Melville's claims of Marquesan cannibalism was an issue that RLS spent a good deal of time researching.

As the CASCO's date of departure was drawing near, misfortune descended upon the Stevensons. Lloyd's one and only camera, seen as terribly important in documenting Stevenson's trip for possible future articles and lecture trips, slipped out of its carrying case and was lost overboard as Lloyd was climbing the ship's ladder on his return from shore.

The farewell visit to the CASCO two days before she was to sail by nine Marquesan friends was dramatic and somewhat puzzling to the Stevensons. Included in the party were Taipi Kikino, the young chief who had initially boarded the CASCO upon its arrival, and Hoka, Anaho's chief dancer and singer, who was the adoptive son of Toma, a man who saw himself as the rightful traditional chief of Anaho village. In the party also were the villagers who had arrived by canoe and attempted to sell food and curios to the Stevensons upon their arrival. Although they appeared insulted at that time by their inability to sell their wares at what the Stevensons considered exorbitant prices, these same objects were now presented to the family as gifts. The only one of their new-found Marquesan friends missing was Chief Ko'oamua, Stevenson's prize example of a once-practicing cannibal. Later it was reported that villagers found him passed out and draped over a low-lying limb of a tree, the victim of trader's rum used as currency for payment for the chief's copra. Ko'oamua would have liked to have been present at the farewell party. He had just started celebrating too soon.

As Louis recalled, this farewell visit was not protracted. He wrote,

> One after another they shook hands and got down into their canoe; then Hoka (the dancer) turned his back immediately upon the ship, so that we saw his face no more. Taipi, [the more acculturated Marquesan] on the other hand, remained standing and facing us with gracious valedictory gestures; and when Captain Otis dipped the ensign, the whole party saluted with their hats. This was the farewell; the episode of our visit to Anaho was held concluded; and though the CASCO remained nearly forty hours at her moorings, not one returned on board, and I am included to think they avoided appearing on the beach. This reserve and dignity is the finest trait of the Marquesan.

What must have been very depressing to Louis who always wanted to do the thing that was culturally correct was that the gifts that he had distributed to the islanders whom he had come to respect and cherish as friends were left on the beach because he still had not learned the proper protocol for gift-giving among these very tradition-sensitive people.

On August 12, with the help of a Marquesan-rowed long-boat, the CASCO eased its way out of the harbor, then hoisted sail and began its progress toward Taiohae along the rocky headlands where the foam and mist of crashing breakers created arching rainbows high above. The passage, with the trader Regler as pilot, was a difficult one, lasting eight hours with high winds and heavy seas. This was taken in stride by the CASCO, but the passengers and crew, who no longer had their sea legs, fared badly. The weather moderated somewhat as their course took them south along the east coast of Nuka Hiva. They now were on a broad reach with the trades greatly aiding the speed and comfort of their passage until they reached Cape Tikapo at the southeast tip of the island. Here they turned west and ran past the mouth of Controller Bay. The bay had long served as a protective haven from the weather for whaling ships. Rocky capes projected into the bay creating three narrow coves, well sheltered from the prevailing winds. With its 40- to 50-foot depths and a good holding bottom of mud and sand, it was ideal for visiting ships.

The CASCO, however, was going on to Taiohae Bay, 5 miles to the west, which was also a safe anchorage. It was here that the whaler ACUSHNET arrived with Herman Melville in 1842 and where he deserted ship escaping to Taipi valley, the notorious land believed by some to be the home of the most hostile of the Marquesan tribes. As the CASCO approached its destination, the voyagers found the mouth of the bay flanked by two gigantic bare rock islets, which appeared on the chart as *Sentinelle de l'Ouest* and *Sentinelle de l'Est.* A mile and a half up a horseshoe-shaped bay, which Stevenson noted was big enough to accommodate the whole French fleet, was located the village of Taiohae on the eastern shore. On the west a rocky slope was capped by a great volcanic lava plug. But here and there, where the soil had lodged in crevices, palms and other tropical vegetation provided a splash of vivid green to the otherwise gray-black of the stone. The setting was breathtaking in its beauty, but Stevenson, like many who would follow him to this spot, was depressed by the silence and the sadness of the scene.

Taiohae, described by Louis as "the civil, religious and market capital of the Marquesas," lay on the eastern shore of the bay and consisted of a thin line of white houses nearly hidden by the foliage of a grove of hibiscus trees and a line of lofty palms which bordered the beach. On the slope of a hill above the town was the residence of the colonial administrator with its flagpole proudly flying the French tricolor. A long pier jutted out into the bay, and a short distance beyond, a government revenue schooner lay at anchor.

As Louis was surveying the magnificence of his second South Sea port of call, Regler came up from below and addressed the author:

> Not a very impressive capital city is it, Mr. Stevenson? Over there on that hill to the right of the wharf is Government House and close beside it are the ruins of old Fort Collet which now serves as a jail. To the left is the home of Queen Vaekehu, who really isn't a queen any more but is still a very interesting old gal. I'm sure that you will get to meet her and her son while you're here. They claim that she was once a powerful force in the islands, some say even a cannibal, before the Catholic missionaries arrived and converted her. After her conversion the priests had her cancel the *tapu* system that applied mostly to women, and the French administration set her up as a kind of royal puppet or figurehead. The only good thing about this burg is that there are a couple of good saloons where a guy can relax and get away from trying to put up with these lazy Kanakas all day long.

As was true of many Marquesan villages, even the capital seemed devoid of native people, particularly children. Later they would learn that the Catholic missionaries established separate boarding schools on different islands for boys and girls, thereby eliminating promiscuity. It did not take long after going ashore for the Stevensons to decide that they preferred Anaho to Taiohae because "here the people were too civilized." When the few European inhabitants were told this they were amused and questioned whether or not the famous writer and his family had themselves "gone native." One European on the island recalled that Mr. Stevenson "used to go about barefoot, with his trousers and shirt-sleeves turned up, and never wore a hat; and 'most everyone thought he was a little crazy." As for Fanny, after initially donning her South Sea *muumuu* and *holaku* dresses she never again wore any other type of garment.

On August 14, Fanny, Louis and Maggie made a pilgrimage to the home of Queen Vaekehu which was perched on the side of a hill overlooking the harbor. It was a pretty little three-room European-style house painted white and surrounded by flowering hibiscus bushes and oceanic rosewood trees. They were met at the door by a young woman who welcomed them in English and ushered them into a dining room area where the queen, dressed in a print gown, motioned for them to take seats. The room contained several chairs and two tables with colorful cloths. The planked wooden floor was spotless and the walls were painted an attractive turquoise blue. Religious pictures and family photographs decorated the walls. Out the front entrance of the house they could view the sea and the surf, and from the verandah in back there was a spectacular view of the mountains. A group of young women who had been working behind the house brought drinking nuts for the guests. The hostess, looking every bit a queen, was at least 65 years old with a refined, dignified aura. Her beautiful gray hair was brushed back off her forehead, and her hands and ankles were elaborately tattooed. Louis later described her as "nunlike," but he surmised that she had not been nunlike in 1842 when the French had installed her as queen of the island of Nuku Hiva. At that time one French official, Max Radiguet, is known to have described her as "the loveliest Polynesian he had ever seen."

Unfortunately, Queen Vaekehu spoke no English, and the only French word in her vocabulary was *Merci.* But the young woman who had ushered them into the house now seated herself beside the elderly lady and served as an interpreter. Through this medium the queen welcomed them to her home and to her islands, which she referred to as *Te henua te enata* (the Land of Men). She apologized for the fact that her adopted son, Stanislaus Moanatini, could not be present, because his position as Minister of Public Works required his presence elsewhere. Then she added that her own government position rarely took her away from home except on rare ceremonial occasions. Queen Vaekehu revealed that she received a stipend of $20 a month and that she was very much a monarch in name only. In a high, almost falsetto voice which was characteristic of Marquesan women of rank, she talked about her life, and responded to Louis's respectful inquiries.

It was rumored in the European community that when she was young she was a spoil of war, being passed from one victorious chief to another and ultimately recognized as the Queen of Taiohae. But as her prestige diminished with the growing influence of the white man, in 1853 Vaekehu turned to Catholicism for peace, recognition, and what the missionaries called "redemption."

In response to Stevenson's questions of what Nuku Hiva was like when she was young, the elderly queen described an island well-populated with healthy men and women in viable communities. Her words, translated by her interpreter, described the Nuku Hiva interior.

> Each valley was the home of a large single tribe, and a man could not venture out on foot beyond his tribal border without many armed companions. In the villages there was ceremonial dancing and feasting and *kava* drinking, and young people made love when it pleased them and old people told tales of great leaders and famous battles, and feasts of 'long pig.' The chief of Taiohae was a man of great strength and cunning, and woe to any man who turned his back on him. Yes, those were the days before the white people came with their greed, their rum and their diseases, and the yellow men brought their opium to destroy our minds and bodies.

And then the old lady suddenly stopped talking and merely looked out through the open door at the harbor and at the CASCO riding at anchor. Her eyes turned misty and she smiled, perhaps thinking of better days and the world she had lost. "I think I have said enough. *Merci.* "

Sensing her mood, Louis quickly thanked the queen and extended an invitation to her and her son to come out to the CASCO for dinner on the following evening. Then the family left the home and walked down to the beach without exchanging a single word. No one knew quite what to say.

The following evening the queen, Stanislaus and his daughter came aboard the CASCO for dinner. Queen Vaekehu was dressed in white, and the contrast between the color of her gown and her extraordinary tattooing was striking. As she sat among the Stevensons eating and drinking champagne she appeared to be enjoying herself, although there were great communication problems. Not understanding either English or French and somewhat deaf to boot, she pretended to hear and be entertained. She made occasional pleasant and complimentary remarks in Marquesan, which her son translated, and she seemed very much at ease and surprisingly alert. Early in the evening Fanny turned to the queen's son and asked him if there was anything special that his mother would like to have. Stanislaus replied, "Kanaka ladies smoke." At this, Fanny started immediately to search for a pipe and tobacco for their royal guest, and then she decided that the old lady might like to try smoking a cigarette. Fanny sat down next to her and showed her how they rolled their own cigarettes, and she successfully followed suit. When her cigarette was lighted she took a puff or two and produced a big smile indicating that she liked cigarettes very much.

Stanislaus was also a delightful guest, quite intelligent and cosmopolitan. He was the holder of a Marquesan chief's title, but as a young man had been sent by the local Catholic Bishop, Dordillon, to South America where he was educated by the Fathers. He spoke fluent French and English but retained much of the traditional Marquesan cultural knowledge and personality characteristics as well as the language. He had a curious pattern of speaking of his country as a land of "savages," and referred to himself as "a savage who has traveled." It was well known that Stanislaus was highly valued by the Administration for his ability to motivate his native workforce to keep the roads always passable.

Obviously very attentive to his mother's needs, Stanislaus at the appropriate hour suggested that it was time for them to say good night. At that point he presented each of his hosts with a large tapa cloth and to Louis he also gave an "old man's beard," an article of ceremonial decor made from long braided facial hair and worn as a headdress or as a decorative collar or shawl. As the queen left the dining saloon she took both of Fanny's hands in hers and kissed her on both cheeks.

After the ship's tender had pulled away, bound for the shore with the dinner guests, Louis examined the gifts they had received and estimated that their value totaled between two and three hundred dollars. The extent of the generosity was evident when he remembered that the queen's annual stipend was only $240.

While the Stevensons were enjoying themselves in the Marquesan capital, Captain Otis was having crew problems. Having sailed from San Francisco without a first mate with knowledge of celestial navigation, Otis was able to sign on Captain M. Henri Goltz, a middle-aged ex-trading schooner skipper, as first officer.

He was especially valued by Otis because of his knowledge of the Tuamotu archipelago waters, an area which was well-known for taking its toll of sailing ships. Goltz was a fine looking man and very capable, but unfortunately a bit garrulous. Louis maintained that his "words flowed like a river" and that he often would have "liked to have dammed that river."

Otis had not anticipated any further crew changes, but the "Japanese" cook, just three days before their leaving Taiohae, went ashore without permission, got drunk and stayed out all night. In the morning Otis notified the gendarmes who found Cousina and put him in jail overnight. When he was returned to the ship he was insolent to the skipper and was immediately dismissed. Otis confided to Louis that he wished he could dismiss the other four seamen as well, but his crew was too small already.

In a village the size of Taiohae very little went unnoticed for long, and the CASCO's cook problem was the talk of the community—native and European alike. It also attracted the attention of a young Chinese man named Ah Fu. When Captain Otis was ashore the young man approached him and in somewhat inadequate English convinced him that he was not only a capable cook but in fact a gourmet chef. And this was in large measure the truth.

Ah Fu had been brought to Nuku Hiva as a child to fill a quota of Chinese laborers, but since he was too small to do any hard agricultural work, the contractor threw him off the plantation. Marquesans took pity on the little fellow and adopted him. He not only survived but flourished among the Polynesians. Nurtured and educated in island ways by his foster family, Ah Fu grew tall and brawny, and looked more Marquesan than Chinese. He retained something of his ethnic identity by shaving his head and wearing a queue, however. Occasionally working for island Europeans he had developed a skill in cooking which RLS acknowledged but said that he lacked something in the skill of stewarding. It is easy to imagine why a young man like Ah Fu would want to sail away on a beautiful yacht like the CASCO, serving a famous author and his family. The Stevensons were equally blessed, for in time Ah Fu became an extremely efficient house man and a faithful companion as well as a wizard in the galley.

The Stevensons' stay in Taiohae was short (12 days) compared to their sojourn in Anaho, but in some ways they were happy to move on to other islands. The only really negative aspect of the stop in Nuku Hiva was the presence of *nonos*, the almost invisible sand flies that often attacked in swarms inflicting extremely painful stings which, if scratched, resulted in raised welts that often became infected. It was generally agreed throughout the Marquesas that Anaho had the best climate in all the islands, but that their next destination, Hiva Oa, was blessed with few mosquitoes and no *nonos*. Island folklore maintained that the inhabitants of Hiva Oa were especially diligent in their service to one of their indigenous deities, and as a reward, the god packed up the stinging insects in a coconut shell and sent them to the less faithful inhabitants of Nuku Hiva.

Just prior to the CASCO's departure from Taiohae Brother Michel Blanc, lay missionary, carpenter, and sculptor from Hatiheu, asked if he might have passage to Hiva Oa, a request Stevenson gladly honored since Brother Michel promised Louis a horseback excursion of the island ceremonial centers. When Brother Michel arrived at the CASCO he had brought several head of sheep and pigs to be given to the mission station at Taahuku. The 12-hour passage to Hiva Oa was unexpectedly rough with the worst waves Captain Otis said he had ever encountered, and even he was seasick on deck, explaining that he had been too long in port. The new cook was barely able to provide an evening meal for the passengers, but this was of little concern because only Louis and his mother arrived to eat, and then one left early in the meal, although neither would reveal which of them it was.

As the CASCO approached the northwest coast of Hiva Oa they shipped such heavy seas that the livestock on the forward part of the deck were washed overboard. And as the wave swept aft along the deck it also caught First Mate Henri Goltz, knocking him down and nearly carrying him overboard as well. His head was cut badly, requiring immediate medical attention from Fanny, although she was incapacitated herself from seasickness.

Once in the lee of Hiva Oa the seas subsided, but as they passed through Bordelais Channel, between the small island of Tahuata and Hiva Oa, CASCO had to fight a strong westerly current until she rounded Point Teaehoa and sailed north by west toward the somewhat more placid water of Traitor Bay. As in other Marquesan ports, the approach to the island was spectacular—a panorama of high mountains with verdant summits which disappeared into the clouds. Ahead was a narrow riverlike inlet to starboard called Taahuku Bay, while to port was the more open and less sheltered Atuona Bay with a curtain of rocky cliffs rising behind a black sand beach. CASCO glided slowly toward the narrower fjordlike Taahuku Bay anchorage and dropped her hook in five fathoms of water. The village of Atuona, which consisted of a cluster of houses, a store, a copra shed, a Chinese "eating house," and a deserted fort, lay approximately a half mile away around a pinnacle of land known as Point Feki. To reach it the CASCO voyagers had to take their tender in through the surf, wade ashore between breakers, and then walk a considerable distance on a narrow path through a coconut grove to the village.

No sooner had the word gotten out that a famous author and his family had arrived than the high chief of the island, named Paaaeua, came out to the ship and announced that he was adopting the Stevenson family. This meant that they should exchange names, and that Paaaeua's property now also belonged to the Stevensons. On the other hand, Louis surmised that it also meant that the chief would share in the ownership of the CASCO. Since the author and his party would be leaving in a matter of days Stevenson played along with the generous offer made by Paaaeua, and in his journal wrote, "Had we stayed at Atuona, Paaaeua would have held himself bound to establish us upon his land, and to set apart young men for our service, and trees for our support."

Since names were exchanged and the Stevensons were officially taken into Paaaeua's family at an elaborate feast, the island guests decided that it was only right that from now on Paaaeua should be affectionately referred to as their "Pa."

The main problem with this situation was that there existed at that time a conflict between two chiefs—Paaaeua, who had been appointed high chief by the French administration, and Moipu, who was recognized by the Marquesans as being the rightful holder of that office, but who had been removed because of "bad conduct." That bad conduct apparently consisted of his being the last of the cannibals. Concerning Moipu, Stevenson recorded, "I met this man . . . in the village, and detested him on sight; when man-eating was referred to, and he laughed a low, cruel laugh, part boastful, part bashful, like one reminded of some dashing peccadillo, my repugnance was mingled with nausea." He apparently had revealed to Louis that his favorite morsel was the human hand.

Not to be outdone by Paaaeua, Moipu took Lloyd aside and declared that he was adopting him as a brother, and that Lloyd now would have the name Moipu and the deposed chief would assume the name *mata kalahi* (glass eyes). One of the main problems which developed for Lloyd, who once again became the official photographer of the trip when he was able to buy another camera from one of the local traders, was that every time he tried to take a picture of Moipu (like when he posed in full battle dress), Paaaeua would insist on being in the picture.

While Stevenson was not particularly interested in Europeans in these South Sea ports, here he was looking forward to meeting a Scotsman named M'Callum who some years ago had managed to acquire a large plantation of some 5,000 coconut trees and had become wealthy growing cotton as well as selling copra. The man's economic successes impressed Louis considerably less, however, than the reputation he had as a poet. Stevenson's first disappointment resulted from his learning that M'Callum, while of Scottish ancestry, was actually born in the United States. What was particularly interesting about him from Louis's perspective was that before succumbing to the lure of the South Seas he had been a ship's carpenter from the Cape Flattery area, and since his arrival in Hiva Oa he had built his own inter-island schooner.

During Stevenson's short stay in Hiva Oa he never was able to meet the Scottish poet/plantation owner M'Callum face to face, since he lived at the far eastern end of the island; but they did manage to exchange letters via the skipper of M'Callum's schooner that made weekly trips to Atuona. A much cherished keepsake of Louis's visit to Hiva Oa was M'Callum's poetic greeting which read,

Sail, Ho! Ahoy! CASCO
First among the pleasure fleet

That came around to greet
These isles from San Francisco

And first, too; only one
Among the literary men
That this way has ever been—
Welcome, then, to Stevenson.

Please not offended be
At this little notice
Of the CASCO, *Captain Otis,*
With the novelist's family.

Avoir une voyage magnifical
Is our wish sincere,
That you'll have from here
Allant sur la Grande Pacifical

While Louis was unable to personally meet this man, whom he labeled the "island poet laureate," he did get acquainted with a most interesting character named Keane. This very British island trader was a former cavalry officer who had served in India prior to settling in the South Seas. He was married to a very pretty and gentle half-Danish, half-Hawaiian woman and was living a lifestyle as close to that of a native Englishman as possible. He proudly stated that he would have nothing to do with native cookery and that he had never even tasted Fanny's favorite pudding, *ka'aku.* While the Stevensons enjoyed the Keanes' English-looking garden and attractive wooden European-style house for a change, they found its owner something of an anomaly. His idiosyncrasies were overlooked, however, when he came to their assistance by selling Lloyd his camera when he learned that theirs had been lost overboard.

The Stevensons thought the island of Hiva Oa was much more beautiful than Nuku Hiva, but they had to admit that it also had Scottish-type mists in the mountains which hid much of the beauty. They could not sit on deck at night because of the heavy dew, but they still enjoyed a few hours respite in the cockpit during the day reading or recounting their personal adventures.

On one occasion they were enjoying lunch on deck when

Lloyd suddenly shouted "Look! Look!" and pointed toward the mouth of the harbor where a schooner under head sails and main was coming around Point Teaeoa. The ship was only slightly larger than the CASCO, but it appeared to have a sizable crew tending lines and preparing to drop anchor off the village of Taahuku. The schooner obviously had the look of a yacht rather than an island trader, and when it anchored within hailing distance of the CASCO it was learned that it was the British yacht NYANZA of Glasgow registry, owned by Captain J. Cumming Dewar, a Scotsman who surprisingly enough came from Louis's own county, Midlothian. Margaret Stevenson had met the captain's father, and Louis had once seen Dewar walking on the shores of the Côte d'Azur in the south of France.

Visits were exchanged by Dewar and Stevenson in the next few days, and Louis was amazed by the size of the NYANZA crew, which numbered nineteen, and included three officers, eight able-bodied seamen, two cooks and three stewards, a signalman and a sailmaker. The CASCO, on the other hand, impressed Dewar very little. He found it "of great beam and little depth" with very limited accommodations and "more adapted for sailing about San Francisco Bay than for a cruise across the ocean." However, in July 1890, CASCO was safely anchored off Oakland in San Francisco Bay after her Pacific island cruise, and the NYANZA was lying shipwrecked off the island of Ponape in Micronesia.

Louis, as an aspiring anthropologist who was determined to return to civilization with artifacts from all the remote parts of the South Seas, was intrigued by the Marquesan treasures known as "old men's beards," which were literally facial hair fastened on men's foreheads by a wreath made of porpoise teeth and worn as ornaments on special ceremonial occasions. Some students of South Seas culture maintained that wearing such human hair as ornaments dated back to the time of cannibalistic feasts where the victim's hair was cut off to make headdresses, arm rings and necklaces which were believed to have magical properties. Stevenson had received several of these, including one from Stanislaus, Queen Vaekehu's adopted son, who presented it when he and the queen were invited to dinner aboard the CASCO. Louis wanted to have them all woven into the kind of wreath which Marquesans had once worn as headdresses. This desire brought to the CASCO one of its most eccentric visitors, a man named Mapiao, who was described by Stevenson as "a great *tahuku*—which seems to mean priest, wizard, tattooer, practiser of any art, or in a word, esoteric person—and a man famed for his eloquence on public occasions and witty talk in private." Mapiao, whom Stevenson should have identified as a *tuhuna* (artist or expert craftsman), arrived on board with a magnificent beard of his own, which Louis described as being tied in a "sailors knot" to ensure its safety. Brother Michel, who was on board at the time, estimated that this magnificent artistic bush was easily worth $100.

While Stevenson appreciated Mapiao for his skill in producing an artifact for them that would be highly valued, his arrogance was insufferable. He spoke no English, but with gestures that made his demands crystal clear, he turned the entire Stevenson family into his servants. When he wanted water he would not go to the ship's scuttlebutt, nor would he even reach for the glass of water if set down before him, but would demand that the glass be placed in his hand when he wanted to drink. Food was brought to him in the morning, but he would not touch it until the sun was directly overhead. This pattern was repeated for several days. On his final day aboard his food was placed before him as usual, and a glass of water was also placed next to the food. When high noon arrived he motioned to Fanny to serve him the water and the food which was definitely close enough for him to reach himself. Fanny misunderstood his signals (or pretended to) and instead of serving him, she threw the water and his dinner overboard. He looked stunned for a brief moment and then began to laugh, whereupon Fanny and Louis followed suit.

When it came time to pay Mapiao for his very expertly woven wreath of old men's beards, Louis got the impression that he wanted payment in fishhooks. Several were laid before him in addition to several dollars—a reasonable payment considering all the food and personal service he had received over the last few days. When Stevenson asked *"Mitai ehipe?"* ("payment good?") the man replied in Marquesan that "Your ship is good. Your food is good and we part friends." With that he left the ship with his head bowed and with an expression on his face of one who has been deeply injured. Once again Louis had become impressed with the fact that Marquesans were an extraordinarily complex and mysterious people. They could be annoying, charming, friendly, shy, abrasive or respectful, depending upon the situation, and Europeans often misunderstood the why and wherefore of it all.

As the time allotted for their stay in Hiva Oa was drawing to an end Louis reminded Brother Michel of the promise he had made concerning a horseback tour to the "high places" where the ancient ceremonial centers could be found. The following morning the missionary arrived at the boat landing area with two "sober nags," suitable for negotiating the precipitous trail leading up the mountain. Fortunately the weather was beautiful, and halfway to their destination they stopped to rest and look down upon the island vista of soaring rock walls, rich tropical vegetation and in contrast to it all, the deep blue of the ocean. In the distance they could see the "whale-like" unpopulated island of Motane, some 15 miles away.

After continuing their ascension of the mountain they suddenly came upon a patch of cotton on a level section of land with a rushing brook, a deep grove of island chestnut trees and a house sitting atop a well-built *paepae* (foundation). As they approached the house, shouts of "Mikael! Kaoha, Mikael!" filled the air, and half a dozen smiling youngsters burst out of the doorway followed by a handsome bare-breasted mother who obviously was well along in years but still had copious coal-black hair and firm youthful breasts. When Louis dismounted she approached him, presented him with two bright red hibiscus blossoms and said, "Goodbye! I speak Inglis." She then informed him that it was "a whaler man who was a plenty good chap" who had taught her the language. Brother Michel and Stevenson were then provided with a cool drink, and as they continued on their journey toward the ceremonial center Louis could not help thinking what a ravishing beauty the woman must have been when she was young; he wondered what might have happened to her lover, and if he ever thought about what he had left behind in the Marquesas.

Further on they came to a pool in the mountain stream where a young woman was bathing completely nude. When she saw them approaching she bounded out of the water and quickly covered herself with her flowered *pareu*, whereupon Louis turned to Michel and naively commented, "Even in these daughters of cannibals shame is eloquent." Brother Michel just shook his head and chuckled.

Soon they realized that they were on an ancient road which led them into the twilight of a forest and to a place where a ceremonial center, called by the natives a *paepae tapu*, could be distinguished in the gloom. The term *paepae* normally referred to the floor or platform on which Marquesan houses were built, and this sacred (*tapu*) center rose above a paved floor of black lava stones so carefully fitted together and so level that Stevenson believed the workmanship was superior to anything that might be done by European stone masons. Built on this foundation were three tiers of terrace, one hundred yards in width and twenty in depth, constructed of huge stone blocks ten to fifteen feet long and five or six feet thick—the sides of which were smooth and bore no chisel marks. The terraces contained rows of benches and individual seats, the latter apparently for honored individuals like priests or high chiefs. On the upper terrace all that remained of a temple was a single joist supported by beautifully carved stone uprights. Along the sides of the terraced section were the remains of small huts which probably housed the custodians of the sacred center. And at the center of the ceremonial *paepae* a great banyan tree, the only tree permitted in the sacred area, spread its protective canopy.

As Louis stood before this once magnificent sanctuary he imagined a time of ceremonial splendor, of clans trooping into this sacred place in a body, each having its appointed seats and special places for the chiefs, for drummers, for dancers, and for priests. He imagined the ceremonial feasting and he wondered how often the magnificent altar was used for consumption of human flesh of vanquished foe.

"Mr. Stevenson, I think we had better start back, " said Brother Michel, arousing his companion from his reverie of festive and possibly brutal yesterdays.

"Yes, yes, indeed, Brother Michel, I was just envisioning another time, another world. Let's saddle up. Fanny always worries if I am not home when I promise."

At that, the two men mounted their horses, returned up the ancient Marquesan thoroughfare, and started their downward trek toward Atuona. After a long, hard day sweltering in the humid heat of the tropic sun and the steaming island vegetation, the descent from the mountain heights was stretching into late afternoon with a setting sun about to plunge into the sea. Now the tradewinds brought a chill from the sea and Louis began to feel ill for the first time in his many weeks in the South Seas. By the time he reached home he was running a temperature and coughing, and that night he was hemorrhaging for the first time since he left San Francisco.

Two days before their planned departure for Tahiti, Louis and Fanny arranged a conference on deck with Captain Otis. Fanny was deeply concerned over her husband's recent health problems and wanted to leave immediately for Tahiti steering the most direct route possible. Louis, on the other hand, asked Otis to head straight for the Tuamotus and call at "some out of the way place." But the skipper vetoed both requests stating that the Tuamotu Archipelago was no place for a sailing ship with its low-lying coral atolls, its dangerous currents and its not-to-be-trusted charts. In no uncertain terms he told them, "It may take longer, but we are certain to get there if we sail around the north end of the archipelago and then come due south through the Society Islands—Bora Bora, Raiatea, Huahine and Moorea." Stevenson firmly held to his position of seeking out new adventures in exotic places and Fanny almost hysterically pleaded with Otis for the quickest and most direct route to Tahiti since Louis's health had declined so drastically in the last few days. Finally Otis shook his head in desperation and said,

> All right folks, it's your funeral as well as mine. But don't say I didn't warn you. I'll admit that we do have a few things going for us. Goltz has been through the area many times, it's early September and we should encounter reasonably good weather with calm seas and light winds. But I can't leave here for at least two days. We have to take on water and supplies and there are some minor ship keeping duties that I must attend to. As for that remote place you wanted to visit next, Mr. Stevenson, I've heard that Fakarava might be an excellent waypoint stop. It's an atoll 32 miles long and 15 wide with two passages into its lagoon. It is the administrative center of the Tuamotus, and there could be a medical person there as well as the government officials.

With that Otis cocked his skipper's cap over one eye, wheeled and strode down the deck in the direction of his stateroom.

Early in the morning of September 4 the anchor of the CASCO was weighed and catted; a whaleboat manned by sturdy Marquesans took the little schooner in tow and headed down the channel of dark green water and rounded Point Teaeoa to a view of the open sea. Behind the ship was what Stevenson described as a "theatre of mountains" some 4,000 feet high standing like a vast wall around what was often called Traitor Bay. Once in open water CASCO climbed the incoming swells and heeled to port as her sails billowed and strained with the force of the tradewinds. Now the line to the whaleboat was released and its coxswain was directed to come alongside where the crew's payment in bread, rum and tobacco was passed down. Then the whaleboat cast off and the crew cheered the yacht's departure as she picked up speed and soon left *te henua te enata*, "the land of men," far astern.

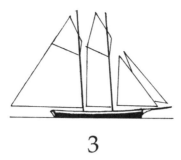

3
The Tuamotus—
The Dangerous Desert Islands

As THE CASCO sped southwest by west on a beam reach with moderate winds and all canvas set and drawing, Captain Otis was clearly troubled about the prospect of entering the vast area of coral atolls known as the Tuamotu, or Dangerous, Archipelago. The term "dangerous" derived from the fact that these islands were mere rings of coral, topped with a bit of sand and a few coconut trees, and therefore not observable more than seven or eight miles away. Furthermore, it was also an area where charts were known to be grossly inaccurate, with islands misplaced or completely missing. It was also extremely difficult to tell one atoll from another. The 300,000 square mile archipelago, lying in a northwest-southeast direction, was rectangular in shape and contained approximately 80 islands, only half of which were inhabited. On the inhabited islands the residents numbered anywhere from a mere handful to over a thousand humans plus a multitude of rats, mosquitoes, flies and land crabs managing to survive on a minimum of greenery and a few rows of towering palms producing coconuts which were sold to the white man as copra.

For the first three days since leaving Hiva Oa the CASCO had covered close to 450 miles with a steady tradewind. Unfortunately, however, the sky had now become overcast and as the schooner drew closer to the Tuamotu region, determination of the ship's position by celestial navigation was impossible. Utilizing dead reckoning, and relying on the experience of First Mate Goltz who had sailed the area for years, Captain Otis had expected to sight the island of Takaroa before nightfall on September 7. What they had not anticipated, however, was that a strong current from the west was carrying them to windward.

Although the first mate spent much of the night on the bowsprit peering into the darkness, and a special lookout watch was set to attempt to find the evasive island, it was not until 5:15 a.m. that the helmsman woke Stevenson, who had spent the night in the cockpit, and pointed in the direction of the rising sun saying, "There it is, Sir." There was indeed a row of palms that represented an atoll, but which one? "It's Tikei," said Goltz, who had just come up from below. "We obviously have been set about 30 miles to the east by the current. Now we can alter our heading, and we should sight Taiaro by about noon." Actually the landfall came at about 11:15 a.m. and the mate commented, "You know, Taiaro means lost at sea—how appropriate." Ironically, Stevenson learned later that a trader, one Mr. Narii Salmon, had watched the CASCO pass his island and wondered if it were lost.

The weather continued to be socked in, preventing any sun sights to monitor their dead reckoning course to Fakarava. Just at sunset they passed Raraka, but then the night closed in and the threat of shipwreck on an unexpected reef was with them for another night. About 10 p.m. the sky cleared, but taking star sights was out of the question with no visible horizon and a sky so filled with stars that the normal navigation stars were almost impossible to delineate. As Louis sat in the cockpit staring up at this display which looked like diamonds in the sky, two lines of an Emerson poem came to mind, and turning to the helmsman he recited

And the lone seaman all the night
Sails astonished among stars.

As they sailed northwest along the Raraka coast, the sound of the surf on its reef was a drowsy monotone but still menacing, because of the constant threat that the current might carry them ashore. Captain Otis worried about current; he worried about whether the wind was strong enough and steady enough to keep them off the northern shore of Raraka; and he worried because the starlit night offered him only a hint of what lay ahead. But then a shout came from the man at the wheel, "Land ahead," and a moment later the first mate cried, "By God, it's Kauehi."

Still not trusting the accuracy of his charts or his own ability to judge the ship's speed and distance made good over the ocean floor, Otis made sure that he was well away from both Raraka and Kauehi and hove to the vessel. Then he threw over the sounding line and sat on the taffrail the rest of the night making sure that the line continued to hang perfectly straight up and down. At daylight, Kauehi, mostly green brush and white sand with very few palms, was clearly visible, and now it was an easy run west to the northern end of Fakarava, where the Garue Pass would take them into the lagoon.

Captain Otis, somewhat blurry-eyed but very relieved, looked toward the huge atoll which lay ahead.

"We made it, Mr. Stevenson. Two hundred miles through a nightmare of islands only because we had a good first mate, thank God, and a hell of a lot of luck. I hope you will find Fakarava the 'out of the way place' you were hoping for. As far as I am concerned, if I never see these damned Tuamotus again it won't be too soon."

The channel between Fakarava and the next island north, Toau, was eight miles wide and presented no hazard, in fact it was a common avenue for most ship traffic to Tahiti. Garue Pass also did not require any special precautionary seamanship since it was roughly a half-mile wide. However, because Goltz advised the captain of the strong outgoing flow in the pass at certain times, Otis waited for slack water and as a result had no trouble entering.

The course through the pass was southeast by south, and one mile into the lagoon they turned 90° to port and on a heading of east-northeast sailed some five and one-half miles across the lagoon to an anchorage in seven fathoms of water just off the village of Rotoava.

Actually the CASCO could have taken one of two channels through the reef, one to windward and one to leeward, which meant that a sailing vessel could leave or enter regardless of the direction of the wind.

While the CASCO was making its way across the lagoon the Stevensons were all hanging over the rail watching through crystal-clear water the ship's progress over the bottom. Although hampered somewhat by the glare of the sun, they watched the color of the lagoon water change from a deep blue indicating 20 or more fathoms, to a lighter blue indicating shoaling, and finally to turquoise where the anchor was dropped. Here and there they could see brown or purple patches marking coral heads, but none of these were close enough for concern. What fascinated the new arrivals most was an absolute spectrum of vivid color exhibited by the schools of fish which were "stained and striped, and even beaked like parrots."

Experiencing the first smooth water since they left San Francisco, the passengers and crew were free to inspect their surroundings from a fairly stationary deck. The village of Rotoava was the residence of the governor of the Tuamotus and its capital, chosen because it was the only safe anchorage in the archipelago, and therefore an ideal port of entry for any ships stopping in the Tuamotus. It was hardly what one would expect of a government seat, however. It consisted only of two small government office buildings, a prison and gendarmerie, a modest governor's residence, a few small whitewashed bungalows set close to the lagoon and shaded by tall coconut palms, and at the edge of town, a Catholic chapel with a steeple and a belfry. The scene was certainly a great contrast from what the Stevensons had encountered in other South Sea ports. While the settlement of Rotoava was no less impressive than Taiohae, the port of entry for the Marquesas, it was the setting that was so different. Instead of a village backed by soaring volcanic peaks there was only the long line of coconut palms lining coral sand beaches in either direction as far as the eye could see, and a blue-green lagoon like a vast placid ocean without distant shores. But like other villages where the CASCO had dropped anchor, there was not a soul to be seen anywhere, and although it was Sunday the area around the church showed no sign of life either.

In front of the government structures a pier with landing steps and a harbor light on a staff jutted out into the water. The light was the first such aid to navigation those aboard the CASCO had seen since leaving San Francisco. They also appreciated the landing steps for it meant that they did not have to climb a steep ladder or wade ashore on the beach from their tender. After a considerable period of time during which an awning over the cockpit was rigged and a boarding ladder was lashed in place, a man came out of what was apparently the custom house. He walked to a tethered boat at the end of the pier and rowed out toward the CASCO. When he arrived alongside he addressed Captain Otis in broken English, *"Bonjour Capitaine.* I am Monsieur Donat Rimareau, Acting Governor of the Tuamotus. I would like to see your papers, *s'il vous plaît."* Captain Otis cordially invited him aboard.

The man who climbed onto the deck was a tall, gentle-mannered, civil servant about 40 years of age with golden-brown skin derived partly from the sun and partly from his ancestry, which was half French and half Tahitian. He spoke Tahitian and French, but his English left something to be desired. Fortunately, Louis spoke fluent French. The official told the new arrivals that he had taught himself English "because the English had been so good to him." This kind treatment had apparently occurred in Europe when, as a young man, the island government had sent him to France for his education.

After looking over their papers, which he found in order, he explained that he and a Mr. Charles were temporarily acting for the governor who was away on government business in Raiatea in the Society Islands, where a native insurrection was taking place. He also explained why Rotoava appeared completely deserted. It seemed that most of the town's inhabitants owned land on other atolls, and periodically they were required to return to the island where their holdings were located and re-register their titles. This was one of those times.

When Donat Rimareau's business with the CASCO was completed he invited the Stevensons and the captain to come ashore with him and he would show them about. Once ashore, he took them to the courthouse where he served them coconut punch and then to the governor's residence where they all marveled at the beautiful garden with numerous varieties of flowers, shrubs and fruit trees. These had been planted in imported soil, 300 bags of which had been shipped over from Tahiti. Rimareau pointed out that the regular soil, consisting of sand and bits of broken coral limestone, was not capable of supporting anything but coconut and pandanus trees, and even then the locals planted a piece of ship's biscuit and a rusty nail with the seed coconuts believing that would supply the required nutrients. Maggie remarked that she had observed fig and banana trees growing throughout the village, and was told that these too depended upon imported soil. There were even small plantations on the island growing sugar cane, sweet potatoes, yams and taro, but always with the help of Tahiti's good black dirt.

After learning of the Stevensons' penchant for shell collecting Rimareau took them across the island to the ocean beach, which was only a ten-minute walk, so that he could show them the best place to look for shells. He said that here the shells would be shiny and colorful while those from the lagoon were dull and often rough. Returning to the village Otis signaled for the tender to come and pick them up, and while they waited, their host asked if they could please come ashore the next morning so that the local citizens who were on the island could meet them. "We don't have a lot of ships dropping in on us, and the people enjoy seeing new faces," he said.

At that moment the tender arrived and the Stevenson party thanked their village guide for a pleasant afternoon and stepped aboard their boat. Last to board was Louis who tipped his somewhat soiled and wrinkled yachting cap to his newfound friend and assured him they would return at 10 a.m. the next day to meet the local citizens.

After a pleasant dinner and several glasses of champagne served up by their new gourmet cook and steward, Ah Fu, and consumed without the annoyance of a howling wind and a heaving sea, the family retired to the cockpit to observe the setting of the sun in their first atoll anchorage. Everyone expected to sleep well that night without the usual motion, but Louis and Lloyd brought their bedding on deck about midnight, deciding that their cabins were just "too stuffy." At breakfast the following morning the author announced that he intended to look for a house ashore which might have a bit more ventilation.

At 10 a.m. Louis looked toward the custom house and there he saw a small cluster of people, mostly Polynesians, waiting for the much anticipated occasion of meeting the passengers of the newly arrived yacht. Monsieur Donat Rimareau was there, and Louis urged his family to quickly board the tender and not keep the local citizens waiting. As the tender approached the pier, they could see that all of the people were holding gifts ranging from pandanus leaf hats to woven coconut leaf baskets and purses to shell necklaces. When they tied up and climbed the landing stairs, they were met by Rimareau who said, "Thank you for coming, Mr. Stevenson. My neighbors have been anxiously waiting to meet the visitors on what they are referring as *Pahi Muni*, 'The Silver Ship'." Somewhat surprised by this new description of the CASCO, Louis turned around and looked at their schooner. Although the hull was painted black, reflections of the sun off the water played upon the topsides and did indeed make it look like they were overlaid with silver.

"You might want to tell your family members that the usual salutation in these islands is *iao ranua*." suggested Rimareau. After the word was passed, the Stevenson clan marched down the pier to meet their newfound admirers. Acting as interpreter, Donat Rimareau introduced each and every islander, and the family greeted them all with a hearty *iao ranua*. Within a short time the Stevensons were standing in the middle of a pile of Tuamotu handicrafts which had been presented by a generous, happy island throng. As the author shook the hands of the reception crowd he thought to himself, "These people are darker and smaller than Marquesans and not nearly so handsome, but they seem better behaved."

Not only had the villagers come laden with gifts, but Donat had been more than generous, presenting all the members of the Stevenson family, and even Captain Otis, with pearls, mother-of-pearl shells lined with gold, and a whole box filled with pink coral and fine shells. He even gave them a large *bénitier* (holy water) shell with branches of coral growing out of it.

When all of the gifts had been presented, Rimareau told Stevenson that everyone had expressed a wish that they might come aboard the beautiful Silver Ship. Of course Louis consented, and the visit was scheduled for 2:30 p.m. the following day. Very pleased, the assembled islanders once again shook hands all around and indicated they would be back tomorrow. Stevenson was also delighted, for a tour of the vessel would give him a chance to reciprocate somewhat for the gifts they had received.

At the agreed upon time on Tuesday, 21 people were waiting on the dock for their promised visit to the CASCO, and Otis sent the ship's tender in for them. The group that came aboard were of all ages from a 4-month-old baby to an old lady of 80. Stevenson proudly showed them about the yacht and then gave everyone biscuits, ginger snaps and jam. The women were given syrup and water and the men rum, but on the second round all chose syrup. Donat, who had arranged this visit, told the author after the people had departed that they all thought the party aboard the CASCO was better than one which had been given earlier by a French admiral aboard his vessel, because Stevenson had given them plates and spoons to eat their jam and biscuits and the admiral hadn't.

After the islanders had gone, Louis and Rimareau settled themselves in the cockpit for a friendly glass of wine, and the author asked the government official if he could help them find a house on the beach to lease for the time they would be in port. Donat responded that there was one house available next to the Catholic chapel on the edge of town. Arrangements could be made he said by contacting the Catechist, a man named Taniera Mahinui, whom Louis later described as combining "the incongruous characters of Catechist and convict," and "well qualified for either part."

It seems that Taniera was born to chief status on the island of Anaa. When the French government foolishly decided one day that the taxes should be collected by the chiefs, this was Taniera's downfall. No one is certain whether or not any taxes were collected, but it is certain that none were turned over to the French authorities. Since Taniera was seen about this time having a wonderful time in restaurants in Papeete, the young man was accused, tried and convicted of embezzlement and sentenced to five-year imprisonment on Rotoava. Taniera slept in the town jail, the door of which was never locked, and he received most of his meals from the gendarme. As long as he returned to the jail every night he was free to carry on the work of the Lord as the Church's Catechist. Regarding his qualifications for the work of a cleric, Stevenson recorded in his journal that "he was highly qualified for his office in the Church, being by nature a grave, considerate, and kindly man; his face rugged and serious, his smile bright; a master of several trades, a builder both of boats and houses; endowed with a fine pulpit voice. I never met a man of a mind more ecclesiastical."

With the help of Taniera the Stevensons leased what they believed was the best equipped private house in Rotoava other than the home of the governor. It was a three-room bungalow with a front and rear verandah. The house was furnished with two tables, six chairs, three sewing machines and two wooden

The Stevenson party prior to departure from San Francisco. From left to right seated: Valentine, Maggie and Fanny. Second row: Lloyd, Captain Otis and Stevenson. Standing behind: Dr. Merritt. The picture was not taken on the CASCO. *San Francisco Maritime National Historical Park*

CASCO in San Francisco Bay. *San Francisco Maritime National Historical Park*

The soaring steeples of Ua Pou. *Author's collection*

Casco's somewhat protected anchorage in Anaho Bay, Nuka-hiva. *Joe Jares*

South Sea atoll lagoon. *Author's collection*

Tautira vista. *Author's collection*

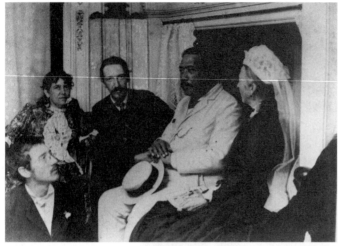

Lloyd, Fanny, Louis, King Kalakaua and Maggie in CASCO's luxurious saloon. Note the decorative carvings on the bulkheads. *The Writers' Museum, Edinburgh*

Luau with King Kalakaua at Manuia Lanai, Honolulu. *The Writers' Museum, Edinburgh*

EQUATOR departing Honolulu. Left to right: Lloyd, Stevenson, Fanny, Joe Strong and deck hand. *San Francisco Maritime National Historical Park, Minto collection*

beds which the Stevensons never used, preferring their boat mattresses laid on the floor. The walls were decorated with hand-tinted photographs and tasteful lithographs by prominent European artists.

The house was owned, Louis found out later, by a French Tahitian by the name of François, who until recently had held a government job as janitor in the governor's residence. After a disagreement with the unpopular Vice-Resident Monsieur Charles the young man quit his job, and with his wife and child, set sail in his half-decked cutter for his small plantation at the other end of the lagoon, where he said he was going to plant cocoa-palms. Normally the lagoon was placid, but a squall with heavy winds developed, causing their craft to capsize. They managed to right the boat, but since it was full of water they could only put the child in the boat and cling to the stern themselves. Although the mainsail had been carried away, the jib remained and moved them along in the direction of Rotoava. After nine hours in the water they reached land and staggered home, only to find the Stevensons installed.

When Louis learned that François had lost the whole cargo of his cutter—half a ton of coconuts, tools and clothing—he offered to pay his rent in advance, but the young man refused, saying that his friend Taniera would collect the rent in good time. Then the family left their house to the Stevensons and found haven among friends elsewhere in the village.

Inspired by sightings of shark fins and giant sea turtles surfacing near the CASCO, Stevenson, the eternal seeker of knowledge and new experience, turned his attention to the underwater microcosm of the atoll lagoon. In this aquatic wonderland multicolored fish—spotted, striped and infinitely structured—darted about the coral heads, sometimes alone and sometimes in regimented formations. Within this realm were also the great *Tridacna* clams resting within the branches of coral. Their shells were so large that mission chapels used them to hold baptismal water, but these same giant clams could also cause death by drowning if a pearl diver's hand or foot should be caught within the closing shells. Below the *Tridacna*, on the snow-white surface of the sandy bottom were found beds of pearl oysters, a major source of income for these atoll people and their colonial administration.

Diving for pearls and mother-of-pearl shell was an important economic activity bringing more income than even the production of copra. But in French Polynesia no one was allowed to dive for pearls and shell without the permission of the French government, for it was a major source of revenue. There were only a small number of guard schooners throughout the Tuamotus riding herd on this industry, and the islanders, parroting the ethics of their colonial role models, managed to get a significant percentage of their harvest past the officials and into the hands of transient traders, thus avoiding profit sharing.

What fascinated Stevenson about the beautiful lagoon fish was the number of them purported to be poisonous or capable of inflicting extremely painful wounds with their fins. This happened to Captain Otis when he was scratched while handling a fish with a parrot-like beak. He suffered the entire remainder of the charter from a numbness resembling paralysis in one of his fingers. From the local divers the novelist learned that all fish with hard, scaleless, box-like bodies, or with parrot-like mouths, small gill opening or with very small belly fins or none at all were to be avoided. Any fish capable of inflating was considered extremely dangerous, and the stonefish with back spines could kill a person if stepped on. Armed with all this good advice, the entire Stevenson party spent literally hundreds of hours, often in waist-deep water, on the shores of the lagoon and on the ocean beaches. They, incidentally, had been warned that some shells also were poisonous. A common taunt from Otis when they returned with bulging bags filled with their day's treasures from the sea was that "next time they should charter a ship with cargo hold."

Louis availed himself of every opportunity to interact with Fakaravans. Donat Rimareau, who identified with the people in spite of his government associations, proved to be an excellent key informant and interpreter. Having been educated in Europe he had insight into Western values and culture as well as those of his island compatriots. He was well-versed in local folklore, and it was from one of Donat's folktales that Stevenson created his short story, "The Isle of Voices." It was a tale of an Hawaiian wizard who traveled on his flying carpet to Fakarava, where he collected shells on the ocean beaches and then turned them into dollars. Rimareau was actually more Polynesian than European in his day-to-day attitudes and behavior. Like other Fakaravans he was strongly supportive of the family and the household, and he very much believed, contrary to Marquesan cultural patterns, that husbands and wives should be united by personal attraction as well as by economic and political alliance. As Stevenson explored the lifeways of the local islanders he could not help but contrast their behavior and values with those of the Marquesans. First of all, he thought he understood the Fakaravans better. He considered them more mercenary, more willing to work, and more frugal, but perhaps less honest than Marquesans. They were more adaptable to cultural change as well. While Marquesans seemed to have lost their will to live and had a dwindling population, the people of the Tuamotus were actually increasing. Rimareau showed Louis government records which revealed that on twelve atolls in 1887 there were 50 births to 32 deaths. Stevenson thought this might be explained in part by the fact that the people had great concern for health and sanitary discipline.

Although upon first meeting these atoll people he was led to believe they were better behaved than the Polynesians he had just left, he soon realized that the Tuamotu folks had somewhat of an ambivalent attitude in regard to fiscal responsibility. They never denied a debt but tended to use every artifice, including flight, to avoid paying it. But when it came to gift giving they were generous beyond reason.

Two religious denominations were predominant on Fakarava, the Mormons and the Catholics. The Mormons believed in being married to only one wife; they read the Protestant Bible and observed Protestant forms of worship, including baptism with immersion; and they prohibited the use of tobacco and liquor.

The Catholic church had conventional forms of worship but this did not keep Mormons from attending their services. In fact, there was a common pattern of members of the two denominations attending each other's services and feeling quite at home in both. The people just liked going to church and didn't get too upset over doctrinal and ritual differences.

Among the entire population there was a strong belief in ghosts, called *tupapahus*. They talked of devils with blue faces and shark's teeth who were transported through the night on the wings of the albatross. They also claimed there were vampires who sucked the blood of children and phantom cannibals who howled on windy nights. And there were supernatural creatures who whistled and were the main focus of the sect known as The Whistlers. This group, which Louis thought resembled European spiritualists, always seemed to cause Donat to look distressed when asked about them. He would lower his voice to a whisper and look around to see if anyone were listening. He maintained that they believed in the souls of the dead returning to mourning relatives and communicating through whistling.

In a letter to his long-time friend Sidney Colvin three days before departure from Fakarava, Stevenson wrote, "My health has stood me splendidly; I am in for hours wading over the knees for shells; I have been five hours on horseback. Withal I still have colds; I have one now, and feel pretty sick too; but not as at home; instead of being in bed, for instance, I am at this moment sitting snuffling and writing in an undershirt and trousers."

A day after writing the above, however, Stevenson's cold worsened substantially and he began to hemorrhage again. Fanny, who doted over her husband like a mother hen, went immediately to Captain Otis demanding that they leave at once for Tahiti since there was no doctor on Fakarava. Otis said a departure on such short notice was out of the question. He explained politely but firmly, "The sky is overcast which could portend squalls. And right now there is no wind to move us across the lagoon and out through the pass. If we raised the anchor now we could drift onto a coral head in a matter of seconds. No, Mrs. Stevenson, I am as concerned about your husband's health as you are, but I must insist on my judgment and knowledge of seamanship to prevail at this time."

Conditions for leaving were no better the following day, but the Stevensons decided that they should publicly say goodbye to all their island friends. The word went out and in the afternoon they all met on the dock where each and every Rotoavan was given a gift, and the village as a whole was given a large sack of flour. The flour was hurriedly taken to a local kitchen where small loaves of bread were baked for everyone. The loaves were then tied with strips of coconut palm leaf, symbolizing chiefly authority and believed to render the gift sacred. With much hugging and weeping the farewell event came to an end. Louis paid Taniera the rent, hoping François would actually see it, and presented him with a carriage clock, the only one they had that worked besides the ship's chronometer. That afternoon the Stevensons moved their mattresses and personal effects back aboard the CASCO. They were now ready to go.

That evening Fanny, feeling a bit of sadness at the thought of leaving this "out of the way place," reminisced in her journal:

> At sunrise we walked from our front door into the warm shallow waters of the lagoon for our bath; we cooked our breakfast on the remains of an old American cooking-stove I discovered on the beach and spent the rest of the morning sorting over the shells we had found the previous day. After lunch and a siesta, we crossed the island to the windward side and gathered more shells.
>
> The close of the placid day marked the beginning of the most agreeable part of the twenty-four hours; it was the time of the moon, and the shadows that fell from the coconut leaves were so sharply defined that one involuntarily stepped over them.

On Tuesday morning at 7 a.m. Captain Otis came on deck, noted the sky and the wind velocity and announced that they would be leaving within the hour. Noticing the activity aboard, Donat rowed out for one last goodbye, and then he went ashore and stood on the dock with a gathering crowd of well-wishers. Out at the church Taniera ran up the Sunday Church Flag although it was Tuesday, and on the pier there was much waving of hats and handkerchiefs as the anchor came out of the water, was secured and the Silver Ship headed across the lagoon for Garue Pass.

On the Rotoava pier Donat Rimareau stood watching the ship carry away a man he knew he would never forget. Around him was a group of villagers talking among themselves about the extraordinary people who had lived among them for nearly three weeks. In talking about Stevenson's hospitality aboard the Silver Ship and the way he related to everyone as though they were cherished friends, one of the men asked Donat, "Why does he do it? No European coming to Fakarava has ever treated us so before."

"It is because he has a good heart," replied Donat.

"But how can he afford to do such things as give everyone

who visits his ship rum, sweet drinks and sugar biscuits? And he even paid us for telling him old Fakarava stories. How can he afford it?"

"He is a writer of books for the rich Europeans," answered Donat. To this the group replied with a perceptive "Ah!" and went away satisfied. Donat stood on the pier until the CASCO went through the pass and disappeared from view. Then he slowly walked back to the custom house wondering what Stevenson might someday write about them.

Having negotiated Garue Pass without difficulty, Otis gave the helmsman orders to take up a southwesterly heading. They rapidly passed Toau and Mau atolls to port and soon saw Fakarava sink out of sight behind them. The wind was fair, the barometer was rising. They were Tahiti bound.

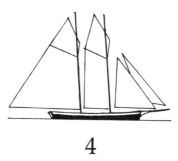

4
Tahiti—The Pearl of the Pacific

IT WAS A glorious day with brisk winds and a cloudless sky. Foam-crested waves dotted a sapphire sea and the CASCO, making better than 8 knots, was laying a white foam trail across a sun-drenched ocean. Sails were popping and spars complaining, and up forward was the happy sound of dolphins cavorting in the tumbling bow waves. It was not the kind of day where Stevenson would be content to stay below. In spite of his nagging cough and cold, he came on deck, drew a deep breath of the clean and bracing sea air, and thought how good it was to be alive.

The anticipated two-day voyage to Tahiti was drawn out into a third when the wind dropped to a mere breeze, and the CASCO lazed along through the tropical night with all sails set but scarcely drawing. Tahiti rose from the sea shortly after daybreak. It was an island fringed by a coral barrier reef which lay a half to two miles offshore with passes, marked by red and white buoys, to lagoon-like waters. The chart revealed that the general outline of the land resembled a figure eight, with the largest portion of the configuration referred to as Tahiti Nui and the smaller portion Tahiti Iti (little Tahiti). The islanders, however, called this small section the Taiararu Peninsula. Both areas contained a pyramidal mass of mountains, rising to over 7,000 feet on Tahiti Nui and and just over 4,000 on the peninsula.

Louis and his mother were the first members of the family on deck, and as they looked ashore, they were impressed by the form and outline of the island, but found it no match for the beauty of the heavily wooded pinnacles of Nuka Hiva. In fact Maggie said the Tahiti peaks were "puny" by comparison.

As the CASCO sailed slowly along the northeast shore they passed the promontory known as Point Venus, where in 1769 Captain Cook built a small fort and observed the transit of Venus across the face of the sun in order to calculate how far the sun was from the earth. Just beyond Point Venus they passed Matavai Bay where Cook's ship ENDEAVOUR was anchored for three months during that sojourn. At Point Taunoa, with the town of Papeete in sight, they encountered a pilot vessel and took a pilot aboard who brought the vessel into Papeete Bay where they dropped anchor about noon.

Stevenson, who was now running a high fever and feeling exhausted, was taken by Fanny to the Hotel de France where he was put to bed and a physician called. When the doctor arrived, he examined Louis briefly, administered a sedative, and told him that if he should experience another hemorrhage before the day was over it might be fatal.

The author listened stoically to the doctor's diagnosis, thanked him, and bid him good afternoon. He then turned to Fanny and asked her to have Captain Otis brought to see him as soon as possible. When the skipper arrived at the hotel, Louis was the only one among the assembled family who did not seem distraught and worried. Years later Otis described the occasion to a Honolulu newspaper publisher as follows,

> When I arrived at the hotel he sat propped in the bed; he appeared to be quite weak, but he greeted me cordially, and I remember that he was smoking a cigarette as usual. He was facing death as he had faced life and sickness, with a smile and a jest. He told me he had sent for me, fearing that he might take a turn for the worse; and he might not live until morning. "You see the doctor does not give me much time, so I have divided what there is left of my assets, into equal portions, one for each, only reserving the last for Mrs. Stevenson." He then proceeded to inform me, as calmly as though he had a century to spend, how I was to dispose of the yacht and settle the business. After that he bade me adieu as quietly as if no danger threatened his life and hopes. The man did not seem to realize that he acted the hero in little things of his life, as well as where he stood face to face with life's greatest evil—Death.

But Louis did not die that day, and by the next morning he felt much better. Now, however, he began to complain bitterly about his accommodations. His room was satisfactory, but it was on the waterfront where there were numerous bars and restaurants, most of which were open all night, with merrymakers singing, playing guitars and shouting as they spilled out into the street with bottles in hand. It was also the area where shops were located, and the Chinese storekeepers were only slightly quieter than the drunks as they shouted orders to their employees and advertised their wares to passersby. Then there was the ubiquitous jingle of bicycle bells and the rumble of buggy wheels on the street below. Not only did the noise make sleeping difficult, but the copra warehouse located on the town dock exuded an acrid stench of drying copra which could make a healthy man ill, let alone a bedridden one.

After a quick search, and with the help of the British consul, Fanny located and rented a small house near the English consulate, next to a London Missionary Society church. It was directly across from the ruins of the *Calabooza Beretanee* (British jail), where Herman Melville had been incarcerated for being part of a mutiny on the whaler LUCY ANN, which carried him out of the Marquesas in 1842.

Shortly after moving into the house they were informed by the doctor that there had been a recent epidemic of influenza which was brought from Chile, and the Stevensons thought perhaps Louis had somehow been infected with it during their stay in Fakarava.

With the fresh fruits and seafood of Tahiti and plenty of rest, Louis gradually made a comeback. He often walked to the hotel for lunch and returned with Fanny for dinner. He made a courtesy call on the widowed sister of Queen Pomare, and began to jot down ideas for a new book which would be called *Ebb Tide*. It would deal with the villainies and misadventures of the beachcomber population, an element which represented a significant percentage of the population of this South Sea port of 4,000. It was the element which frequently wound up in the calabooza.

After two weeks in Papeete, none of the Stevensons had much positive to say about Tahiti, and Maggie seemed to express their feeling best when she stated, "I don't like Tahiti. It seems to me a sort of halfway house between savage life and civilization, with the drawbacks of both and the advantages of neither." Louis, in like mind, announced to Fanny one evening that Papeete was "too depressing a place in which to end their happy marriage, and that he had decided therefore not to die just yet."

While Louis recuperated, Otis, Lloyd and Maggie made a day trip to Moorea on the little inter-island steamer—taking their lunch and renting a horse and carriage for an island tour. They agreed that the island was beautiful, particularly around Oponohu Bay, with Mount Muaroa rising like a volcanic dagger 3,000 feet in the air at the end of the inlet. But still, Maggie stuck to her guns, declaring that nothing around here was "as spectacular as the Marquesas."

Louis's mother, with her indefatigable energy level, seemed unable to just sit on the verandah and look at the scenery, and while she waited for her son's recovery she decided to make herself useful and learn to type, because "it might be a good thing to have another typewriter in the family besides Lloyd." After taking her first lesson from Lloyd she spent her time practicing by writing to all her friends in Scotland.

It had been nearly a month since they dropped anchor in Papeete Harbor, and Louis was anxious to complete his physical recovery in some setting less urban. He had read about the *maeva marae* (ceremonial centers) on the island of Huahine in the Leeward group of the Society Islands and wanted Captain Otis's input on what navigational problems might be involved in visiting the island. Otis checked his charts and Sailing Directions and reported that Huahine had dangerous surrounding reefs which would make a night approach out of the question, but they did have an excellent anchorage and an adequate pier. However, the Sailing Directions also stated that the island received excessive amounts of rainfall, and therefore, mosquitoes were a major problem.

Then Otis reported on a conversation he had with a local trading schooner skipper on the previous day. When he told the man that his passengers on the CASCO wanted to escape the hustle and bustle of the Papeete area, the captain of the schooner informed him that the other side of the island of Tahiti was extremely beautiful but, unfortunately it was inhabited by "a people almost as wild as the people of the Marquesas." This was all that Louis wanted to hear, and he said, "Captain, that sounds like just the spot for me. When can we leave?" After a few moment's deliberation Otis replied, "I believe we can leave on the 24th if you are able to travel. There is a good harbor at Taravao and we should be able to make it there in just a few hours. It's only about 30 miles."

With a pilot aboard and all flags flying—Stars and Stripes and Union Jack from the masthead and a courtesy tricolor on a starboard halyard—CASCO sailed out of Papeete Harbor bound for Taravao on the southeast side of Tahiti Nui on the peninsula where it joins with Tahiti Iti. An eager Stevenson family was in high spirits, anticipating yet another exciting South Sea adventure. It wasn't long in coming, and it wasn't exactly the kind of adventure they would have preferred. As the ship left the shelter of the harbor it was hit by extremely strong headwinds, which swirled around Point Venus and funneled through the 12-mile channel between Tahiti and Moorea, consequently creating heavy head seas. For nearly 12 hours the schooner was forced to beat up the channel, tacking frequently as they fought for headway and maneuvered to keep their distance from Tahiti's barrier reefs with their thundering surf. On one occasion Otis even had to execute a dangerous jibe to save the ship from disaster on a lee shore. After rounding Point Venus they were able to proceed close hauled, but the weather continued so foul that the one day trip envisioned by Otis took nearly 30 hours and caused Louis to threaten to write an essay exposing the fallacy that this ocean was "Pacific."

At one point during their beat down the east coast of Tahiti Otis noticed that the main topmast appeared to be out of line, and the helmsmen, who had already noticed it, were afraid to stand their watches for fear the spar might come crashing down on them while at the wheel. Otis told them that they should keep alert but that he doubted that there was any real danger. He also promised to check out the problem as soon as they reached their destination.

It was early morning, a day and a half after its departure from Papeete, when CASCO approached the break in the barrier reef which served as a portal to Taravao Harbor, also known as Port Phaeton. Range beacons, which indicated the center of the channel, had been installed on the hill behind the harbor, but the entire width of the break in the reef was white with crashing surf. It promised to be a hair-raising experience at best, and Otis had the ship's boats run out, ready to be lowered in the event of an emergency. As the CASCO approached the harbor entrance the wind suddenly died, leaving the ship without the power to shoot the gap. The pilot, who had come aboard in Papeete, shouted at Otis, "We're not going to make it, Captain. We're doomed." But as quickly as the lull had come, a sudden squall produced a blast of air which filled CASCO's canvas and sent her surging through the gap, riding the crest of a wave for a moment, then plunging down into the trough, and finally gliding peacefully across a placid harbor. Louis turned toward Otis and with a mischievous grin said, "I guess that was the calm before the storm, Captain." At that moment Fanny entered the cockpit from below, and seeing that the boats were run out ready for lowering remarked, "Isn't that nice? The captain has already made preparations so that we can soon be going ashore."

As the schooner's anchor went down Stevenson casually approached Otis and said with a very straight face, "Captain, don't you think such yachting gymnastics as we just performed amounted to rather risky sport for invalid authors to engage in?" Without a second of hesitation Otis replied, "Well, Mr. Stevenson, you have known from the very beginning that sailing isn't for sissies." Then with a twinkle in his eye he lightly patted Louis on the back and moved on to the business of having a tender lowered for going ashore.

The Stevensons had not been ashore for but an hour or so when they returned to the ship with the news that this was not the place for them if Louis was to properly recover his health. While Taravao appeared beautiful and picturesque from the sea, the village was wedged between two mountains and surrounded by a dense forest of immense trees, and because of its location and oppressive vegetation, the village was extremely humid with little in the way of a cooling breeze. Consequently the mosquito population was unbearable, and Fanny had decided that they must go elsewhere.

At this point Captain Otis stated that some of the old trading schooner captains that he had met had talked about a kind of paradise tucked away at the end of the road on the north side of Tahiti Iti about 10 miles away. He said that the village was called Tautira and that he had heard that Captain Cook had visited the village in 1774 and again in 1777. The village was apparently out on a point of land and there was a protected anchorage not far away. There was a problem, however. Otis explained,

"They say the place is beautiful with as good a climate as can be found on Tahiti. However, I am afraid to take the CASCO to sea again until I have inspected that topmast which is obviously out of line. The plunge we just made coming through the breakers may have damaged that spar badly."

"Well, that settles it," broke in Fanny. "Have the boys row me ashore. I am going to find transportation to Tautira somehow."

Otis immediately called for the boat crew, knowing better than to try to talk Fanny out of something this important that involved the health of her husband.

Within an hour's time Fanny was back, and waiting on the shore were a team of horses, a wagon and a driver. As she came aboard she said, "Everyone get ready. Have Ah Fu pack us lunch. We have to have the horses and wagon back to the Chinese gentleman I rented them from by tonight, so let's get started. We will need everyone, including you, Captain, as I understand there will be some streams to ford, and we may need the extra muscle in case we get stuck." With that she disappeared below and started putting together a few things she and Louis might need in the next couple of days.

The trip to Tautira was a difficult one, but then very little was going right that day. The distance was only about 10 miles, but the road was almost non-existent and they had to ford streams at least a dozen times. On one occasion the wagon was stuck mid-stream and everyone but Louis had to get out and push. Because of the heat, the horses could not be driven faster than a very slow walk. Stevenson lay on a mattress brought from the CASCO, but as the wagon bounced along over rocks and into potholes he gritted his teeth and wondered if the torture would ever end. When they finally reached the village he was coughing up blood, and his face was pale in spite of the fact that he was running a high fever.

As the Stevensons entered the village they were received by a curious crowd of villagers, since white visitors were a rarity. Out of the crowd stepped an impressive looking Tahitian whom Maggie described as "a very fine and dignified man, over six feet three, and broad in proportion, and he looks more like a Roman emperor in bronze than words can express." Identifying himself as Ori a Ori, sub-chief of the village, he welcomed this extraordinary group of tourists. Then a gendarme stepped out of the welcoming party, and seeing the very sick author, offered his assistance in finding accommodations for the new arrivals. With his help Fanny negotiated a semi-European style house and put Louis to bed where he immediately fell asleep, exhausted and feverish. Fanny was determined to stay by Louis, but the rest of the party set out for Taravao. They would return later aboard the CASCO.

With Stevenson in bed and fast asleep, Fanny took stock of their surroundings. The house had one large, stuffy, clapboard-walled room and two bamboo-walled rooms which seemed to provide some circulation of air. It was sparsely furnished and had cost her more than she thought appropriate, but the place was clean, and she figured it would do until something better could be arranged. When she walked out on the verandah she had her first real look at Tautira. She could hardly believe what she was seeing. The scene was absolutely breathtaking. Tautira was an untouched paradise, a toy village in the midst of a flower garden. There was a broad village green like a public park through which a fresh water stream flowed gently from its origin in the Haavini Valley above to an indigo-blue sea below. There was a riot of color everywhere—the rich green of swaying coconut palm fronds blending with the white and yellow blossoms of the frangipani and the red, yellow and white blooms of the hibiscus. The fragrance of ginger and *tiare* filled the air.

Returning to the room where Louis was sleeping, she looked fondly at her loved one and said quietly, "Mr. Stevenson, I think I have a surprise for you. We have finally reached that South Sea utopia you have been seeking all your life. Sleep well my darling, a lovely new world awaits you."

The trip back to Taravao by horse-drawn wagon seemed easier since Maggie and the others no longer had Louis to worry about, but it was well after sundown when they saw the anchor light of the CASCO, which promised a good meal from Ah Fu's galley, a glass of wine and a well-deserved slumber.

Early the following morning Captain Otis began his inspection of the out-of-line topmast. Climbing 65 feet to the top of the mainmast he checked the section where the topmast overlapped the main by 10 feet and was secured to it by two metal bands, called caps. Seeing what appeared to be small cracks in the upper spar he began prodding the timbers with his rigging knife. To his horror the knife easily penetrated both the topmast and the upper portion of the mainmast. Both spars were obviously damaged beyond repair by dry rot. If he had flown a topsail from that topmast as he was tempted to do at one point during the trip from Papeete to Taravao, the topmast would have surely come crashing down on the deck. What infuriated the captain most was the fact that prior to leaving San Francisco, Dr. Merritt had assured him that the CASCO's preceding skipper had surveyed the ship and had sworn that it was seaworthy in every respect and capable of an extended sea voyage. But Otis knew that that much dry rot could not develop in a matter of a few months.

There was only one solution to the problem. Otis would have to take the CASCO to Tahiti and try to find a replacement for the damaged spars. But first Otis and his crew set about stabilizing the topmast with shroud lines port and starboard and lines forward to the peak of the foremast. With the topmast thus supported and lashed, the skipper took CASCO and his charges down the coast and anchored in Vaitepiha Bay just west of Tautira. Since the weather was favorable, Otis wanted to leave for Tahiti immediately, and the tender was sent ashore with Maggie, Lloyd and Valentine, their clothes, and enough food, wine and other supplies to last for at least a month, the amount of time the captain estimated the repairs would take. Although well-supplied, it was a somewhat forlorn little cluster of refugees who waved goodbye as the CASCO weighed anchor and headed north.

With the help of the sub-chief Ori a Ori and young men from his family the new arrivals and their gear were moved into the house that Louis and Fanny were occupying. No sooner had they settled in than Ori arrived at the front door accompanied by a tall, handsome and regal young woman who introduced herself in English as Moë the *matea* (matriarch) of Tautira. Actually she was the ex-Queen of Raiatea, the island where, in that very year, the French had deposed the island royalty after a native insurrection. Now she was living in exile in Tautira and serving as its *matea* because the area had been conquered by King Moë of Raiatea many generations ago and was still considered by Tahitians to be a colony of that island. Moë's mother was a Tahitian princess of the old royal family of Teriirere and had married an English trader named Salmon.

After introducing herself and giving a brief explanation of her role in Tautira she stated, "I have received word that a very sick man arrived in our village with you yesterday and I have come to see if I might help. We island people have many effective remedies which have returned our ill and impaired to good health. May I see the person who is ailing?"

In response to her request Fanny invited her into the house and took her in to see Louis, who was awake but appeared very weak. As ill as he was, he was his usual gracious self. Always a man who appreciated a beautiful woman, Louis savored her large laughing eyes, her attractive little mouth, her turned-up nose and her full little cheeks which revealed dimples whenever she smiled—which was often. In spite of her royal status there was an air of gentle charm about her and a quaint naiveté. And when Moë suggested that she might have a remedy for his condition, Stevenson smiled broadly and commented that he was delighted to have such a considerate and attractive nurse, and that he hoped he could be a cooperative patient.

In reply, Moë said, "Good. I will return shortly with something that I am certain will make you well again. But I also want you to prepare to move to a better house. This one is much too small for a sick man and his whole family to live in. I am arranging to have you all moved to Ori's house which is the largest in the village. It has many rooms, even one for Ori, who will watch over you and make sure that you and your family have everything you need."

With that she took her leave, and the Stevensons just looked at each other in amazement at their good fortune.

True to her word, Moë returned in less than an hour with a carved wooden vessel, much like one from which *kava* was served. It was filled with the traditional remedy she had promised. The bowl contained strips of raw mullet soaked in seawater with coconut cream, lime juice and red pepper. Fanny propped up Louis in bed with pillows, and Moë handfed the ailing man, who seemed to enjoy the experience and who thought to himself that in his long history of poor health he had certainly been given worse tasting medicine and by less attractive practitioners. Moë returned several times daily to feed Louis what turned out to be her elixir of life, and she had him up and walking again within a week. As the author's health improved he began spending long hours relaxing on the verandah, drinking in the beauty of the village setting and writing friends about Tautira, which he described as "the Garden of the World." To one he revealed, "We are in heaven here. I should prefer living among the people of Tahiti to any other people I have come across."

During his early days of convalescence Stevenson composed a poem honoring the princess to whom he owed his life. One afternoon he asked her to stop by. When Moë arrived he handed her a beautiful red hibiscus blossom and recited,

> *I threw one look to either hand,*
> *And knew I was in Fairyland.*
> *And yet one point of being so,*
> *I lacked. For Lady (as you know),*
> *Whoever by his might of hand*
> *Won entrance into Fairyland,*
> *Found always with admiring eyes*
> *A Fairy princess kind and wise.*
>
> *It was not long I waited; soon*
> *Upon my threshold, in broad noon,*
> *Fair and helpful, wise and good,*
> *The Fairy Princess Moë stood.*

As Stevenson acknowledged his affection for his Tautira hosts, they in Polynesian fashion returned his gift of love in more than equal measure. Ori immediately assumed the role and duties of a brother, insisting that he and Louis exchange names. Stevenson became *Teriitera* and Ori a Ori became *Rui*, which was as close as his language could come to the name Louis, since it had no "l" or "s" sounds. Later, Louis once again also became known as *Ona* (owner of CASCO) as he had in the Marquesas. Moë and Fanny exchanged names as well, but in time Fanny became known as *Tapena Tutu* (Captain Cook) because she claimed that she was a distant descendant of that famous navigator.

In fulfilling his role of a brother to Louis, Ori a Ori completely took charge of the Stevenson family welfare, and Fanny's journal records that he

> took charge of the sack containing our money . . . mostly half and quarter dollars. To Ori a Ori the sum seemed a vast fortune, and we spendthrifts. . . . I remember once asking him for a quarter for a chicken I had bought on credit while he was gone to a distant valley. He spoke to me with much severity, showing me the great bunch of cooking bananas he had carried on his shoulder all that distance for our subsistence. He scolded, "Here have I been tramping through the heat of the day mile upon mile to get food for the family—good, wholesome food, at no cost beyond my own exertions—and I return to find that you have been wantonly wasting your husband's substance in buying luxuries only suitable for feast days." After that, I asked permission before venturing on any extravagance.

The Stevensons' reputation of being spendthrifts was based to a large extent on their outlay for a feast that was given for the whole village after the Stevensons had been in residence in Tautira for three weeks. Its purpose was to thank the people for the many kindnesses the family had received. It cost nearly $80, an absolute fortune from Ori's perspective. The guests included some five factions of residents— Protestants, Catholics, "irreligious," school children, and a small group of Mormons. They roasted four large pigs and distributed four cases of ship's biscuit, which the CASCO had offloaded before leaving for Papeete. The people came with flower wreaths on their heads, laughing and singing, and dressed in colorful pareus made of trade cloth with flower and leaf designs against either a red, yellow, blue or white background. As was the custom on such occasions, guests arrived with chickens, fruits of all kinds, handicrafts and a few little pigs of their own, which were meant to be consumed by the Stevensons at some future date. From that day on pareus were also the uniform of the day of their European hosts, who loved the comfort of the Tahitian wraparounds but joked about "finally going completely native at last."

It was a wonderful party, and Louis, now feeling well enough to exert himself, danced a brief but humorous Tahitian style dance. The new foreigners, recently arrived from the sea, were now a part of the village, and they anticipated a more than pleasant four- or five-week stay until the CASCO would reappear with a new main mast and topmast.

For weeks the Stevensons had lived almost entirely on native foods, the most popular of which was poi with coconut cream, a dish much like Fanny had learned to prepare in the Marquesas. Louis never tired of fish, poi and pork but the rest of the family often yearned for a more varied diet. However, Ori a Ori was in charge of the bank and Fanny soon learned that one must not go over the head of a Tahitian family chief. Louis, who had cast off his shoes and shirt and had exchanged trousers for a flowered wraparound, found Ori a valued ally in his attempt to learn the Tahitian language and in collecting Tahitian songs, folktales and legends.

The Stevensons' thank-you party was followed several days later by a visit of Louis and Fanny to the village of Papara to pay their respects to Tati Salmon, the chief of the Teva clan which was the dominant kin group in the Tahiti-Iti area. On this particular occasion Tati was in his vanilla plantation when his house boy ran to tell him that he had European visitors asking for him. The boy described the male caller as "being barefoot and dressed in a pareu with his shirt on the outside" and "a woman whose hair hung down her back wearing a Mother Hubbard." Tati's immediate reaction upon meeting the man was that the emaciated looking white caller with long hair hanging down over his collar was "the illest man he had ever seen and the most eager to learn about Teva traditions."

All in all the couple visited Tati in Papara three times, once for a whole week. Louis spent about half this time in bed working with Tati and later in Tautira with Ori and Moë, on a ballad written in hexameters, the style in which Latin and Greek epics were written. The ballad, which he called *The Song of Rahero*, was derived from a traditional legend about how the villainous chief Rahero tricked a naive young fisherman named Tamatea from the village of Paea into insulting the despotic chief of Taiarapu (Tahiti Iti) whom Rahero hated. When Tamatea is put to death by the district chief for the insult, the boy's mother, Ahupu, vows revenge. She spreads the news that her village has accumulated a great surplus of food, thereby luring the district chief, his warriors, and Rahero to Paea where they demand the hospitality of this village which has so much food. The greedy guests overeat and consume great quantities of *kava*, and as a result fall fast asleep. The feast house is then torched by Ahupu and the Paea villagers, and all the guests are killed except Rahero who escapes, kills a local fisherman, abducts his wife and announces that he and his captured wife will now begin to produce a new tribe of warriors which will someday return to Paea for revenge. Once completed, Stevenson dedicated the ballad to Ori a Ori, writing as follows

> *Ori, my brother in the island made,*
> *In every tongue and meaning much my friend,*
> *This story of your country and your clan,*
> *In your loved house, your too much*
> *honoured guest,*
> *I made in English, Take it, being done;*
> *And let me sign it with the name you gave.*
> *Teriitera*

Besides penning the lengthy Rahero ballad Stevenson also wrote *The Feast of Famine* which drew on the author's impressions of Marquesan culture and traditions. Both seem to have been written as a welcome departure from the tedium of trying to finish his novel, *The Master of Ballantrae*, which had long resisted completion.

The clan chief Tati became very fond of Stevenson but thoroughly disliked Fanny, because of her "rude, bossy" ways. He believed the author to be completely managed by Fanny, who was not above sending him off to bed when she believed he should rest. Tati also objected to the fact that there were times when she would scold her husband for smoking or drinking too much wine, and showed little courtesy when she interrupted conversations between Stevenson and the clan head. He felt that Louis was completely dominated by what Tati described as a "tyrant" and a "bully." But then in his culture males were superior and females mostly chattel.

Fanny's reputation fared much better with Tautirans, however. With the help of the local women she learned to plait hats from pandanus fibers, and on her own produced a form of art work which became Ori's most prized possession. Using a lamp to cast shadow profiles on the wall she cut out silhouettes of Ori a Ori and the whole Stevenson family.

Her efforts so thrilled Ori a Ori that he pasted them on his wall, and when the party finally departed Tautira he had Fanny write an accompanying card which read, "Robert Louis Stevenson and party came ashore from the yacht CASCO, November 1888; and were two months the guests of Ori, to whom, having little else they gratefully bequeathed their shadows in memoriam."

The entire family tried their hand at being Tahitian. Even the maid Valentine was determined to learn how to cook Tahitian style, but after several failures at roasting fish over an open fire she returned to the more familiar oil stove. Lloyd hung out with the young men, took pictures of every typical Tahitian activity imaginable and began work on *Ebb Tide*, a book about beachcombers in Tahiti which Louis promised to co-author with him. Some evenings the family just sat on their verandah and enjoyed the perfume of the night or listened to the singing of the Tahitian chorus coming from the village assembly hall. According to Fanny, when the music ended they would go for a walk through the village "in a cloudy moonlight, on the forest lawn which is the street of Tautira. The Pacific roared outside upon the reef. Here and there one of the scattered palm-built lodges shone out . . . the lamplight bursting through the crannies of the wall."

Meanwhile, Captain Otis was having great difficulty solving his problems with the CASCO's damaged spars. Ordinarily the job should have taken about a week, had he been able to find the right kind of timber and an experienced work force. But Papeete was a pretty remote port to have the proper shipbuilding materials readily available, and Otis was only able to find one ship's carpenter among the beachcomber population, and he was not as committed to the task as Otis would have liked.

The problems of searching for a mast replacement had also been complicated by still other adversities. First Mate Goltz, who had signed aboard in the Marquesas, had succumbed to the many temptations of Papeete, particularly rum, and was continually drunk. Since he was of little or no use to Otis, he was replaced as first mate by a Dutchman named Reuter. Seamen Charles Wallin and Fred Schröder, who also had problems staying sober, proved equally useless for the task at hand, and the captain replaced them with a lad named Henry from Honolulu, a capable but somewhat elderly deckhand named Louis, a native Tahitian named Atta, and an English boy, Jack, who had originally found his way to the South Seas as a stowaway on a ship to New Zealand. Seaman Charles Olsen, who was also part of the original crew leaving San Francisco, had to return to the United States because of illness. Ah Fu, however, was loyal as always and a great comfort to Captain Otis, who could always depend on an excellent meal after a hard day's labor.

Much to Captain Otis's irritation, several weeks passed with no prospect of finding replacement spars for the schooner. But then he heard that a whaling barque lay shipwrecked on the reef not far from the port of Papeete. While the ship was much larger than the CASCO, its shorter mizzen mast, which was rigged with fore and aft sails, had only to be altered a bit to provide the needed spars for the CASCO. Fortunately the timbers were solid, without a trace of dry rot.

At the very beginning of the project the ship's carpenter told Captain Otis he really didn't need the money, and throughout the entire undertaking he worked when he felt like it and quit when the weather was not to his liking. When the sun would begin to bear down in the late morning, the carpenter would proclaim "Only mad dogs and Englishmen go out in the midday sun," and he would pack up his tools and head for the nearest waterfront saloon to spend his morning's wages. Otis did manage to keep most of his new crew sober and on the job, however, but in the tropical climate the men could only work a few hours in the morning and then again in the late afternoon.

When the new spars were finished, Otis and his crew set up a load-bearing frame on deck consisting of two spars (called sheerlegs) lashed together at the top where a line was secured and blocks attached to provide a mechanical advantage in lifting the mainmast. The new spar was then hoisted until its base could be guided into a hole on deck, lowered, and secured to the step plate on the keelson. The topmast was then hoisted into place and made fast in a mast cap. With the masts in place, new standing rigging was tarred and installed as main and topmast stays, shrouds, backstays and ratlines.

The month of November passed before Stevenson received any communication from Captain Otis about the status of the CASCO. Then a short note, recounting Otis's problems finding the right sized spar and the difficulty of getting laborers to work full time on the project, was delivered to him by the Tautira village chief Areia, who had gone to Papeete on village business. In his letter Otis estimated it would take at least another three weeks before the CASCO would be ready for sea.

When the news of additional delay arrived in Tautira Louis's mother saw the positive side of their dilemma and wrote her sister in Scotland that "the long detention has proved a blessing." She reported that Louis's appetite was splendid, he was a little fatter than he had been in the Marquesas, and that she had not seen him "so well since 1879." Louis was, to be sure, using the time wisely. He spent long hours bathing in the cool fresh water stream that ran through the village; he continued his efforts to learn Tahitian and expand his collection of native songs and legends; and he grudgingly worked a bit on *The Master of Ballentrae*, but that proved to be an onerous undertaking and he set it aside for later. RLS also spent considerable time horseback riding and exploring the environs with a one horse gig. He often ventured deep into the verdant valleys behind the village, and on one exceptionally beautiful day he was returning to Tautira when he observed a scene which so enchanted him that his prose description excelled in charm anything he had formerly written about the South Seas. He wrote,

> Presently we came to a house in a pretty garden, quite by itself, very nicely kept, the doors and windows open, no one about, and no noise but that of the sea. It looked like a house in a fairy-tale, and just beyond . . . we saw the inhabitants. Just in the mouth of the river, where it met the sea waves, they were ducking and bathing and screaming together like a covey of birds: seven or eight little naked brown boys and girls as happy as the day was long: and on the banks of the stream beside them, real toys—toy ships, full rigged, and with their sails set, though they were lying in the dust on their beam ends. And then I knew for sure they were all children in a fairy-story, living alone together in that lovely house with the only toys in all the island; and that I had myself driven in my four-wheeled gig, into a corner of that fairy-story.

Obviously back in the counterpane fantasy world of his childhood, Stevenson seemed as happy and carefree as these little Polynesian people at play. But the fantasy world was short-lived, and soon the real world was presenting problems not easily overlooked. It would be close to a month before they could expect to see the CASCO again, and the stores originally brought ashore from the ship had been expended and their money was nearly gone. When Fanny and Louis had received the note from Otis outlining his problems and predicting it would be close to Christmas before he could pick them up, Fanny had burst into tears and Moë had followed suit. But Ori a Ori said, "Rui, you are my brother: all that I have is yours. I know your food is done, but I can give you plenty of fish and taro. We like you and wish to have you here. Stay where you are till the CASCO comes. Be happy—*et ne pleurez pas*." And then Louis too wiped away a tear.

The Tahitian diet suited Stevenson well, while others in the party longed for coffee, jam, ship's biscuit and wine, but there was plenty of poi with coconut cream which was still looked upon by the family as their favorite desert.

Early in the morning of December 1 Ori approached Louis with the news that he and a crew of three were preparing to row the village whaleboat into Papeete to bring back news of the CASCO and some of the CASCO provisions the Stevensons so badly wanted. While Louis objected strenuously, stating that the trip was too difficult and too dangerous, Ori insisted that he had made the trip many times, and he wanted to help his brother who would surely do the same for him if needed. Put that way Louis wished him Godspeed and accompanied him down to the beach, where he watched the men launch the boat and make their way up the coast. Ori had promised he would be back in three days, and he said he hoped news of an early CASCO arrival would please Louis, although he said that it would be a sad day for him when his brother would sail away.

The chief and his crew rowed steadily, putting up a bit of sail where possible, and they managed to complete the 35-mile journey by late afternoon. As they entered to harbor Ori sighted the CASCO at the inter-island schooner wharf.

Captain Otis was on the dock supervising the hoisting of the main topmast when a noble and dignified Tahitian approached and introduced himself as Ori a Ori, the sub-chief of Tautira, and said, "I have just come from Tautira where your passengers are waiting for your return. Mr. Stevenson asked me to find you and inquire about the work on the sailing ship and when you might return for them. They no longer have any white man's food, their money is gone, and they say they have almost forgotten what wine tastes like. The young men of my family and I have rowed a whaleboat here so that we can take back provisions from your ship and news of its possible arrival in Tautira."

Captain Otis recognized Ori a Ori immediately as Stevenson's Tahitian benefactor and asked him to his cabin where he wrote a long letter describing the status of the CASCO repair and predicted that he would probably be able to pick up the party about Christmas Day. Ori and his crew were fed and housed on the CASCO for several days until the weather would permit a return passage. After the chief's first meal aboard, which he ate with the captain in the forward cabin, Ah Fu remarked to Otis regarding Ori's hearty appetite, "Him must leave dam quick, or else bust um bank."

A week later, with the bank still relatively solvent, the weather broke and the whaleboat was loaded with a case of champagne and several boxes of tinned beef and ship's biscuit and a large can of jam. With their cargo safely stowed under the thwarts, the Tautira chief and his crew rowed quickly out of the harbor singing a lively Tahitian melody to provide cadence for their rowing. Ori was in a buoyant mood, for he knew that Louis would be happy with the stores, and the chief was delighted with the news that he would have the company of his newfound brother for at least another three weeks.

When the whaleboat arrived back in Tautira there was considerable excitement and relief, as it was four days overdue. The three-day trip Ori had anticipated had actually taken a week. But as the whaleboat was beached the Stevenson clan was front and center among the villagers with broad smiles on their faces expressing their joy at Rui's safe return.

The day after the whaleboat arrived with their much anticipated stores the Stevensons gave a small dinner party in the chief's honor and poured glasses of champagne for everyone including Ori, who claimed that he had never tasted the drink but had heard that it was "a drink for chiefs." After downing his first glass of the wine he held out his glass for a refill stating, "I shall drink it continually, since it truly *is* a drink for chiefs." He casually inquired of Louis, "What is the cost of it by the bottle?" When the author told him, Ori returned his full glass to Stevenson and said, "It is not fit that even kings should drink a wine so expensive." But fortunately the Stevensons noticed later that the shock did not affect his appetite.

As evening approached on December 16, there was great excitement in Tautira, for a schooner had been sighted by the young men of the village, but then it disappeared out to sea again. When the Stevensons received the news, they were certain it was the CASCO and that Captain Otis had decided not to attempt to enter the harbor, as it was too dark to safely negotiate the passage through the reef. Undoubtedly he would be arriving early the next day. But when morning came there was no schooner to be seen, and everyone disappointedly accepted the fact that it was not the CASCO that had been sighted after all.

The following week was eventful, however, for although it did not bring their schooner, it did bring an old friend to their village. Two French school supervisors arrived to conduct an oral examination of the Tautira pupils, and acting as their interpreter was none other than Donat Rimareau, whom the Stevensons had left in Fakarava approximately three months earlier. Since the school officials spoke no Tahitian, Donat had very little time to spend with the Stevensons, which was somewhat of a disappointment to the family. The results of the examination were also disappointing, as the students did poorly in everything except arithmetic. Maggie suggested that the officials could hardly expect better results, since no one could read, because the only book in the village was a Bible owned by the Tahitian mission pastor.

At 9:30 a.m., December 21, the children of the village began shouting, *E pahi, E pahi* (a boat, a boat) followed by the equally exuberant response in the Stevenson household, "Hurrah! a sail in sight. It must be the CASCO." They watched and waited, but to the dismay of all the white speck on the horizon disappeared only to be replaced by another late in the day. The next morning it was still there and growing larger until about 11 a.m. when the CASCO did indeed enter the bay and anchor just offshore. "Now at last," Maggie put it, "we are no longer shipwrecked mariners."

Lloyd, Valentine and Maggie immediately went aboard so that the Ori a Ori family could start repossessing their house, but Louis and Fanny wanted to remain with their host until the last possible minute. Captain Otis came ashore to tell Louis that he needed a couple of days to adjust the rigging and generally make the ship ready for the 2,300 mile trip to Hawaii, so he was planning their departure for Tuesday, which was Christmas Day.

Ori then invited everyone to Sunday dinner, saying he wanted to entertain the captain to thank him for his hospitality while in Papeete. Everyone ate heartily what they realized would be their last Tahitian feast, and then the Stevensons toasted Ori a Ori, Moë and the whole village who had made their stay their most cherished South Sea memory.

On Christmas Day the entire population of Tautira lined the beach to bid their European friends farewell. The French gendarme, Monsieur Tebeau, stationed in Tautira, fired a twenty-one gun salute with his army rifle as the CASCO's anchor was brought aboard, and then Captain Otis returned the honor with his Winchester. The schooner's sails now filled with wind as she turned toward the open sea, and soon the CASCO was but a white dot on the horizon. The Tautira well-wishers walked slowly home feeling that something very interesting had just gone out of their lives.

Heartbroken by the departure of his beloved friend and ceremonial brother, Ori sat down the day after Stevenson's departure and wrote the following touching letter which Louis received shortly after his arrival in Hawaii.

Tautira, 26 December 1888

To Teriitera (Louis) and Tapina Tutu (Fanny) and Aromaiterai (Lloyd) and Teiriha (Maggie)
Salutation in the true Jesus.
I make you to know my great affection. At the hour when you left us, I was filled with tears; my wife, Rui Tehina, also, and all of my household. When you embarked I felt a great sorrow. It is for this that I went upon the road, and you looked from that ship, and I looked at you on the ship with great grief until you had raised the anchor and hoisted the sails. When the ship started, I ran along the beach to see you still; and when you were on the open sea I cried out to you, "Farewell Louis": and when I was coming back to my house I seemed to hear your voice crying "Rui farewell".... I did not sleep that night, thinking continually of you, my dear friend, until the morning.... I looked into your rooms; they did not please me as they used to

do. I did not hear your voice crying, 'hail Rui.' I thought then that you had gone, and that you had left me. Rising up I went to the beach to see your ship, and I could not see it. . . . I will not forget you in my memory. . . . But now we are separated. May God be with you all. May His word and His mercy go with you, so that you may be well and we also, according to the words of Paul.

Ori a Ori; that is to say, Rui.

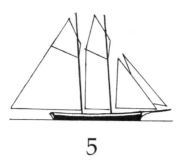

5
Hawaii—Crossroads of the Pacific

WHILE THE BROKEN-HEARTED Ori a Ori stood watching the CASCO disappear over the horizon the Stevensons sat in the cockpit gazing back at the mountains of Tahiti as they grew smaller and smaller and finally disappeared from view. Everyone seemed to be entertaining bittersweet feelings which they were attempting to sort out. The Tautira experience had brought them more intimately into contact with South Sea people and their ways than they had experienced in either the Marquesas or the Tuamotus. On the other hand, they relished being back sailing again with the CASCO lazing along through a moderate sea with all sails drawing, heading for new unimagined adventures in this vast ocean world of royal blue water and sky and distant emerald isles.

The Hawaiian chain lay 2,300 miles away, and they were anticipating a two and one-half or three week voyage to that destination, which had come to be known as "the crossroads of the Pacific." For Louis, crossroads meant mail and bank drafts, arriving from the outside world, and there promised to be a six-month supply, which he jokingly referred to as "Pandora's Box," awaiting them at the home of Belle Strong, Fanny's daughter, who had been living in Honolulu since 1882. They were expecting letters from friends in Europe and America, and more important, checks from publishers which would replenish their badly eroded finances. The Stevenson family figured the crossroads would be an excellent location from which to decide if, when, and where they might head for further South Sea sailing adventures. For now it was good to hear the bow wave rushing by CASCO's hull and watch the dolphins racing alongside and frolicking under her bowsprit. A frigatebird soared overhead, easily keeping up with the CASCO which was traveling at a leisurely 5 knots. It was comfortable sailing, and after a light lunch of fresh pork and island fruits and vegetables everyone came back to the cockpit and returned to some of their pre-Marquesas activities such as watching flying fish, reading Gibbon's *Decline and Fall of the Roman Empire* aloud, and generally enjoying the warm summer sunshine and refreshing sea air.

On December 27, they passed Makatea, the upthrust atoll whose name had been given to all such islands. The only high island in the Tuamotus, Makatea, consisted of a plateau with precipitous cliffs 260 feet high ringing the entire island. Some 60 miles north they passed Tikehau, an oval shaped atoll; they would have entered the lagoon through its single pass, but the winds were so light that Captain Otis was afraid to attempt an entry. The next day brought a bit of excitement—the sighting of the Honolulu-Tahiti mail steamer. CASCO ran up signal flags as a salute, but the steamer maintained her course and soon was out of sight. It would be the only sighting of another ship until they reached Hawaii.

Although the good weather continued to prevail, the CASCO was making slow progress north toward the doldrums, and the sun beat down so unmercifully that soon it was too sweltering to sit in the cockpit. The deck was so hot that it nearly burned hands or bare feet. Brass fixtures such as rails or the ship's binnacle could not be touched at all. But the nights were beautiful, and because there was no moon the stars seemed brighter and more numerous than the Stevensons had ever remembered. They thought Venus had the appearance of a small moon, and the star gazers reluctantly commented that soon they would no longer see the Southern Cross which they had become so used to associating with their beloved southern seas.

Luncheon on January 1, 1889, marked the end of the fresh meat, which was stewed duck. Then for dinner, rations of salt pork, salt beef and ship's biscuit returned to the menu, plus what fresh fruits and vegetables from Tahiti had not yet spoiled. There were still plenty of coconuts, however, and this meant that everyone still had the pleasure of having coconut cream in their coffee. Louis, who always seemed to enjoy himself at sea, remarked concerning the rations, "It seems then, that we are between the devil and the salt horse, and the deep green sea." This brought a chuckle from the rest of the family but not from Captain Otis, who had developed an earache.

The first two weeks in January brought such terrible weather that the passengers equated their situation with the tribulations of Job. There were constant squalls with violent winds and often with lightning and even hail, followed by days of dead calm with occasional puffs of wind which were not even strong enough to ripple the sails. There was just the constant creaking of the masts. Day-long downpours of rain were not unusual and when there was enough wind to move the ship, it came from dead ahead and required constant tacking to make any headway at all. The day that CASCO crossed the equator, January 13, however, a steady dependable wind allowed the ship to log 130 miles in a 24-hour period.

January 17 brought a drastic change in the weather. They had picked up the long anticipated northeast tradewinds which blew with a vengeance, permitting 24-hour runs between 170 and 230 nautical miles. Given their course for Hawaii, the wind permitted the CASCO to sail on a beam reach, the best possible point of sailing, but it also brought a beam sea that caused rolling and made life miserable for both passengers and crew. The northeast trades then blew without ceasing all the way to Hawaii, and the motion of the ship was so violent that the passengers were restricted to their cabins where they were thrown about in one direction and then another. When the crew went on deck to handle sails or lines they tied ropes around their waist to keep from being washed overboard. In spite of the use of fiddles as well as keeping the tablecloth wet to prevent dinnerware from sliding off the table, Ah Fu was unable to serve little more than soup and coffee to what few diners chose to arrive for meals.

Fanny, who always suffered the most from rough weather, declared about this time that this would be her last voyage, and that when and if they ever reached Hawaii she would go ashore and stay there. Not only was it difficult to impossible for any of the family to get any rest either night or day, but there were also little unpleasant surprises like the night when a bucket of sea water came through the open cabin skylight and pored straight down on Maggie's head, bringing her awake with a scream. Completely soaked, she took refuge on the cabin floor just as a similar dousing happened to Lloyd.

It was during this tradewind-driven passage north that Otis

approached Louis with the news that the barometer was falling dangerously fast and that he believed that a hurricane might be approaching.

"What do you want me to do, Mr. Stevenson?" he asked. "Do you want me to heave to and ride it out or run for it?"

"By all means, Captain, I think we should run for it," Louis said with a big grin on his face.

Otis, who was still suffering from an earache, shot back, "Mr. Stevenson, do you always have to be so damn cheerful?'

During the next few days of "running for it," which proved to be the right thing to do, the CASCO veritably flew along under double reefed fore and main sails and a small storm jib. But there was one day which Stevenson would long remember. He had bravely ventured on deck by way of the after companionway and had found green sea splashing over the cockpit coamings and pouring down the companionway until he slammed the hatch shut. At this same time the foresail sheet jammed on a cleat in the process of tacking, and the captain had no knife to cut it free. Stevenson rushed forward shouting to the helmsman "Pinch her well," and when he arrived amidships he and Captain Otis in a combined effort managed to pull the line free. It was the first time that Louis had ever taken an active part in working the ship, but he explained his actions to Otis later: "I worked like a Trojan, judging the possibility of hemorrhage better than the certainty of drowning." And if this was not enough for one day, when Louis went below he found the hatch in the after cabin sole open and three crewmembers frantically bailing and carrying buckets of seawater out of the bilge. The pumps were temporarily out of order.

Meanwhile Fanny wedged herself in her bunk with pillows. While chronically ill of *mal de mer* on every voyage she rarely complained, but did occasionally express her anguish in letters to friends back home. With a chamber pot close at hand in case of emergency, Fanny Stevenson wrote to Fanny Sitwell

> I have more cares than I was really fit for. To keep house on a yacht is no easy thing. When Louis and I broke loose from the ship and lived alone among the natives I got on very well. It was when I was deathly seasick, and the question was put to me by the cook, "What shall we have for the cabin dinner, what for tomorrow's breakfast, what for lunch? and what about the

sailors' food? Please come and look at the biscuits, for the wee-vils have got into them". . . . I do not like being 'the lady of the yacht' but ashore—oh, then I feel I am repaid for all!

As the CASCO neared the island of Hawaii the wind was gale force with 15-foot swells now on the ship's starboard quarter, which exposed them to broaching and possible capsize. Louis later described the situation in a letter to his cousin Bob Steven-son:

> It blew fair, but very strong; we carried jib, foresail, and main-sail, all single-reefed, and she carried her lee rail under water and flew. The swell was the heaviest I have ever been out in. . . . We had the best hand—old Louis—at the wheel; and, really, he did nobly, and had noble luck, for it never caught us once. At times it seemed we must have it; old Louis would look over his shoulder with the queerest look and dive down his neck into his shoulders; and then it missed us somehow, and only sprays came over our quarter, turning the little outside lane of deck into a mill race as deep as to the cockpit coamings. I never re-member anything more delightful and exciting.

When the CASCO sailed past Kailua-Kona they were in the lee of the island and the winds died entirely and the sea flattened out. Then a light breeze developed taking the CASCO past the is-lands of Maui and Molokai. It was Wednesday, January 23, and the anticipated two and one-half to three week duration of the Tahiti to Hawaii passage had already taken 30 days. Rations were down to a bit of salt beef and ship's biscuit. There was no wine, no coffee and worst of all for chain-smokers like Louis and Fanny, no tobacco. Honolulu, with its luxury hotel dining rooms and its cornucopia of fresh victuals, seemed so near and yet so far. With the lights of Honolulu in sight, the wind died com-pletely.

At dawn on Thursday Louis came on deck and discovered that the sails were filling and the CASCO was moving slowly but surely toward Honolulu.

During this stressful voyage to Hawaii, Louis and Otis spent a good deal of time together on deck and at this stage of the cruise both men had come to have a great deal of respect for each other. In a letter to Charles Baxter Stevenson wrote, "I be-lieve I poured forth my sorrows over my captain in your ear. Patience and time have quite healed these conflicts; we do what we want now, and the captain is a trusted friend. It did require patience in the beginning, but the seed has borne a most plentiful crop, and I feel quite fond of our captain, and (as I say) really like the man."

The feeling was definitely mutual. Otis, who originally was repulsed by Stevenson, made no attempt to disguise his low opinion of writers and poets. He considered RLS a bohemian scribbler who knew very little about the sea and ships but wrote about them at length anyway. This opinion was based on the one book he had read, *Treasure Island.* But throughout the cruise Otis came to have real respect for him as a competent sailor and a valiant adventurer. RLS took great interest in everything occurring on or around the CASCO, but was never in the way. He even loved rainy days on deck and was anything but the invalid Otis had anticipated being stuck with. Shortly before returning with the CASCO to San Francisco Otis told the Honolulu publisher Arthur Johnstone that when the CASCO was being chased by 15-foot swells off the island of Hawaii and was in danger of broaching-to, Stevenson was on deck observing all the action, and "How did Stevenson take it? Why, man, he never turned a hair; in fact, I am convinced that he enjoyed it. . . . When I was in my stateroom for a few minutes, he came in, holding against the walls to avoid falling, and told me in a tone of enthusiasm, and with sparkling eyes, that it was 'a new experience and a desirable one which he would certainly find a place for'." Otis later found that place in the novel *The Wrecker.*

The thing that impressed the captain most was the way Louis faced his possible death in Papeete, and Otis doubted that he himself could have been as casual and courageous as the man had been.

As Otis anticipated the end of his charter, he knew he would miss this invaluable companion who was first up in the morning walking the deck barefooted in a cotton shirt and trousers and a white yachting cap. According to Belle Strong, Fanny's daughter, the captain was so taken with Stevenson that the family began to notice that he had started to use many of the author's expressions at the dinner table. He also "copied his frank engaging manner and was evidently one of his warmest admirers," and when recounting events of their South Sea cruising adventures, he often quoted Louis and described many of the author's daring exploits.

On January 24 the CASCO was sighted off Kawaihoa Point and the news was telephoned to the port authority which in turned notified Belle Strong, who had been very concerned because the ship had been reported "missing at sea," since a 31-day passage from Tahiti to Hawaii was unheard of. Belle had been living in Hawaii for six and one-half years with her artist husband Joe and son Austin. Both she and her husband were working at King Kalakaua's court, and the harbor authority was very much aware of her concern.

Upon hearing the news she arranged for a skiff to take her and her eight-year-old son Austin out to the entrance of the Honolulu Harbor, where she could meet the incoming schooner and present *leis* to her long-lost family. The only complication was that as the CASCO rounded Diamond Head winds picked up sending the vessel hurtling toward its Honolulu anchorage at thirteen knots, an experience which Lloyd later described as "flying round Diamond Head with the speed of an express train, flashing past the buoys and men-of-war." As they entered the harbor the lookout forward reported an open boat with two people waving wildly directly in the schooner's path. As they drew closer the Stevenson family recognized Belle and her son Austin. Otis immediately relieved the helmsman and altered course mumbling an oath under his breath. As the schooner passed the skiff, the boatman threw a line aboard, and the boat was towed alongside at alarming speed. Austin, who was in the bow was easily snatched aboard, but Belle was hoisted on deck with somewhat more difficulty in a scene which featured a flurry of a brightly flowered cotton frock and eyelet petticoats. She somehow made it aboard without a scratch or a bruise. It all happened so fast that Belle hardly knew what happened to her, but she did remember her mother scolding, "Now that was a foolish thing to do. You could have been killed." When Belle regained her composure, she threw her arms around each member of the family and asked, "How is everybody?" The answer was a unanimous "hungry!"

On Friday, January 24, the CASCO anchored just off the Oceanic Steamship Company's dock not far from another schooner with which they were very familiar—the British yacht

NYANZA, which they had met in the Marquesas. Somewhat earlier Belle had gone out to meet the NYANZA, thinking it was the CASCO. Unfortunately, before the NYANZA left Hawaii six days later there was bad feeling between the two crews, as the *Honolulu Bulletin* printed a letter, presumably written by Lloyd, describing the meeting of the two ships in the islands, wherein he referred to the NYANZA as an "ugly" yacht. That ship's crew was deeply offended, and believing Otis was the author, the captain was nearly involved in fisticuffs.

As CASCO's anchor clattered out of its hawse pipe Louis turned and surveyed the city of Honolulu. His initial reaction was that he was not much impressed. There were paved streets bustling with carriages and street cars; electric light poles; residential areas with white frame houses and whitewashed picket fences; the urban sprawl of office buildings, hotels and an assortment of retail stores was not his idea of a Polynesian paradise.

Belle also had some first impressions of her vagabond family. Louis, she thought, was almost as brown as a Polynesian, and he was healthier than she had ever seen him. Maggie looked as prim and proper as always. Fanny was looking brown as an islander but "peaked," having just spent several days suffering from seasickness. Belle was particularly struck by her baby brother Lloyd who seemed to her "very English in speech and manner," and his "witty talk, his fine manners and his unusually musical voice" made a deep impression on her. She especially noticed that he wore a gold earring like a sailor. But what seemed to be a common characteristic of all the family members was their obsession with food "of which they could talk of little else."

When everyone was together in the after cabin Belle said, "I think we can solve your hunger problems. Joe and I have made arrangements for all of us to eat at the Royal Hawaiian hotel this evening. It will be a celebration of your safe return back to civilization with a roast beef and champagne dinner, and Joe and I will even pay the bill, because in addition to having no food aboard, I'm sure you don't have much money either. Tomorrow morning we will start inquiring as to where you can stay as I am sure that you would like to have a change of scene from this schooner."

Meeting people at Butaritari, Gilbert Islands. *Charles Scribner's Sons, New York*

King Tem Binoka at Abemama Island.
Scribner's Magazine

"Equator Town" on Abemama Island.
Charles Scribner's Sons, New York

The arrival of the Stevensons in Apia, Western
Samoa. *Painting by Loy Neff*

Samoan village.
Author's collection

JANET NICOLL in New Zealand port. *Wellington Maritime Museum collection, Photograph Inksters Ltd, Greymouth*

The crew of the JANET NICOLL. *Charles Scribner's Sons, New York*

The king of Manihiki (standing center) with island judge on his right and Tin Jack on his left. Man in the foreground is one of the island beachcombers. *Charles Scribner's Sons, New York*

Figurehead on Penrhyn Island which will later appear in *Ebb Tide,* the book Stevenson wrote with his stepson Lloyd. *Charles Scribner's Sons, New York*

Trader Tom Day of Naukanau Atoll.
Charles Scribner's Sons, New York

Vailima Mansion. Author's collection

It was a glorious evening for all. Everyone dressed for the occasion, including Otis who wore his captain's cap and dress blue uniform with gold stripes on the sleeve, and Louis was even wearing shoes, something he had not done for months. Everyone was adorned with orchid *leis* and danced to the dulcet strains of commercial Hawaiian music. When the evening was over Maggie declared that the meal had been "the finest banquet of which I have ever partaken. But, oh dear me, this place is so civilized."

The following day Belle brought word that a Mrs. Caroline Bush, mother of a local politician, and a great admirer of Stevenson, had invited the family to stay at her home in Honolulu. Bags were quickly packed and ferried ashore to a carriage which Belle had rented for the transfer.

Belle and her artist husband Joe Strong had come to Hawaii in 1882 after an elopement of which Fanny greatly disapproved. Joe's father and mother had originally come to the islands as missionaries several years earlier, but they had retired and returned to Oakland several years before Belle and Joe decided that Hawaii would be an excellent place for a promising young artist to make a name for himself. Joe Strong did manage to obtain a commission from the Spreckels Sugar Company of San Francisco to produce an immense painting of the Pali on Oahu. The chief executive, Claus Spreckels, was a close friend of the Hawaiian king and was an occasional participant in Kalakaua's all-night poker parties.

When Joe and Belle first arrived, Charles Warren Stoddard found them a place to live and educated them regarding the political and social situation which involved two feuding social sets or castes—the "Missionaries" and the "Royals." The Missionaries were actually the sons and grandsons of the early proselytizers of which it was often jested that "they came to do good and did very well" (financially of course). And the Hawaiians added that "when the missionaries came, we had the land and they had the Bible. 'Let us pray,' said the missionaries. We closed our eyes. When we opened them again, they had the land and we had the Bible."

Shortly after their arrival, the Strongs were invited to the king's Coronation Ball in the newly constructed Iolani Palace in

February 1883, eleven years after Kalakaua had ascended the throne. At that event Joe and Belle were introduced to the king, and the sovereign was quite taken with Belle, with the result that she entered the monarch's employ where he depended on her for all manner of services, mostly artistic but some political. And by the time the Stevensons arrived Joe and Belle had long been solidly in the "Royal" camp (often described as "the drinking crowd"), which made it possible for Belle to set up an audience with the king for Louis and Lloyd just two days after their arrival.

Belle enjoyed being included in the king's social events, but she had other responsibilities such as caring for her son Austin and designing royal ceremonial paraphernalia like flags and banners for the palace and even a special coat of arms. Joe did some portrait painting for the royal family but mostly he found the palace social whirl so much to his liking that he became addicted to alcohol, occasionally used opium, became a womanizer not unlike Belle's father, and was a complete spendthrift. When the Stevensons arrived in Hawaii Belle had been seriously considering leaving him. This came as no shock to Fanny, who had always opposed the union. Joe was once described by Fanny in a letter to Charles Baxter, the man who handled Louis's financial affairs, as "refined, artistic, affectionate, as weak as water, living in vague dreams. One needs to be a millionaire to support him and a philosopher to love him."

When Louis and Lloyd arrived at Iolani Palace on January 26 for the audience Belle had arranged, they were ushered into a well-appointed drawing room where the king was seated on a couch upholstered with gold brocade. As he rose to greet them Stevenson was immediately impressed by his appearance—tall, stocky but not fat, with a kind and sensitive face framed by a heavy mustache and beard. He was dressed in a well-tailored white linen suit. His demeanor immediately put his guests at ease.

The king prided himself on being somewhat of a man of letters, having published a volume on Hawaiian folklore and having written the words to the Hawaiian national anthem. He was well acquainted with Stevenson's literary achievements and had read both *Treasure Island* and *The Strange Case of Dr. Jekyll and Mr. Hyde*. The two men were immediately taken with one another, sharing a common interest in Polynesian art, culture, archaeology, history and language, and Stevenson was much impressed with this sovereign's cosmopolitan interests. He learned that in 1881 the king had made a 10-month tour of the world, visiting the crowned heads of Japan, China, Siam, Egypt, Italy and England and had even called upon the Pope in the Vatican and President Grant in the United States.

Before the audience was over, Louis had invited the king to tea aboard the CASCO and the king had extended an invitation to the author to join him later in the week at his "boat house," where the king and his cronies played poker and hoisted a beverage or two. In addition to hosting high-stake card games, Kalakaua revealed he was also an enthusiastic sports fan, promoting yachting, horse racing and, worst of all from the missionary point of view, he supported troupes of hula girls, whose dancing the righteous contingent thought obscene. In fact the *Hawaiian Gazette* described native dancing as "representative of all that is animal and gross, the very apotheosis of grossness." Such sentiments, Louis soon would learn, were part of an orchestrated attempt by anti-Royalists to have all Hawaiian arts and traditions stamped out and forgotten.

Two days after Stevenson and Lloyd met with the king in the palace, Kalakaua came aboard the CASCO for tea. The king arrived wearing immaculate white linen slacks and tunic with touches of gold braid on the shoulders and a military-type cap with gold leaves on the bill to match the braid. While his appearance was formal, his demeanor was casual and genial, and the king had much to share with Louis.

Tea turned out to be champagne and biscuits; after an initial round, Stevenson entertained by reading his recently finished ballad *Ticonderoga* which the king enthusiastically applauded. This event was followed by a rousing rendition of a sailor's hornpipe by Captain Otis on his accordion while Belle danced. After several more rounds of champagne, Lloyd sang the song *The Fine Pacific Islands* which His Majesty maintained was "most appropriate for the occasion." Following what had been a delightful afternoon Kalakaua stated that he "unfortunately had another engagement" and with great dignity thanked his hosts and departed in the royal steam-powered barge.

After his departure, Louis, having observed Kalakaua drink five bottles of champagne and two bottles of brandy with no apparent affect, turned to Belle and asked, "Does the king always drink that much?" And Belle, who had been to numerous parties in the palace and had spent considerable time working for the king, laughed and said, "Oh yes, he is famous for having an extraordinary capacity. It is said that his secret for staying sober is that he drinks a glassful of *poi* mixed with milk before social engagements where liquor might be served. Incidentally, I happen to know where the king was going when he left here. It was to a cocktail party to which he had been invited aboard a newly arrived man-of-war in the harbor." Louis chuckled and shook his head thinking of how his friend Charles Stoddard had described Kalakaua, as "a king as one reads of in nursery tales. He is all things to all men, a most companionable person. Possessed of rare refinement." And Ah Fu's assessment of the king, as the royal barge carried him ashore, was "He son-of-gun fine fella."

Before leaving the CASCO that afternoon Kalakaua reciprocated with an invitation for the entire family to have breakfast at Iolani Palace the following morning at 8:30. Upon their arrival for their breakfast date the guests were somewhat surprised to be welcomed at this early hour by the boisterous tones of the Royal Hawaiian Band, the musical ensemble which the king was quick to pronounce "the pride of his heart." While the guests secretly thought the breakfast musicale somewhat inappropriate and even bizarre, Maggie was the only one of the group forced to evaluate the performance. When asked by the king how she liked it, she politely said, "It was very nice and it didn't disturb me in the least."

After lavishly entertaining her guests for several days, Caroline Bush arranged for them to have use of her son Henry Poors' beach bungalow, called Manuia Lanai, on Waikiki beach. This retreat was just an hour from town on the mule-drawn tramcar line, but it was a lovely spot near Diamond Head, overlooking the surf-washed beach, and it was far enough off the beaten path that Louis was not unduly annoyed by celebrity seekers. Actually the place consisted of just a single room lanai open to the seaside—hardly a place to accommodate a family for an extended visit. It was, however, quite suitable for a major social event about to take place.

On February 3, Henry Poor, who was a close political ally of the king, hosted a luau at Manuia Lanai for some 25 guests in honor of King Kalakaua and Princess Lili'uokalani. The feast featured roast pig, poi chicken, raw fish, seaweed (limu) roasted Kukui nuts and the king's favorite—baked dog. When the latter was brought out the king made a special point to recommend the delicacy to Stevenson, who had little choice but to partake as gracefully as possible while the king described the elaborate process involved in the preparation. He described how the so-called poi-dog was delicately pampered by being raised in solitude on a diet of carefully selected vegetable food designed to give the meat a sweet and delicate taste. On feast day the dog would be killed and bled, wrapped in Ti leaves and baked in an underground oven on hot stones. Never one to denigrate Polynesian customs, Stevenson pronounced the exotic delicacy definitely "fit for a king" but maintained that at this late point in the luau he "just couldn't eat another bite." He then announced that he would like to make a special presentation to the king for the extraordinary hospitality the Stevensons had received from His Majesty. After proposing a toast, Louis produced a black velvet bag from which he took a perfectly shaped Tuamotu island yellow pearl, which he presented to the king and read the following sonnet:

> *The Silver Ship, my King—that was her name*
> *In the bright islands whence your fathers came—*
> *The Silver Ship, at rest from winds and tides,*
> *Below your palace in your harbour rides:*
> *And the seafarers, sitting safe on shore,*
> *Like eager merchants count their treasures o'er.*
>
> *One gift they find, one strange and lovely thing,*
> *Now doubly precious since it pleased a king*
> *The right, my liege, is ancient as the lyre*
> *For bards to give to kings what kings admire.*
> *'Tis mine to offer for Apollo's sake;*
> *And since the gift is fitting, yours to take.*
> *To golden hands the golden pearl I bring:*
> *The ocean jewel to the island king.*

Fortunately a property nearby known as the Frank Brown Place became available a few days after the luau, and the Stevensons settled in for what would be nearly a five-month residence. The Frank Brown Place was a cluster of buildings consisting of a small house with a large verandah or *lanai* with venetian shutters which served as a dining room and a gathering place for the family at night, three sleeping rooms and a kitchen. The walls of the *lanai* were covered with tapa cloth tapestries, decorative mats and a variety of Polynesian artifacts. Outbuildings included a fine arts studio for Fanny's writing activities and Lloyd's painting and photography, and a hut referred to by Louis as "a dirty little cottage," which served him as a bedroom and workroom. Mosquito nets were a necessity for all beds, and Fanny complained that she had "never seen so many ants, lizards and bugs in her life" as she found at the Frank Brown Place. She had tried to improve the appearance of Louis's "dirty little cottage" by papering the walls with the pink pages of the *Police Gazette,* but soon discovered that the result was that the walls began producing a loud scratching sound like someone furiously scribbling with a pen. The noise, they soon discovered, was made by beetles feasting on the paste that Fanny had used.

The cottage was often used for writing early in the morning, and while Louis would write propped up in bed, Ah Fu would serve him tea and toast at the first light of day. When the breakfast tray was removed, Stevenson would place a slice of toast on a shelf above his head on which he would nibble from time to time as he worked. One day he discovered that a little mouse came out to share his snack with him. Soon it became so tame that the little fellow would come down off the shelf for his breakfast. One morning Fanny peeked through the window and there was Louis drinking his tea and beside him was the little mouse nibbling on the corner of a piece of toast. One of the author's favorite photographs was a picture of himself in bed playing his flageolet for a very attentive mouse.

Not all visitors were treated as cordially, however. While Stevenson enjoyed spending time with stimulating visitors, his celebrity was definitely beginning to cause him problems and restricting his ability to work. He did entertain the king now and then for a pleasant afternoon of conversation about Hawaiian history and folklore, and he did have a number of naval officers, sea captains and men of letters with whom he enjoyed spending time, but there were often high society folks who dropped by to meet him. These *haoles* bored him with inane comments about his books, and their racial attitudes toward Polynesians annoyed him; they did not seem to have enough sense to realize that he needed time alone to work. For example, Louis had been struggling with the book *The Master of Ballantrae* for over two years and now he almost hated the sight of it. A magazine, *Young Folks,* had been publishing it in monthly installments, and he still had not brought himself to finish the last chapters. As he described it, "the magazine was already on my heels, when desperation helped me; and in a few days of furious industry the novel was, for good or evil, rushed to its last word."

Fortunately, Fanny was there to protect Stevenson's time and health, as well as his sanity, by suggesting that guests should leave when she believed him fatigued or bored. This was often done in spite of pleas from Louis that guests should stay a bit longer. Since Louis had suffered a few minor setbacks healthwise due to Hawaii's more temperate climate Fanny felt fully justified in her actions.

Fanny's extreme dedication to the welfare of Louis greatly irritated Belle, who was jealous of the fact that her stepfather seemed to completely dominate her mother's life, leaving little time for her. It was also Belle's perception that her mother was not even as interested in her grandson Austin as she had been in San Francisco, and while Fanny appeared not to be aware of it, Belle's hostility included ideas that the Louis/Fanny bond was poisoning the Osbourne family relations.

Stevenson had expected that there would be royalty checks waiting for him in Honolulu, but in late January he wrote E. L. Burlingame, editor of *Scribner's Magazine:*

"Tomorrow the mail comes in, and I hope it will bring me money either from you or home. . . . Not one word of business have I received from the States or England, nor anything in the shape of coin; which leaves me in a fine uncertainty and quite penniless on these islands."

To Charles Baxter, who was handling Louis's financial affairs in Edinburgh, he wrote:

"No money, and not one word as to money! However, I have got the yacht paid off in triumph, I think; and though we stay here impignorate, it should not be long, even if you bring us no extra help from home."

Indeed, Captain Otis was paid off early in February, and on the 14 the Stevensons sadly watched the CASCO weigh anchor and head for home. This was also followed by the Stevensons and Valentine parting ways. The young maid had decided she had taken about all the abuse from Fanny that she could endure and informed Louis that she wanted to take the next steamer for California. Stevenson, who was grateful for all her years of faithful service, knowing that the suspicious and jealous nature of Fanny would sooner or later lead to this, gave Valentine money for transportation plus a handsome bonus to support her until she could find other work in America. Fanny, on the other hand, hinted to family and friends that the young woman had become involved sexually with a CASCO crewmember and that she also had "very sticky fingers."

In Stevenson's next letter to Baxter in March 1889, he acknowledged receipt of considerable funds, and consequently he and Fanny began thinking about future travel plans. Without question the matter of finance had played a significant part in these future plans. Lacking adequate capital the family would have had to return to San Francisco on the CASCO, but they realized it would be a long, rough voyage in cold and possibly foul weather.

Both Louis and Fanny realized that if they did return to Europe they would never be able to return to the Pacific again, and Louis believed his health was completely dependent on the benign South Sea environment. Even Hawaii had proved to be too temperate. Having received adequate financing, Stevenson now began to think in terms of another South Sea island voyage. Even Fanny, who said she would never go to sea again once they arrived in Hawaii, seemed ready to try again. In a letter written to Fanny Sitwell late in March she wrote, "Louis has improved so wonderfully in the delicious islands of the South Seas, that we think of trying yet one more voyage. We are a little uncertain as to how we shall go, whether in a missionary ship or by hiring schooners from point to point, but 'unregenerate' islands we must see."

They had decided they would like to visit the Gilbert Islands and then go on to Ponape and perhaps then by steamer to the Philippines or China. Louis had heard that the missionary vessel MORNING STAR would soon be departing for the Gilberts, the Marshalls and the Caroline Islands, and he wrote Reverend Dr. C. M. Hyde, an administrator in the American mission in Honolulu, inquiring about booking passage. The MORNING STAR was a large barquentine steamer and would have been physically comfortable, but Stevenson was uncertain how philosophically comfortable they would be with their pietistic fellow passengers.

On March 14 a powerful hurricane with winds over 100 miles an hour had struck Apia in the Samoan Islands driving three German and three American warships anchored in the harbor onto the reef, resulting in the death of 146 sailors. The only ships that survived the blow were the British warship CALLIOPE, which managed to sail out of Apia, and a small 69-ton trading schooner named EQUATOR, which rode out the storm several miles at sea. The EQUATOR was the first ship to enter Apia Harbor after the storm and they volunteered to transport the mail and a group of American naval cadets to Pago Pago, Eastern Samoa, where connections for San Francisco could be made with the steamship ALAMEDA. John Wightman, the American owner of EQUATOR, was aboard the schooner, having made an inspection of his company's trading post, and he booked passage on the ALAMEDA as far as Honolulu. On April 6 the ship arrived in Hawaii with the news of the Apia tragedy. Louis, who had heard much about the Samoan Islands from Charles Warren Stoddard who praised its healthy environment and the very traditional lifestyle of the people, read in the newspaper about Wightman and his now-famous little schooner. Discovering that the vessel made regular trading trips among the Gilbert and Marshall Islands, Stevenson made arrangements to meet with Wightman the next day. The ship owner very obligingly agreed to a six-month charter for five thousand dollars, with the proviso that "whenever the ship's anchor went down, if for no more than five minutes, the Stevensons had the right to hold the ship there for three days without extra charge."

The EQUATOR was typical of the inter-island traders commonplace in the Polynesian and Micronesian island groups in the latter part of the nineteenth century. In 1856 the J. C. Godeffroy Company of Hamburg, Germany, established a network of agents and trading stations throughout the area with headquarters in Apia, Samoa. John Wightman had also established headquarters in the Northern Gilberts. Numerous trading schooners like the EQUATOR called regularly at the various islands, trading occasionally for pearl shell but mostly for copra (dried coconut), whose oil was a valuable commodity in the manufacture of soap and cosmetics.

Copra was for most islands their sole source of revenue and one that required little technical expertise to produce. Mature coconuts which had fallen from the trees were collected and the outer husk pried off on pointed sticks driven into the ground. The nuts were then halved by a swift stroke of a machete and the meat extracted with a smaller sharp knife. The pieces of coconut were spread out on mats in the sun and protected from rain until they turned brown and began to exude oil. This product, known as copra, was placed in burlap bags for transport to trading schooners, where it was weighed and traded for money or goods.

In the early afternoon Stevenson burst into their Waikiki residence somewhat out of breath shouting "I've chartered a schooner! I've chartered a schooner!" When the family had gathered around he announced, "I've arranged the details, and the trading schooner EQUATOR will pick us up in a couple of months to take us to the Gilbert Islands and beyond. She's a seaworthy little craft, a bit smaller than the CASCO, but able to take the worst kind of weather imaginable."

At that point Louis produced a photograph of the ship that Wightman had given him and asked, "Isn't she one of the finest little sailing ships you ever saw?"

"I'll drink to that," shouted Lloyd as he ran to get a bottle of champagne.

As Louis popped the cork and filled glasses all around, he said, "And we don't have to go to sea with missionaries," referring to the MORNING STAR mission supply ship they thought they would have to take. "We can smoke on this blessed ship!" he exclaimed raising his glass.

"And drink," added Lloyd with his glass raised as well.

"And swear," laughed Fanny, who had never said so much as "damn" in her whole life.

Stevenson, who by April 1889 had already had his fill of civilization Honolulu style and "beastly *haoles*," boarded the steamer W. G. HALL bound for the "big island" of Hawaii with stops at Kailua, the summer residence of His Gracious Majesty, and at Kealakekua, where Captain Cook was killed on the beach by hostile Hawaiian warriors in 1779.

RLS's final stop was at the small village of Ho'okena, where he spent a week as the only European among what he referred to as "God's best—at least God's sweetest works—Polynesians." Here he collected material for the short story *The Bottle Imp*, and spent two days exploring the region on horseback. He was particularly interested in the City of Refuge, the ancient sanctuary at Honaunau where he visited the temple, the House of Keawe, which was a repository for royal skeletal remains. Criminals, slaves, people marked for sacrifice, and in time of war, children and the elderly, could find asylum within the walls of the City of Refuge where they were under the protection of priests and safe from even high chiefs and kings.

The day after his ride to the sanctuary, when he declared "he was aware of muscles he had never known he possessed," Louis was on the beach at Ho'okena with many of the villagers as a whaleboat from a schooner anchored offshore was beached. It had arrived to take a fugitive 19-year-old girl with leprosy to the leper colony on Molokai. The girl and her mother had been hiding in the mountains for two years, but now the police were holding her and were about to send her away. There was also an elderly woman leper whom the villagers helped into the whaleboat followed by the girl dressed in a red *holoku* with a red ribbon in her broad-brimmed Sunday hat. As she embraced her friends for one last time a flood of tears ran down her swollen face. Then the girl's mother entered the boat as well and it returned to the schooner which promptly sailed for Molokai. The lepers could never return to their village again and the girl's mother would remain with her daughter if permitted as a "clean" *koku* (aide).

As Stevenson watched the schooner sail out of sight he thought to himself, "Isn't it a tragedy that Hawaii has no City of Refuge for two lepers and a devoted mother." And again, he said to himself, as he had in the Marquesas many months ago, "I must go to Molokai." But the meeting with Father Damien which he had long planned on would be impossible. The priest had himself succumbed to leprosy some two weeks earlier.

On May 10 Stevenson wrote Charles Baxter: "The care of my family keeps me in vile Honolulu, where I am always out of sorts, amidst heat and cold and cesspools and beastly *haoles*. What is a *haole?* You are one; and I am sorry to say, so am I. After so long a dose of whites, it was a blessing to get among Polynesians again even for a week." And to Sidney Colvin he wrote, "Honolulu does not agree with me at all; I am always out of sorts there, with slight headache, blood to the head, etc. I had a good deal of work to do and did it with miserable difficulty; and yet all the time I have been gaining strength."

His week on Hawaii was a welcome break, but even the island of Hawaii depressed him and he did not even attempt to ascend to the volcanic region or visit the soaring mountain areas with peaks so high they were obscured by clouds. Upon his return to Honolulu he complained of the "decadence of the natives who have lost their identity and graceful, primitive charm."

Sometimes when Louis had spent an arduous day of writing and was not anxious to entertain any visitors, he would walk over to the Cleghorn estate, where he enjoyed passing a pleasant hour or two with Princess Kaiulani, the 13-year-old daughter of Governor Cleghorn and the late Princess Likelike, the sister of King Kalakaua. The little girl was heir apparent to the throne, and soon would be leaving for boarding school in Great Britain to acquire an education befitting a queen. Because Kaiulani was somewhat uneasy about going abroad, Stevenson did his best to ease her anxiety by describing the beauty of England and the highlands of Scotland, the wonderful things she would learn in school, and the fun she would have meeting new friends. Their periodic conversations, held under a gigantic banyan tree, also turned to accounts of Stevenson's travels in America and through French Polynesia and to fictional creations by the author about pirates, wild Indians, and handsome princes and beautiful princesses in fairytale lands. He loved her innocent ways, the creative intelligence of her mind and her grace and beauty, so like the ladies in his fairy fantasies.

When Louis heard that the little maid would be leaving on the same ship his mother would be taking for her return to Scotland he wished her bon voyage, a "meritorious matriculation" and he presented her a poem for her red velvet-bound album:

Forth from her land to mine she goes,
The island maid, the island rose,
Light of heart and bright of face:
The daughter of a double race.
Her islands here, in Southern sun,
Shall mourn their Kaiulani gone,
And I, in her dear banyan shade,
Look vainly for my little maid.
But our Scots islands far away
Shall glitter with unwanted day,
And cast for once their tempests by
To smile in Kaiulani's eye.

In early May the family went to the dock to see Maggie and Princess Kaiulani off, with a dozen or more *leis* which they placed about their necks until they could barely see and hardly breathe. As the steamship UMATILLA departed, the Royal Hawaiian Band, sent down specially by the king, played *Aloha Oe.* Maggie waved from on deck to Louis, whose delicate health meant that she might never see him again; she shed not a tear but gallantly waved and smiled to her loved ones as the ship pulled away from the dock.

Drawing on their experiences in Tahiti, Louis and Lloyd decided to collaborate on a South Sea island book which would be titled *Ebb Tide* and would focus on characters such as the beachcombers they had encountered in Papeete. After a hard week's work on the first three chapters, Lloyd approached Stevenson one morning sitting alone in the lanai and asked him to read and evaluate his manuscript. Then Lloyd left the room, not wanting to endure the suspense of waiting for the master's judgment. After what seemed an eternity to Lloyd, but was actually only a half-hour or so, Stevenson shouted "Lloyd! Lloyd!" and when the young man hurriedly entered the room Louis had nothing but "unstinted praise," which Lloyd, a rank amateur at novel writing, was thrilled to receive from his famous stepfather. But suddenly his euphoria was interrupted by a knock on the door and the arrival of what appeared to be a very troubled young Frenchman about 35 who identified himself as a physician. Since the man obviously wanted to talk with Stevenson alone, Lloyd excused himself and left the two men engaged in a discussion which lasted for several hours, much to the irritation of Lloyd who saw the young doctor as an interloper.

After the man left, Louis appeared very depressed and told his stepson they would have to continue their discussion of the book some other time. The following day Stevenson announced that the morning paper carried the account of the suicide of the young doctor with whom he had spent the previous afternoon. The young man had blown his brains out and left a note stating that he had been diagnosed with leprosy and rather than endure confinement in the isolated Molokai leper colony he had decided to solve his problem his own way.

It was on that very day that Stevenson began making plans for visiting the leper settlement which had occupied his thoughts for so many months. Early in May he obtained official permission to visit the colony on Molokai, where government policy required that all with the malady must go. Fully expecting to find a situation much like a penal institution, where patients would be "out of sight, out of mind," Stevenson boarded the steamer KILAUEA HOU bound for Kalawao-Kalaupepa so he could experience the colony first hand. While there he also hoped to learn something concerning the life and work of the Belgian priest Damien who had devoted his life to the welfare of the lepers, but had died just three weeks earlier of their disease. Damien, whom Stevenson had heard about for years, had been a very controversial celebrity. When Louis had asked about the man in Honolulu he had received very mixed opinions. He was highly criticized by Protestants, who thought him crude and boorish, but he was much admired by the Catholic community, who saw him as something of a saint.

Also aboard the ship bound for Molokai were Sisters Crescentia and Irene of the Sisters of Saint Francis Order from Syracuse, New York, who were going to the colony to attend and comfort the patients. The passage aboard the KILAUEA HOU was extremely rough and the Sisters were terribly seasick, while Louis suffered only in not being able to sleep. Consequently, he was out on deck very early surveying Molokai with its leper promontory, which was a ten mile tongue of land separated from the rest of the island by a very high and sheer *pali*. The colony, therefore, was accessible only from the sea or via a narrow and dangerously steep trail leading up the 2,100 foot high face of the Pali.

Since there was no harbor, passengers for the leper sanctuary had to be taken ashore in the ship's whaleboat. The first trip carried a dozen lepers—one being a horribly disfigured child. The second boat ashore carried Stevenson and the Sisters, one of whom was shedding a silent tear beneath her veil. Deeply moved by what he considered the sacrifice of the Sisters and not knowing quite how to express his admiration for them, the author said very quietly, "Ladies, God Himself is here to give you welcome. I'm sure it is good for me to be beside you."

When the boat reached the landing stairs a crowd of lepers greeted the passengers and extended their hands to help them get ashore. Louis had brought gloves but when he saw the eager, friendly faces he could not put them on, and at first he considered not extending his hand, but then bravely reached out his bare hands for assistance in disembarking. Later he told Fanny that as he moved through the crowd and set off in the direction of the nearby village of Kalaupapa, he realized that "All horror was quite gone from me; to see these dread creatures smile and look happy was beautiful." As he passed through the village he found himself exchanging *alohas* and stopping to swap pleasantries with people who had come out of their houses to observe the new arrivals.

As Louis left the village and continued on toward his destination, Kalawao, where he would be quartered, he thought to himself, "I am happy here, only ashamed of myself that I am here for no good." Kalawao was still two and one half miles up the road, but fortunately the colony superintendent, also a leper, met him with a horse. But the horse was so unruly and difficult to manage that when RLS finally reached Bishop Home, where he would stay, he was so exhausted that he went to his room and slept the clock around.

Stevenson stayed in Molokai for seven days under the watchful care of Mother Superior Marianne and he rode over to Kalaupapa daily to meet with patients, observe the activities and learn about the recently deceased priest Damien he had so longed to meet. On his first day he met and was charmed by a delightful coterie of seven little girls who asked him if he liked to play games. He said, "Indeed I do," and the next day he brought over a croquet set which he had brought from Honoulu to present to the settlement. Since the girls had never played the game before, he was the player/coach for the group every day, rain or shine.

Louis also spent long hours talking with the elderly, the blind and the disfigured, always inquiring about Father Damien—asking about his faults, his virtues and his sacrifices. Some of what he learned about the priest he communicated to lifelong friend and art critic Sidney Colvin in a letter after he returned to Honolulu. He wrote, "Of old Damien, whose weaknesses and worse perhaps I heard fully, I think only the more. . . . A European peasant: dirty, bigoted, untruthful, unwise, tricky, but superb with generosity. . . . A man, with all the grime and paltriness of mankind, but a saint and hero all the more for that."

On the day of his departure Stevenson stopped by to say goodbye and thank you to Mother Marianne for her hospitality, and handed her an envelope containing a poem which read:

> *To see the infinite pity of this place,*
> *The mangled limb, the devastated face,*
> *The innocent sufferers smiling at the rod,*
> *A fool were tempted to deny his God.*
>
> *He sees, and shrinks; But if he look again,*
> *Lo, beauty springing from the breast of pain!*
> *He marks the sisters on the painful shores,*
> *And even a fool is silent and adores.*
>
> *Kalawao, May 1889*

Louis's next stop was in Kalaupapa where he said farewell to his little croquet clan and then went to the boat landing where he boarded the whaleboat that would take him out to the steamer anchored offshore.

This ship was the MOKOLII—not the vessel that brought him. Although Stevenson had obtained official permission to visit the leper colony, he did not realize that he was also required to have permission to leave. Since the steamer had once been fined for accepting a passenger without an exit permit, and since neither the captain nor the purser knew this somewhat emaciated stranger who claimed to be Robert Louis Stevenson, for a while it looked like the author would have to remain on Molokai. But Louis, who had a way with words and with people, showed them his official permit to visit and by exaggerating his Scottish accent a bit, soon convinced them that he was the Scotsman who had written the famous sea yarn *Treasure Island*.

Louis arrived back in Honolulu on June 1, 1889, and immediately bought a beautiful $300 Westemayer grand piano to be delivered to Bishop Home with instructions to the Mother Superior that it was a present to his seven little croquet companions who he said should learn to play something beside just croquet. Along with the piano was also a crate containing toys, games, clothing for all the children and tools for the adults.

Something of his impact on the lepers of Molokai can be gleaned from a letter found among Stevenson's papers after his death. It read, "I cannot suppose you remember me, but I won't forget you, nor God forget you for your kindness to the blind white leper at Molokai."

On the evening of his arrival back in Honolulu the family gathered in their lanai to hear about Louis's adventures on Molokai. He told them of the croquet games and how he had shared mallets and also tennis rackets with the lepers in their games. At this point Fanny anxiously asked, "Louis, you did wear gloves, didn't you?"

"Of course not. The Sisters advised me to, but as they didn't, how could I?"

When Stevenson had finished describing his adventures in Molokai, Fanny turned to him and with a little smile on her face informed him that they had received news that might interest him. "We have received news that the EQUATOR has left San Francisco and will arrive in Honolulu in a matter of a few days. So once more it is time to start assembling things for life far from civilization." The Stevensons were about to be vagabonds once more.

The assembling of "things for life far from civilization" suddenly became a primary activity of the household, and as Fanny reported to Sidney Colvin, the following items were included:

"Our barrel of sauer kraut, our barrel of salt onions, our bag of cocoanuts, our native garments, our tobacco, fish hooks, red combs, and Turkey red calicoes (for trading purposes), our hand organ, photograph and painting materials, and finally our magic lantern. Lloyd, also, takes a fiddle, a guitar, a native instrument something like a banjo, called a taropatch fiddle, and a lot of song books."

There was also the stockpiling of canvas hammocks for each person, revolvers, potassium permanganate, liniment for the head, sulphur, and fine-tooth combs for possible lice infestation. And then there were the supplies that Lloyd and Ah Fu were bringing, for use in case of shipwreck—garden seeds and carpenter's tools.

Shortly after Stevenson had made the charter arrangement with John Wightman for the EQUATOR, Honolulu newspapers published the news, and within a few days three young men appeared at Stevenson's Waikiki residence. Two were Belgians, whom Fanny described as "demanding and persistent," and the other was an "anemic Englishman." They said they had read of the Stevenson family's trip and they begged to accompany the party in any capacity possible. The Belgians, who gave their names as Alexandre and Joseph Rorique, claimed that they were excellent seamen, and Alexandre boasted of having captain's papers. Louis, who prided himself on being a good judge of character, did not like the cut of the men and told them that the EQUATOR already had a full compliment of crew, and that he did not have the authority to hire them anyway, even if there were positions available. And as far as joining them in some other capacity such as personal servants or cabin stewards, he stated that the EQUATOR was only a 69-ton vessel; too small for any additional passengers, and that he did not wish to be discomforted by additional people. However, the men seemed not to want to accept "no" for an answer, and finally Stevenson sharply asked them to leave. What the author did not know at the time but would find out later, was that the Rorique brothers were very dangerous criminals who would be brought to justice for signing on as crew aboard two different trading schooners, poisoning the crew, and then selling the ships and cargoes. Had Stevenson given permission for the Roriques to join them, that cruise might well have come to an end for passengers and crew somewhere between Hawaii and Makin Island in the Gilberts.

As the sojourn of the Stevensons in Hawaii was drawing to a close it was marked by several family problems. First there was the problem of Belle's husband Joe, who would be traveling with the family aboard the EQUATOR. Louis was hoping to develop a set of magic lantern slides on Polynesia for possible future lectures, and Joe had agreed to join the party as official photographer and to add coloration to the normally black and white photographs. The trip was also seen as therapy for Joe, who had just been released from a sanitarium where he had been recovering from illness precipitated by a riotous lifestyle which involved alcoholism, drug addiction and promiscuous sexual behavior. Being included in the cruise would remove him from the temptations of the Honolulu fast set, and hopefully reestablish his health. However, just days before the ship's departure date there was a major family blow-up and Joe was "thrown off the trip" because of his irresponsible expenditure of Louis's funds which were now the sole support of Joe, Belle and Austin.

Shortly after this row, however, Joe appeared at Waikiki "hat in hand" and made a humble and soulful apology, thanking Louis for helping him get his life together, and his health back, and swearing to reform. Declaring that his association with Louis and Fanny had been the happiest days of his life, he kissed them, told them he wished them a pleasant cruise and walked away. His performance was so convincing that Louis, who normally was a better judge of character, ran after him and told him he had changed his mind. He could go along after all. It was a decision Stevenson would often regret.

There was also a problem involving Belle. Considering herself fortunate to be rid of Joe for several months, she was looking forward to more pleasant days in Honolulu where she valued her relationship with the king and queen. Here she also had been involved with the indulgent and extravagant palace social set, and had even been guilty of an occasional extra-marital affair herself. Therefore, Belle was very upset when she was summoned by Louis and told that she and Austin must go to Sydney on the next steamer where there would be funds deposited at a local bank to support them until the EQUATOR cruise was completed. It was a decision that would cloud the Belle/Louis relationship for several years.

Finally, there was a rather serious disagreement between Louis and Fanny concerning the nature of the book he was writing about their South Sea experiences. The problem began when the editors of the *New York Sun* complained about the nature of the articles which Stevenson had been contracted to provide, and they canceled his contract. They did print 37 out of the 50 letters that he had agreed to produce, but as the voyaging proceeded he found the commitment more and more burdensome, especially since it had only netted him a mere thousand pounds. The *Sun's* action gave Fanny an opportunity to express her dissatisfaction with what Louis had been writing about their South Seas experiences. She thought that, when it came to describing their day-to-day experiences, his style lacked the charm characteristic of his earlier biographical writing.

On May 21st Fanny wrote their family friend, Sydney Colvin,

> I am very much annoyed by one thing. Louis has the most enchanting material that anyone ever had in the whole world for his book, and I am afraid he is going to spoil it all. He has taken into his Scotch Stevenson head, that a stern duty lies before him, and that his book must be a sort of scientific and historical impersonal thing, comparing the different languages (of which he knows nothing, really) and the different peoples, the object being to settle the question as to whether they are of common Malay origin or not.

Rather than try to produce an objective anthropological treatise, she thought he should write about South Sea islanders as people, for she believed "there is no one living who has got so near or who understands them as he does."

Stevenson never was able to produce such a documentary volume on Polynesian language and history as Fanny envisioned, although his book *In the South Seas*, published in 1890, contains a small amount of this scientific data.

On the afternoon of June 20, 1889, the schooner EQUATOR raised the island of Oahu—just 11 days out of San Francisco. The wind was brisk from the northeast and the little vessel was logging a frisky 9 knots. Leaning against the rail outside the deckhouse that served as the galley was Thomson Murray MacCallum, the ship's new cook. "Murray," as the crew called him, was a 20-year-old New Zealander who, at age 17, had stowed away on the topsail schooner/steamer, JANET NICOLL, and had subsequently knocked around the islands as a trader until joining the EQUATOR crew in Samoa.

By 5 o'clock the EQUATOR had arrived just off Honolulu Harbor and had dropped anchor to wait for morning before entering the port and tying up at the wharf. Shortly after the anchor was down an inter-island steam packet, which the EQUATOR streaked past just off Diamond Head, came alongside and hailed the EQUATOR, asking its 23-year-old Captain Reid if "that was a greyhound or a race horse he was sailing."

If Reid's seamanship had impressed the steamer captain that afternoon, he certainly would have been awed by his performance the next morning, when the young captain refused a tug and entered the inner harbor under sail, rounded the end of the steamer dock, and brought the EQUATOR alongside the dock as skillfully as if he were piloting a motor launch. The performance brought applause from bystanders on the dock, and a Honolulu newspaper reported the incident stating within the article that "The captain is a mere boy, but he certainly knows how to handle his ship." When shown the article later, the captain ignored the complimentary reporting but was incensed at being called "a mere boy."

Shortly after the ship's arrival Louis, Fanny and Lloyd went to examine their home for the next several months. Captain Reid feared that his ship might not meet the expectations of a famous author and his party, and before leaving San Francisco he set to work making improvements which would make the vessel more comfortable for the chartering party. Consequently, the Stevensons were more than pleased with what they saw.

First of all, he had the ship fumigated by burning sulphur in the hold, as copra-carrying schooners were notorious for harboring giant cockroaches and rats. Then there was the problem of trying to utilize space more efficiently to accommodate five extra passengers. Two pullman-type bunks were built for Lloyd and Joe Strong in the trade room where islanders negotiated for goods or money in exchange for their copra taken aboard. Captain Reid's cabin was fitted with another bunk to accommodate Louis and Fanny; he would move into the first mate's cabin, and the first mate would share what was designated as the second mate's cabin with the cook. Ah Fu and two passengers for

Butaritari would have temporary accommodations in the trade room or in the mess room.

The charter agreement stipulated that the EQUATOR would remain at the Honolulu wharf for a period of no more than three days to permit the Stevenson party to get their gear aboard. And it would have taken considerably less time than that had it not been for their social engagements. Friends were constantly dropping by to inspect the vessel and its accommodations, and on June 23, the king and two of his ministers came aboard for lunch all dressed in white, and gave farewell speeches while the champagne flowed freely.

On the following day, shortly before the EQUATOR's departure, the king was back again with his Royal Band which played a medley of Hawaiian favorites while His Majesty draped everyone with numerous *leis*, and then presented Louis with a beautifully crafted model schooner with sails of silk and a hull bearing the carved inscription "May the Winds and Waves be Favorable."

The sails were set, the lines were cast off and the EQUATOR, again without the help of a tug, left the dock and picked her way out through the anchored vessels in the harbor amid cheers from crews and passengers on their decks and the waning strains of *Aloha Oe*. Captain Reid, wearing his tartan tam-o'-shanter, was at the wheel, and standing beside him at the weather rail was Fanny holding fast to a backstay, her hair streaming out in the wind, and strangely enough laughing with delight. Her resolution to never go to sea again was apparently long forgotten as she looked forward to a new South Sea island adventure.

As Stevenson sailed out of Honolulu on the EQUATOR he gave a huge sigh of relief. He did not like Hawaii and in April had written an old friend from Skerryvore, Adelaide Boodle, "The Sandwich Islands do not interest us very much, we live here, oppressed with civilisation, and look for good things in the future." Louis believed Honolulu in particular, and all *haole* Hawaii in general, to be a very racist place, where negative attitudes toward all Polynesians were commonplace, and little respect was accorded the king, a well-traveled and highly intelligent man of letters.

While Fanny had stated that there was "no one living who understands Polynesians as well as Louis does," the prevailing attitude in this so-called outpost of civilization was that this scribbler of popular novels and children's poetry was very misguided and unrealistic. An example of the ethnocentric bigotry of the media may be seen in the remarks of Arthur Johnstone, a Honolulu publisher, in his book *Recollections of Robert Louis Stevenson in the Pacific*. He wrote,

> Now, the Polynesians are very lovable creatures, but they must be treated with that protecting and correcting love that a father has for his children, if any benefits are to result to the Polynesian. And it is here that Stevenson's kindness of heart and chivalry of nature caused him to shift the faults and weaknesses of Polynesians to the shoulders of a broader civilization, which at times he clearly underestimated. . . . Now, those who have studied the Polynesians are well acquainted with the difficulty of securing reliable testimony from native witnesses on any matter. . . . A perusal of his writings about the South Seas clearly shows that Stevenson *did* idealize the Polynesians, and that his views of them were too often disturbed by sentiment or prejudice.

Honolulu's final farewell to Stevenson was hardly calculated to endear the community to the author. On the day of the EQUATOR's departure for the remote Gilbert Islands the *Honolulu Advertiser* carried a story which included the following somewhat disrespectful closing sentence: "It is to be hoped that Mr. Stevenson will not fall victim to native spears; but in his present state of bodily health, perhaps the temptation to kill him will not be very strong."

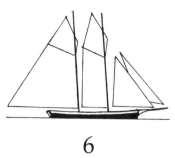

6
The EQUATOR Chronicle—Copra and Kings

As THE EQUATOR cleared Honolulu Harbor and assumed its southwesterly course for Butaritari Island in the Gilberts, Stevenson was on deck watching Oahu's mountainous skyline disappear into the haze and clouds. Once more he was on his way to good health and adventure—compass course 237°, speed 8 knots—on a stout little ship heeling to the pressure of the wind on the sails while the bow's cutwater bit deep into each oncoming swell, throwing a fine mist of spray back along the deck. Louis filled his scarred lungs with this delicious sea air and thought how good it was to be at sea again. Just then Fanny came on deck and stood beside him, gently taking his hand in hers. Stevenson jokingly asked her if she thought they should wash their Hawaiian Sodom and Gomorrah dust from their feet before returning to the wholesome life of the out-islanders. Fanny only laughed and affectionately squeezed his hand more firmly. And then Louis turned to her and said, as though he were reciting a sonnet, "This climate; these voyages; these landfalls at dawn; new islands peaking from the morning bank; new forested harbors; new passing alarms of squalls and surf; new interests of gentle natives—the whole tale of my life these days is better to me than any poem."

Surprisingly enough, Fanny took to the EQUATOR as she never had to the CASCO, although the latter was a luxury yacht and not just a humble copra schooner. She had remarked to Louis that the EQUATOR seemed to float lower in the water, and this made her uneasy, but it also made her feel "more intimately in touch with the sea and that is something you don't experience on larger ships."

A 72.21-ton, 70-foot vessel has very limited accommodations for 14 men, including the crew, and one woman. The crew ate in relays in a mess room on deck next to the galley after the passengers had dined, and while the crew slept in the forecastle, most of the passengers had cabins, but a few slept in the trade room or on the floor in the mess room. The Stevenson party at least had bunks, although they preferred their hammocks in rough weather. But even in calm weather sleep was not always possible for passengers and crew. Giant cockroaches, a common menace on copra schooners, shared their bunks with them, gnawing on fingernails and noses and tugging at eyelashes. In addition to this there was the major hazard of head lice, particularly for Fanny, which forced her to make good use of the fine-tooth comb she had brought aboard. The rats were supposed to keep the cockroaches in check, and the ship's cat was supposed to keep the rats in check, but the system didn't operate as planned. And on top of all this there was the oily-sweet odor of the green copra which gave off a steam that made the cabin floors so hot it was difficult to stand on them barefooted.

The EQUATOR was very typical of copra schooners of the times. Most were about this size and tonnage, and therefore ideal for seeking out small villages on remote islands where there were no trading stations, but where islanders were anxious to sell their only export—the meat of the coconut, extracted from the nut and sold for its oil content. The quality of this commodity was usually above average in these remote locations. It could also be acquired at a relatively low premium, since the islanders traded their copra for inexpensive yard goods, clothing and costume jewelry, poor quality tobacco, cheap whiskey or hardware such as machetes, shovels, nails or fish hooks.

Captain Dennis Reid, the EQUATOR's skipper, was a 23-year-old Scotch-Irishman who had been a sailor since he was a boy and an island trader for several years. He was a charming companion, and an eccentric but even-tempered ship's captain popular with his crew which he handled as adeptly as he did his schooner. He had done well in the trade, being respected by island traders, both native and European. He never utilized a supercargo but chose to do all the trading himself, leaving his first mate to do the weighing and stowing of the copra.

Captain Reid loved to sing and although he did it well, his repertoire was definitely limited. He knew but two songs, "In the Gloaming" and "Annie Laurie," the latter being his favorite as well as his "private property," not to be sung by anyone else but him. He was also somewhat autocratic when he insisted that every evening, without fail, all members of his crew line up for a dose of Kennedy's Discovery or Mother Siegel's Syrup. After receiving the patent medicine each crewmember had to answer a question from the captain so he could make sure they had really swallowed his medicine.

For some reason, which none of the Stevenson party could explain, Reid seemed to be completely bewildered by Ah Fu. In a letter to Sidney Colvin written after they had left the EQUATOR, Fanny Stevenson described the puzzling relationship: "I wish you could have seen the countenance of the captain of the schooner when Ah Fu issued orders to him; between surprise, anger and bewilderment he was absolutely dumb, and to the last day on board he was still unprepared and at Ah Fu's mercy."

The first mate was a Norwegian from Stavanger named Anderson but who was called "Sou'wegian" by the crew. He was several years older than the captain and an excellent seaman, but since he had never learned how to navigate, he was not likely to ever have a command of his own. Fanny was not much impressed by the man, and once wrote a friend that "our mate was in a quiver of fear all the time, and yet slept through all his night watches."

The seamen who stood wheel and lookout watches in pairs while at sea included: Sir Charles Selph (his actual given name and not a royal title), age 16, a kind of adoptive son and protégé of the skipper who was teaching him navigation; Tatoma, a tall well-seasoned Hawaiian; Boston Tom, a husky young man who was on his maiden voyage and often seasick; and La, a young Hawaiian who, like his fellow countryman, was an excellent sailor. And then there was George Muggery Bowyer, "Muggeree" for short, a little Hawaiian lad who served as cabin boy and was a kind of foster child of Captain Reid. The skipper had a nightly ritual involving the youngster: Every evening after dinner Muggeree was called aft and required to sing "Shoo, fly, don't bother me" and take his Kennedy's White Discovery. He then was taken over the captain's knee, given a pretend spanking, and sent to bed.

The ship's cook, identified by fellow crewmembers as "that wizened little rat of a Chinaman," had jumped ship just prior to their departure from San Francisco and had been replaced by

Thomson Murray MacCallum. This 20-year-old New Zealander at that time knew absolutely nothing about cooking, but through trial and error, advice from the captain, and the patient goodwill of the crew, was managing to get by. Fanny's assessment of his performance was that he had "an indifferent hand with the pots and pans," and after a few days she went to Captain Reid and suggested that he be replaced by Ah Fu. However, after a week of Ah Fu's rich French cooking, and in response to the crew's complaints, the skipper put Murray back to work, and from then on the two worked alternate weeks as cook and then as steward, with Fanny Stevenson, Captain Reid, Murray and Ah Fu serving as a "Committee of the Whole" to plan meals.

Ah Fu's weeks as steward were memorable, to say the least. He always dressed in white—his head shaved, with his queue braided and tied with a bright red cord. He was extremely proficient and agreeable, always laughing at every joke he heard, good or bad, but his English left something to be desired, having been learned mainly from sailors and beachcombers. As Fanny wrote a friend back home, "He makes a very economical use of English, one word serving for many purposes. He has learned camphor-wood trunk, so 'camphor' is naturally used for camera. 'Cocalet' means either coconut, chocolate, or cockroach. Sometimes a little confusion arises, but we guess his meaning from the context." He had a bad habit of joining in on conversations with or without a bit of encouragement. For example, when those he was serving began discussing the pirate Bully Hayes, and Stevenson said "I'm afraid he was a very bad man," Ah Fu concurred, offering: "Him son-of-a-bitch."

While Captain Reid was certainly a more humane ship master than Otis, there were times when his passengers were somewhat put off by his bizarre antics. On one occasion when the ship was becalmed, Fanny heard loud splashing out in the water and came on deck and observed the skipper swimming, surrounded by a circle of crew who were there to ward off any sharks that might be in the area. When he came out of the water a few minutes later Fanny berated him for his lack of concern for the lives of his men. To this reprimand he responded, "If the captain should be lost, think how much worse it would be for all on board than if it were a mere sailor. I'm the only one who can navigate."

The first festive occasion aboard the EQUATOR occurred on the Fourth of July. It was an event which included everyone aboard—crew as well as passengers. For the latter's consumption there was a generous supply of fine European wines, followed by a special toast to American Independence made with Louis's private stock of Hennessy's Three Star cognac. Then the crew had their first official "Splicing of the main brace" (a seaman's reference to having an alcoholic drink) which as Murray noted, "added to the holiday spirits of the crew, in a literal as well as figurative sense of the word."

There were other good times on the EQUATOR. Evenings were pleasantly passed playing cards and gambling, using cowrie shells as chips. The captain and Lloyd often sang, and Lloyd would participate with Joe in guitar duets. Even the crew joined in the singing, and Captain Reid told sea stories that were often hilarious.

The weather on the Honolulu to Butaritari passage was pleasant for days on end. Stevenson and Reid spent long evenings sitting on deck swapping yarns and discussing such South Sea island topics as blackbirding, piracy and the copra trade. One evening Louis conceived the idea that he and the captain should be partners in an island trading company. Stevenson saw it as a means by which he could financially prolong his stay in the Pacific islands where the climate had been so beneficial to his health and where he had found such high adventure and peace of mind.

He thought the company should have dual headquarters—on an island and aboard the trading vessel. Captain Reid would serve as naval architect, supervisor of construction and master of a vessel larger than the EQUATOR, a 90-ton topsail schooner with a squaresail on a yard above the fore-and-aft foresail. The topsail rig was a condition demanded by Reid who had first gone to sea in an old square-rigger and was nostalgic about the old days when there were "real sailing ships." The vessel would be half yacht, half trader and have every convenience—gun racks, patent davits, a steam launch, and even a library. The ship would be named the NORTHERN LIGHT, and its cost was estimated at $15,000, which Stevenson believed could be obtained through his writing royalties. Lloyd and Fanny were enthusiastic about the scheme, and Joe Strong was not even consulted.

After several days of intensive discussion the only thing they could not agree upon was a name for the company. Louis thought it ought to have an English flavor to it, but no one could come up with anything that everyone liked. In desperation one night, they asked the cook/steward Murray what he thought they should name their proposed business. After a few minutes contemplation, and with a devilish grin, he suggested *Jekyll-Hyde and Company*. Murray was applauded for his creativity and humor, and a round of claret was drunk to "Murray's loyalty," but his suggestion like all the rest was rejected, and in fact Louis and Reid never did agree on what their company should be called. Nothing ultimately came of the whole scheme. When the Stevenson party landed at Butaritari on Makin Island the trading company was an "assured fact," but after six months in the Gilberts, observing the methods involved in island trading by Reid and others, Stevenson decided his conscience would not allow him to carry through with the plan. In the preface to a later book Fanny wrote, "South Sea trading could not bear close examination. Without being actually dishonest, it came a little too close to the line to please us. Our fine scheme began to fade away."

It was at one of their after-dinner palavers in the stern of the EQUATOR that Louis turned to Reid and said, "Tell me about the Samoan hurricane, Captain, I know it must have been a pretty awful experience, and I'm glad you're here with us and not with Davy Jones."

"Well, Mr. Stevenson, if you really want to hear all the gory details, it happened pretty much like this. We were about 200 miles north northwest of Samoa returning from the Gilberts when the glass began to fall as fast and as far as I had ever seen it. The wind started to blow from the northwest and grew stronger by the minute. When we were directly to windward of Samoa I tried to heave to, but the seas had increased so much in size that I couldn't get the ship's helm balanced so she could be left to her own devices. I then rigged a huge canvas sea anchor, but the force of the winds and seas was so great that the line to the drogue parted. Realizing that our only chance lay in running before the wind, we set a double reefed forestaysail, but as we attempted to come about we suffered a knockdown. I thought we were done for, but the ship righted herself and answered her helm, and soon we were running before hurricane force winds at breakneck speed in torrential rain. For 24 hours we were driven before the gale with no knowledge of our position, but knowing that somewhere ahead lay 200 miles of reef-fringed islands, broken only by a 50-mile gap between Upolu and Tutuila. We knew that at any moment the EQUATOR and her crew could meet their end on a coral reef. We figured we had about one chance in 50 of passing between the islands since we had not been able to fix our position by a sun sight. We just plowed ahead and trusted to luck.

"After a night that seemed to never end, daylight revealed that the wave size had been reduced somewhat, although there was still heavy rain, and the wind was still blowing at close to hurricane force. I guessed that the reduced wave size indicated that we had passed the eastern tip of Upolu and were now in the lee of Tutuila. So we hoisted the mainsail, double reefed, and headed east to stay in the shelter of that island. By noon the seas were greatly reduced, and the sun burst through the clouds just long enough for me to get a good sight, which established our position as just west of Tutuila. And as the weather continued to improve, there to port, emerging from the clouds and mist were the peaks that surround Pago Pago Harbor. A welcome eastern tradewind carried us into the sheltered anchorage, and after two days rest we sailed over to Apia where we had the distinction of being the only sailing ship afloat."

"Well, Captain, that is quite a story," said Stevenson, obviously impressed with the account and its narrator. "I had heard something of your heroic exploits from John Wightman, and that is why we are sailing with you now. There is nothing like voyaging in a stout ship with a veteran 'old man' if you will pardon the expression." At that Captain Reid chuckled quietly and then excused himself so that he could go forward to get his sextant and shoot evening stars.

It was during this passage to Butaritari that Louis and his stepson first conceived of the plot for a book to be titled *The Wrecker*. This South Sea mystery novel was inspired by an actual wreck of a ship with which some very mysterious events were associated. The story, as crafted by the novelist and his protégé, involved a storm at sea, a shipwreck on Midway Island of a vessel they called the FLYING SCUD which was possibly involved in opium traffic, a castaway family on an island with a murderer, and a massacre of one crew by another. It was not one of Stevenson's better works, but it served as a vehicle for utilizing experiences and characters encountered in his own South Sea adventures. And it did in the long run net him a considerable amount of money in royalties which greatly helped finance his extended search for health and new horizons in the South Pacific.

Since the purpose of the EQUATOR cruise was in large part the continued maintenance of Stevenson's health and ability to work at his craft, he wasted little time getting down to serious production. Most of his writing was done propped up in his bunk with pillows supporting his head and shoulders. Here he had plenty of light and fresh air, as there was a porthole aft at the head of his bunk and one window at the side of the cabin, giving him an unobstructed view of both sea and sky as well as cross ventilation. He would often appear to fix his eyes on what lay outside a porthole for several minutes and then hastily scribble a page or two of manuscript. Then he would return once more to his trance-like concentration. His attention to seafaring details was extraordinary, and as he worked on *The Wrecker* he constantly sought out the skipper for information concerning proper procedures and terminology in the operation of a sailing ship.

It was perhaps during these sessions that Captain Reid became inspired to write a novel himself. It became such an obsession that he spent much of his time below struggling with his plot and characters. He would often read what he had written to the passengers, and was elated or depressed, depending upon their reactions. Murray was often his final critic before taking a chapter to RLS. Long after he deposited the Stevensons in Samoa, Reid continued his efforts. Murray also caught the writing bug and many years later published a book titled *Adrift in the South Seas*, wherein he described his charter trip with the Stevenson family.

The voyage from Hawaii to the Northern Gilberts had featured ideal sailing, with tradewinds directly astern, permitting daily runs of between 190 and 215 miles a day. But then progress was impeded by 10 days of calm. Occasionally there was a slight breeze, but mostly the sea had not a ripple and the ship rose and fell on long swells, and the gaffs of the main and foremast swung lazily back and forth groaning with the motion. From time to time a gentle wind would belly out the sails, and then they would once more hang limp as if all life was gone. It was a frustrating time for Captain Reid because he knew that the vessel should soon raise Butaritari and yet he could not see it.

The Gilbert Islands were much like the Tuamotus, in that they were all atolls, and the charts of the region were far from accurate. Consequently some of the charts which Reid was forced to depend upon had warnings such as "The geographic and relative positions of these islands have not been accurately determined." On the chart on which Butaritari Island appeared the captain had observed that there was a note: "Caution—This passage has been reported to lie five miles east and two miles south of this position." With the many atolls in the group, and the fact that such islands could not be seen more than 7 miles away from the deck of an approaching sailing ship, it is not surprising that the Gilberts, like the Tuamotus, were often referred to as "The Dangerous Archipelago."

At 4 p.m. on July 13 the captain appeared on deck, shot the sun with his sextant, and then went to his cabin to work out their position. He returned in a few minutes and told Murray to go aloft and report anything in sight. The young man went to find a spy glass, but when he returned with it the skipper said he wouldn't need it, but that he should take a hand compass up with him.

The EQUATOR had no ratlines on the shrouds of either mast so Murray had to climb up the wooden hoops on the luff of the mainsail and then straddle the crosstrees. As he looked forward he could hardly believe his eyes, for there on the horizon was a line of green palms along a snow white beach. He reported the land to Captain Reid who then asked him to take bearings of the two terminal points of the island so he could plot their position. This done, Murray slid down the backstay, but when on deck he could see nothing ahead but sea and sky. Noting the puzzled look on Murray's face, Reid said, "Young man, you have just seen for yourself that the world is round, and that its curvature means that you can't see a coral atoll or even its palm trees from the deck until you are almost on top of it. That was Makin Island, better known as "Big Muggin" you saw, and from the bearings you took it plots out that we are 15 miles away. Butaritari lies just to the south of it and that is where we will drop anchor."

By the time the EQUATOR reached the Butaritari lagoon entrance it was too late in the day and they had to lie "off and on" until morning when the wind and the tide would be right for them to enter. Early the next day, with the first mate perched on the foremast crosstrees, and with Murray taking soundings with the lead line at the lee rail, they entered the lagoon, tacked to avoid shoals and coral heads, and finally put down the anchor about a mile from shore in three fathoms of crystal clear water. As the passengers looked across the sun-mirrored waters of the lagoon the town of Butaritari appeared as a cluster of drab, brown roofs of houses, while the king's palace and summer house, with their corrugated iron roofs, glittered and were conspicuously dazzling. The community, which Louis perceived as "rustic and yet royal," had houses of all dimensions—some almost as tiny as toys and others which could hold "a battalion." Some were mere open sheds, others had walls and windows, and some perched on pilings in the lagoon. Upon closer examination they found saloons, stores and a church.

Within minutes the ship was surrounded by canoes, and the Stevenson party was introduced to a new variety of South Sea islander. The Gilbertese were darker in color than Marquesans or Tahitians but not as dark as Melanesians, and they were not wearing pareus but *ridis*, small fringe skirts made of the smoked fiber of coconut leaf, the lower edge not reaching mid-thigh. Since the Stevensons thought "a sneeze would leave a lady destitute," they labeled the raiment "the perilous, hairbreadth *ridi.* "

When the islanders shouted their greeting *konamouri demidong*, it seemed harsh and guttural, not a bit like the mellifluous *aloha* of the Hawaiians, the *ia ora na* of the Tahitians, or the *kaoha* of the Marquesans. Louis and Fanny found the women less attractive than those of Hawaii or French Polynesia, but both sexes were admired for their fine physiques. None were tattooed; however, nearly all the bodies of the mature men were covered with ugly ragged scars which Louis learned later were made by slashing with knives edged with shark's teeth. The slashing, but never stabbing, occurred during fights over women. The younger generation of men did not exhibit evidence of such mayhem and this was attributed to the influence of missionaries who had arrived on the island only ten years earlier.

Butaritari was 25 miles long including islets. It was located approximately three degrees north of the equator and had a climate that Stevenson found to be "superb," with "days of blinding sun and bracing wind," and "nights of a heavenly brightness." The islands of the Gilberts were coral atolls much like the Tuamotus, and therefore the land consisted mostly of sand and coral debris with a thin strata of humus which could only support sparse vegetation. There were breadfruit trees, coconut palms, *uri* trees from which they could fashion canoes, and a small variety of pandanus. They also cultivated a taro-like plant called *babai*. But other than these there was only a handful of shrubs and creepers which managed to survive in this arid climate. Mosquitoes and flies were the main agents of discomfort, but fortunately the mosquitoes did not carry malaria or filiriasis.

Butaritari was the headquarters of the Wightman Brothers Trading Company, and here a Mr. Ricks operated a store and served as local agent for the company as well as being the American consul. It was the Wightmans' only trading station in the Gilberts, but the EQUATOR called at all 12 islands taking on copra and selling merchandise to approximately 50 traders.

Butaritari was also the headquarters of the Crawford Company which operated a store and a saloon called "The Land We Live In," run by a bartender who was described by an EQUATOR crewmember as "being badly afflicted with a disease known as 'running off at the mouth'." Mate Anderson maintained that "he could pay out more cable without coming to an anchor than any man in the islands."

There was also another watering hole, the "Sans Souci Saloon," run by Norwegian Tom, who had formerly been a mate on a trading schooner. The only other symbol of Western civilization was a large stone church presided over by a Hawaiian missionary named Maka.

The town was in somewhat of an uproar when the EQUATOR arrived, and it appeared that a considerable proportion of the population was drunk and disorderly. Islanders who could afford it were staggering in and out of the bars, and those who didn't have the price were swilling down sour toddy, a home-brewed concoction made from the sap of the coconut blossom.

It was traditional that the lid on alcohol consumption be lifted for the celebration of the Fourth of July, Butaritari being mostly an American commercial center, but this year the holiday spree had been going on for better than a week. The Sans Souci Saloon had attempted to close, but a drunken mob, yelling and pounding on the door, forced them to reopen. King Tebureimoa, the ruling monarch of the Northern Group of Gilbert Islands, had not breathed a sober breath since the holiday, and no one appeared to be able to establish order.

Upon arrival, the Stevensons managed to rent the home of the Hawaiian missionary next to the church, but unfortunately, it was also close to the Sans Souci Saloon, and they were more than worried about the state of affairs. So was Captain Reid, who had posted a double anchor watch and was not allowing any canoes to approach the ship. The men on watch strapped on revolvers and Louis had them bring him his brace of six-shooters. Reid came ashore and spent the first night with the Stevenson party when he heard that there had been a free-for-all fight among the islanders during the day.

Rocks were thrown at the Stevensons' house during the night, so the following day Fanny and Louis went down on the beach, where all could see them, and carried on pistol practice with the dozens of empty liquor bottles that had been strewn about. Since Fanny was a crack shot as a result of her frontier experience in the West, and Louis was nearly as accomplished, the pair undoubtedly sent a message to the boisterous rabble that they were not to be tampered with.

The king's palace was a large wooden structure in the middle of town, not over a hundred yards from the church. Tebureimoa was the monarch, but no one knew exactly who governed the Makin/Butaritari area—His Majesty or Maka, the Hawaiian missionary. Most of the time the king, pot bellied and slovenly, merely lolled on mats, wearing pajamas that were quite inappropriate for someone of his bulk. He always appeared drowsy, which most attributed to the abuse of drugs, probably opium. He was much chagrined over the fact that he had but one wife while Tem Binoka, the sovereign of the Central Gilberts, had three dozen. Maka had induced Tebureimoa to discard all but one of his wives at his conversion to Christianity when the missionary arrived several years earlier. Now the king regretted it, for with that action he had earned the contempt of his advisory court of old men and he had lost the copra from his former wives' plantations.

About the Hawaiian missionary and his role in the affairs of Butaritari, Louis wrote in his book *In the South Seas,* "I love the man as a man; as a legislator he has two defects: weak in the punishment of crime, stern to repress innocent pleasures."

Tebureimoa also was aided and abetted by Mr. Williams, the black American bartender of The Land We Live In saloon, who served as the king's self-appointed interpreter. While not particularly good at Gilbertese Stevenson believed "he never knew a man who had more words in his command or less truth to communicate" than Williams.

After several more days of debauchery, Maka managed to intervene. The king sobered up, the *tapu* on alcohol sales was restored, and on Sunday July 28, the king and queen, wearing European clothes and accompanied by armed guards, attended church for the first time since the Independence Day holiday. Before the sermon was delivered Tebureimoa walked to the raised platform at the front of the church and renounced drinking. The queen followed his example, and all the men in the church were asked to join them, which they did by raising their right hand. The sorry episode was ended, and the Throne and the Church were once more in accord.

Believing that the crisis on Butaritari was past, Captain Reid felt that it was safe for him to leave the Stevenson party for a few weeks to carry out trading operations on the smaller islands of the area. Comfortable in the house they had leased from Maka, the Stevensons were learning about this new variety of South Sea culture which seemed so different from those to which they had been exposed.

Louis, who had come to pride himself on being a kind of amateur anthropologist, was intrigued by what he observed in the Gilbert Islands' culture in regard to religion. The islands had only been introduced to Christianity ten years earlier, and their belief system now consisted of a strange combination of Christian and traditional Gilbertese beliefs. For example, on the island of Apiang there was a mission school and also a well-attended church, but the ocean side of the island was dotted with numerous altars to the god Chench, who controlled the winds. The people also had traditional religious specialists called *ibonga*, who dealt with the supernatural as prophets, soothsayers, doctors, magicians and miracle-workers. There was a god of the thunder and lightning who sent good weather and prevented people from stealing other people's pandanus fruit upon pain of death. In spite of Stevenson's respect for traditional island culture, including indigenous religions, he had this to say:

"Those who have a taste for hearing missions, Protestants or Catholics, decried, must seek their pleasure elsewhere than in my pages. Whether Catholic or Protestant, with all their gross blots, with all their deficiency of candour, of humour, and of common sense, the missionaries are the best and most useful whites in the Pacific."

For nearly a month the EQUATOR worked the Northern Gilberts. Many of the smaller islands did not have a navigable entrance or pass into the lagoon and the ship had to stand off while whaleboats went to and from the shore with copra and trade merchandise. If the wind were off the beach, Reid and his crew could come in close and anchor just outside the reef, or run a long bowline ashore and secure it to a coconut palm if the water was too deep for anchoring. When the EQUATOR called at Marakei, approximately 60 miles south of Butaritari they were surprised to see a large vessel there ahead of them, but as they came closer they realized that the schooner, the H. L. HAZELTINE, was not anchored at all, but was on the rocks and everything of value had been removed from the wreck. Later they learned that several of the crew had been lost in that shipwreck. While island trading was a lucrative business, it also was a dangerous one.

Whether standing offshore or anchoring in the lagoon, it was immediately open house for all traders, European, Asian or Gilbertese. Reid had a reputation for paying a bit more for copra than other captains and consequently had an edge over them. However, copra was always weighed on board the EQUATOR rather than on the beach in case the bags of coconut should increase in weight by being water saturated in transit from the beach. In Reid's trading transactions everyone's credit was good, and none of the traders had ever failed to make good on their debts. The moment the trading began on an island there was a bottle of "squareface" on the trade room table and the more the trader drank, the easier and more profitable was Reid's job. There was always a noon meal for the traders aboard ship, and it was customary for them to invite the schooner crew ashore at night for a party with plenty of spirits and obliging women.

Over the several months that Stevenson was aboard the EQUATOR he came to see these island traders as a special breed of men, and in his book *In the South Seas* he would write:

"Few men who come to the islands leave them; they grow grey where they alighted; the palm shades and the trade-wind fan them till they die, perhaps cherishing to the last the fancy of a visit home, which is rarely made, more rarely enjoyed, and yet more rarely repeated."

It was late August when the EQUATOR returned to Butaritari to pick up the Stevensons, who by this time were ready for new venues and more challenging adventures. In the process of leaving the Butaritari lagoon they took the anchor aboard and headed for the passage, but as Stevenson put it, "the EQUATOR was unwilling to leave. She hung on to a reef, and not until she had parted with her false keel would she push on and gain the open."

This was not quite the end of their problems. They had planned to sail south, making trading calls at the islands of Nonouti and Tabiteuea, but the wind shifted, making it more favorable to change course and sail for the island of Abemama. In anticipation of that next port of call, the capital of the Central Gilberts and the home of King Tem Binoka, Reid had his crew turn to cleaning the ship from top to bottom and even holystoning the decks with sea water and sandstones.

It was Sunday, September 1, 1889, when they sighted their destination. On the larger atolls like Abemama, there were usually several passages or entrances into the lagoon, invariably on the lee side of the island. About midday the EQUATOR entered the northern passage and anchored just off a crescent shaped white coral terrace topped off with a collage of assorted buildings which constituted Tem Binoka's palace compound. The main village lay well to the south. It was a jumble of houses, which according to Fanny, "were something like bird cages, standing on stilts about four feet off the ground." Lloyd, on the other hand, described them as somewhat resembling "clothes baskets."

No sooner had the anchor gone down than a captain's gig was launched ashore and a crew rowed out with the king's ladder. Tem Binoka had once been dunked in the lagoon when the rope boarding ladder of the trade schooner H. L. HAZELTINE broke under his considerable weight, and not being willing to take further chances with ship's ladders, he now brought his own, which would remain lashed to the side of the schooner as long as it stayed in port.

The boat which brought out the ladder returned and the beach was suddenly black with attendants to the king who helped him and approximately a dozen of his wives into the gig which now served as "the royal barge." The boat was alongside in a matter of minutes and the king hoisted his 300-pound bulk carefully up the foolproof royal ladder. His wives, which Stevenson thought remarkably attractive, remained in the gig where they would sit all day in the hot sun with no shade.

Once on deck the king presented quite a spectacle. He was a man about 50, of medium height, with a flabby chest and a double chin but, all in all, he was more robust than he was fat. He moved slowly and deliberately, his gait being somewhat stumbling and elephantine. Tem Binoka's hair was long and shaggy, his nose hooked like a parrot's beak, and from first impressions his demeanor was arrogant and autocratic. He wore an elegant jacket of red and green silk, and white cotton pants, both well-tailored. This was a surprise, since Captain Reid had warned Louis in advance that the king might appear only in a *ridi* or even in a woman's frock.

Reid was on good terms with the sovereign. The captain was one of the few traders whom Tem Binoka really trusted. In their transactions the king spoke a curious variety of pidgin English, which he had learned from a missionary several years before. However, at the time of Stevenson's visit, Abemama and the islands of Kuria and Nanouki, over which Tem Binoka had control, were the only islands in the Gilberts having the reputation of being heathen. During his reign the king had permitted only one European missionary to settle on the island, and the monarch had even claimed to accept Christianity himself at that time, but it was only a ruse to acquire something he wanted—an opportunity to learn to speak English. The missionary would be allowed to stay only if he would serve as a tutor to the king. After Tem Binoka acquired sufficient fluency for his purposes, the missionary was put on the next schooner out. The king and his subjects returned to traditional gods like Chench, the god of the winds, which the king claimed were good enough for "My fatha" and therefore good enough for him.

The king spent the entire day in the ship's trade room talking with Captain Reid and drinking his Hennessy cognac. They discussed everything from the price of copra to the state affairs of the outside world. The king, who was the sole owner of all the coconut plantations in his kingdom, was a shrewd bargainer and generally did not trust any Europeans traders, Reid perhaps being the sole exception. Only one European had ever been permitted to settle on any of Tem Binoka's islands, a Scotsman by the name of George McGhee Murdock who now worked as supervisor for copra production on His Majesty's thousands of acres of coconut lands. He also served as a kind of secretary of foreign affairs, dealing with copra schooner and whaling captains who used Abemama as a hub of operations.

Stevenson joined the two men in the trade room and was generally impressed by the king. In a letter he wrote sometime later to Sydney Colvin he described the monarch as

> a great character—a thorough tyrant, very much the gentleman, a poet, a musician, a historian, or perhaps rather more a genealogist—it is strange to see him lying in his home among a lot of wives writing the History of Abemama in an account-book; his description of one of his own songs, which he sent to me himself, as 'about sweethearts, the trees, and the sea—and no true, all-the-same-lie,' seems about as compendious a definition of lyric poetry as a man could ask.

After Stevenson had excused himself so the two men could continue talking business, Reid diplomatically shifted the topic to the possibility of the Stevensons living ashore for a few weeks while the EQUATOR engaged in inter-island trading. He told the king that Stevenson was a famous writer of books and poetry and that he was "one of the Old Men of England;" and he implied that Louis was a counselor to Tem Binoka's favorite royal celebrity, Queen Victoria.

When Reid had concluded his appeal for accommodation for the Stevenson party, Tem Binoka responded, "I think about what you ask. I give my answer tomorrow. But for today—when chow?"

As he waited for his dinner, which was a bonus Captain Reid always provided when dealing with the king, the monarch spent his time looking over what marvelous trade items the schooner was carrying. While inspecting every single item, he caught sight of Fanny's somewhat worse-for-wear dressing case that was being stored at one end of the cabin. Since the king was always compulsive about buying anything he didn't own already whether he needed it or not, he made an offer of 20 pounds for the case, but was told it belonged to Mrs. Stevenson. Reid summoned Fanny, and Tem Binoka held out the money while the captain explained the king's request. She very gracefully declined to take the money and told his majesty that she would like it to be a gift to him. As a consequence, the king was now obligated to the newly-arrived foreigners. He sighed, and said under his breath, "I shamed."

At that point Ah Fu, whose week it was to be steward, announced dinner. The meal consisted of soup, rice, peas, salt beef, lobscouse (made of ship's biscuit, navy beans and salt meat), and plum duff—all of which the king seemed to enjoy immensely. When he was finished with his plum duff Captain Reid said that the cook also had some American pancakes, and Tem Binoka responded, "Good, I likum," and proceeded to devour 37.

The indebtedness which the king felt toward Fanny because of her gift to him undoubtedly had a great deal to do with the fact that on the following day he came out to the EQUATOR and told the Stevensons that they were welcome to stay on the island until Captain Reid returned. Another factor, however, that led to the king's decision was never told to the family but was revealed in a book by Colonial Administrator Arthur Grimble many years later. The Scotsman, George McGhee Murdock—who managed many of the king's affairs—heard of Stevenson's arrival on the island and the fact that he was cruising the South Seas for health reasons, and interceded on the author's behalf. While Stevenson met Murdock only once during their stay—and was not particularly taken with him—he never knew how much they had in common or what the man did for him. The story goes something like this.

Murdock had been sent to sea from Greenock, Scotland, at age 13 as a cabin boy by his parents who were told that a sea voyage was the only hope for curing the child's illness (which was very similar to that which plagued Stevenson). The ship's captain was a drunken sadist who abused the boy terribly and caused him to desert ship in Auckland. There he was told that the warmth of the tropics would definitely cure his coughing and spitting of blood, and at age 14 he sailed for the Gilbert Islands, again as cabin boy, on a barquentine trading ship. On the island of Maiana, 60 miles north of Abemama, a kindly trader, Benjamin Corries, befriended the boy. Horrified by the seriousness of his bronchial problems, he managed to hide the boy until his ship departed. Corries educated Murdock and ultimately made him bookkeeper and manager of his store. After several years Murdock decided to go into business for himself in Abemama, and somehow he convinced Tem Binoka that he needed an economic advisor and secretary of foreign affairs to deal with Europeans wanting to do business in his area.

When the EQUATOR arrived, and Murdock was informed of the fact that Stevenson was there to cure an infirmity like that which he himself had suffered with as an adolescent, he interceded for the author so that he might be able to live ashore for several weeks.

While Tem Binoka was extremely gracious in supplying the Stevensons with a place to live, he had five conditions. They were:

1. The king's people should work for them as servants, but only he could give them orders.

2. One of the king's cooks was to help Ah Fu and learn from him how to cook Western dishes.

3. If the Stevensons' stores ran out, the king would supply them, but he must be repaid from the EQUATOR's stores when she returned.

4. The king would have the right to come to dinner any time he chose, and if he didn't come they would have to send him a plate of food from their table.

5. The servants supplied by the king were not to be paid with liquor, tobacco or money.

The king had four houses moved from elsewhere on the island to a spot where the sea water filtered through the coral and made a brackish pool which rose and fell with the tide and could be used for washing clothes and bathing. The site had been selected by the Stevensons and was "out of the wind, out of the sun, and out of sight of the village." This was the nature of the compound the Stevensons affectionately labeled "Equator Town." The houses, which stood on stilts four feet off the ground, were little basket-work affairs with peaked roofs. Lloyd described the strange scene of their being delivered by "48 pairs of legs," with the king, Winchester in hand, firing in the direction—but over the head—of any of the house movers who appeared to be shirking in carrying their share of the load.

After the houses had been delivered Tem Binoka invited Fanny and Ah Fu to his palace storehouse so that they could pick out furniture and whatever else in the way of tools or appliances they might need. As they were escorted through the collection of royal treasures, Fanny tried to commit to memory an inventory of what the king had managed to hoard. Besides a small quantity of tinned beef and pork, flour, rice, sugar and tea, which she didn't think they would need, and some furniture which they borrowed, there were "crates of mirrors, a large rocking-horse, French clocks with gilt cupids, baby carriages, cut-glass bowls and vases, hand cultivators, plated-silver candelabra, silk parasols, framed chromos, toy steam-engines, ornate lamps, surgical-instruments and tea-baskets." Fanny walked away amazed, understanding a bit better why Tem Binoka might also want her used dressing case—he didn't have one in his collection.

The king had assigned several servants to assist the Stevensons. There was "Uncle Parker," who in time became known as "Uncle Barker," because his speech was more canine than human. His job was bringing green coconuts for drinking every day. Two young women, who soon received the aliases "Guttersnipe" and "Fatty" from Lloyd, were assigned to the family to do the washing, but mostly they frolicked in the pool.

For security, the king had drawn a *tapu*-line in the sand around the buildings thereby forbidding anyone other than himself and the Stevenson family and staff to enter on pain of death.

The basket-weave houses provided excellent protection from the sun, but the main threat to the family's comfort was the flies. According to Lloyd, "Never were there so many flies. Flies, flies, flies in thousands and millions; and no place to escape them outside your mosquito net."

Fanny, who was learning to cope with just about everything, created an immense mosquito net shelter in the house over the dinner table which between meals became the family study. Each of their beds was enclosed by smaller nets, as was the cooking area.

After the EQUATOR had departed in search of copra, the family made themselves at home, and each pursued their particular artistic interest. Fanny and Joe Strong went off sketching, Lloyd and Louis hammered away at their new book, *The Wrecker*. Joe and Lloyd took dozens of photographs in the daytime and even at night with flash powder. In the evening everyone huddled inside their mosquito net sanctuary and played cards, read Gibbon and Carlyle aloud, and played on flageolets and guitars.

One day when the king dropped by for dinner he mentioned that he had always wanted a national flag like those of the United States, France or England, and he asked if everyone would submit designs for one from which he could choose. The family agreed and several days later he dropped by to make his decision. Fanny's design appealed to him the most. It consisted of three vertical stripes of green, red and yellow with an appliqué black shark with white teeth and eye, swimming across the multicolored background. The design which would henceforth be the national flag, would be sent to Sydney where flags could be manufactured in quantity. The king was particularly proud of his new ensign, because it included a likeness of the shark, from which his royal line had descended.

When Tem Binoka stated that he wished he didn't have to wait for the flags to come from Australia before he could fly one over the palace, Fanny suggested that if it were possible to find a sewing machine on the island she would make him one. The offer was scarcely out of her mouth when Tem Binoka offered her a sewing machine as a gift. "Me got plenty," he said, and informed her that he had 22 of them in his storehouse, and that she must not have seen them when she was there. When she asked him why he had so many, he told her they made excellent anchors for his fleet of canoes.

Equator Town was the only place where Ah Fu ever exhibited vulnerability. Invariably the master of every circumstance, his behavior here was very atypical. He became seriously ill, but went on with his duties like a martyr. Once when Stevenson finally confronted him about his sullen behavior, Ah Fu replied with all the dignity he could muster, "Yes, Mr. Slevens, I very sick, more better you get a knife and come kill me now. I no can work." He then retired to his kitchen and wept bitterly.

Within a day or two he had recovered, and it was a good thing, for the king's cook, who was assigned to aid Ah Fu and learn from him was, according to Stevenson, "lazy as a slave, and insolent as a butcher's boy," and the cooking lessons he had received from Ah Fu had produced products which were "at times difficult to stomach."

It was Stevenson's practice to stroll on the beach when the moon was full, enjoying the cool night air and the panoply of a thousand stars. Upon returning to his house one night RLS was told by Fanny that someone had been lurking about outside. When Louis went to investigate, a dark figure, which he recognized as the cook, started to run away, but as he passed him, Louis gave him a swift kick. As he related to Fanny later, "I suppose I am the weakest man God made; I had kicked him in the least vulnerable part of his big carcase; my foot was bare, and I had not even hurt my foot."

The man did not show up for work for several days; and when he did return, Stevenson told him he would not report to the king that he had crossed the *tapu*-line late at night, but if he ever found him there after nightfall again he would shoot him on the spot, and then he pointed to his revolver which was laying on the kitchen table.

When Captain Reid left to do inter-island trading, he promised to be back in three weeks, and he left sufficient stores with them for that period of time. However, three weeks came and went, then four and five, and still no EQUATOR. Their supply of ship's stores had long been expended and the king's European food resources were meager. Fanny had brought packets of onion and radish seeds with her, and surprisingly enough, she actually harvested a few much-appreciated vegetables from the barren soil. Ah Fu managed to shoot wild chickens from time to time, and the king's fisherman came by with a turtle from which they made steaks. For some strange reason, however, Abemama seemed to have a dearth of edible fish. Mostly the Stevensons longed for coffee and European canned foods.

After the EQUATOR had been gone nearly six weeks, a trading schooner, the H. L. TIERNAN dropped anchor just off Abemama, and the Stevensons were able to purchase a small supply of canned food from its trade room inventory. Louis asked the skipper, Captain Sachs, if he had seen or heard anything of the EQUATOR, but the answer was in the negative.

Suspecting that the EQUATOR might have met with some misfortune, since it was so long overdue, Stevenson was tempted to charter the H. L. TIERNAN to take them to Samoa. But the price the captain wanted for the charter was too high, and Louis and Fanny thought it would also be unfair to Captain Reid if he should eventually arrive and find them gone. The decision to wait for Reid turned out to be a very wise one, for the H. L. TIERNAN capsized shortly after leaving Abemama with the loss of 16 lives, and of the survivors who spent several weeks in an open boat, all but three died of starvation and thirst before reaching an inhabited island.

At one of the family's evening chats with the king, they got into a conversation concerning the relationship between him and his subjects, and Louis asked him if he gave his people any kind of a dole. "No; I no pay them; I give them tobacco. They work for me all the same brothers." And it was Stevenson's impression that almost to a man his subjects were loyal and dedicated. True, he carried a big Winchester, but as Louis suggested, "By terror you may drive men long, but not far. Here, in Abemama labourers have holidays, when the singing begins early in the afternoon. It is impossible to doubt the beneficence of that stern rule."

By this time in his travels the author had become an astute student of South Sea islander culture and personality, and he was intrigued by the national character of the Abemamans. He found "a curious politeness, a soft and gracious manner. . . . Violence, so common in Butaritari, seems unknown. So are theft and drunkenness. I am assured the experiment has been made of leaving gold sovereigns on the beach before the village: they lay there untouched."

Stevenson's only derogatory comments seemed reserved for the royal cook, whose insolent behavior and laziness were, he believed, devious traits of his own and were not characteristic of the majority.

The EQUATOR finally sailed into the Abemama lagoon on October 11, three weeks overdue, having been delayed by calms and extremely light winds on the passage from Arorae, which lay some 300 miles to the south. The family quickly packed their belongings and had them taken to the ship by some of the king's "volunteers." It would be good to be aboard again, but in a way they had become quite fond of this quaint little desert-island kingdom with its heavy-handed king. But now they were looking forward to cool sea breezes and to the advent of a new group of high islands rising out of the sea with their green slopes and cloud-covered peaks.

The next morning as the crew was preparing for departure the king took the family out to the EQUATOR in his own royal gig, dressed in a beautifully tailored naval uniform complete with white cap and loads of gold braid. He had very little to say and he refused refreshments. But he warmly shook each hand, wished them well, wiped away a tear, and departed for shore.

It was a good day for sailing, and the EQUATOR glided quickly across the lagoon and out the passage to the open sea which welcomed the little craft with favorable winds and frolicsome dolphins.

After leaving Abemama the EQUATOR experienced about three weeks of heavy seas, rain, squalls, and occasional periods of calm. During the times of tranquillity it was not unusual for the seamen to relax a bit and let down their guard. That was exactly the state of affairs on November 6 when, without warning, the ship, with all sails set, was hit by a white squall and thrown on her beam ends, completely submerging the lee rail. The initial impact of the hurricane-force winds carried away the fore topmast, ripped the headsails, and made an horrendous tangle of the rigging.

The ship righted itself almost immediately, but the foresail downhaul was hopelessly snarled, making it impossible to lower the sail. The young men on watch seemed confused about how to correct the situation, but at that moment Ah Fu emerged from the forward deckhouse, which served as his galley, and after assessing the problem, climbed on top of the cabin and cut the tangled lines with a butcher knife, allowing the sail and gaff to plummet to the deck.

Below deck Mr. and Mrs. Stevenson were sitting on the berth on the lee side to the vessel, which meant that when the ship suffered the knockdown they were merely thrown back against the bulkhead and not injured. In fact, no one aboard suffered bodily injury. During the excitement Fanny packed a parcel of shawls and medicines in anticipation of being ordered to take to the boats to abandon ship. She also held the ship's cat tightly in her arms, fearing that it might be forgotten in the confusion. But within a matter of time the crew managed to clear the tangle of lines and broken spars, and the EQUATOR proceeded safely but somewhat more slowly on her way. With everything in order Captain Reid ordered Murray to serve all hands coffee with a shot of rum, and for the hero of the day, Ah Fu, the reward was a gold coin valued at one British pound.

When it appeared that everything had completely returned to normal, Stevenson asked Murray to come to his cabin. There he told the young man, "I wish you would present my compliments to Captain Reid, and tell him how much I appreciate his thoughtfulness in having the squall strike us while on the starboard tack and thus save Fanny and myself the inconvenience of being thrown out of bed."

When the message was communicated to the skipper, he laughed and said,

"All right, Murray, give him my love and tell him to go to the devil."

While neither Louis's or Fanny's writings ever even mention that Joe Strong was aboard, Murray recorded in his book that "Mr. Strong didn't seem to fit in," and that it was rumored that he was taken on as a passenger primarily to get him away from his Hawaiian drinking buddies. He also commented that Joe was the only one who ever caused the crew any problems.

While on Butaritari and Abemama Strong had apparently painted a number of canvases which he rolled up and stored in tubes in the EQUATOR trade room where he slept. When the ship made a trading stop shortly after leaving Abemama the whole Stevenson party went ashore for the day. First Mate Anderson and Murray, who had a rather low opinion of Joe as a person and had long wondered about his ability as an artist, removed some of his paintings from their tubes and inspected them. They found them "very pretty" but mutually agreed they didn't know much about art. They then returned the paintings to the tubes. When Joe returned aboard he discovered that the paintings had been disturbed, and he maintained that $500 worth of damage had resulted. Stevenson became involved in the situation and told Joe to drop the whole matter. Meanwhile, Murray and the mate contended that they had been very careful handling the paintings and commented that while they were not art critics, they doubted if the whole collection was "worth more than five dollars." But they had taken so much abuse from Joe Strong that they vowed somehow to get revenge.

This took place some two weeks later when the EQUATOR sailed into a circle of more than a dozen sharks. When one leaped high in the air, less than six feet from where Fanny was sitting reading on the fantail, Louis suggested that they should catch one. A baited line was rigged with a noose, and soon they had a shark lassoed by the tail. It was hoisted out of the water and dispatched by the first mate's revolver.

Several days earlier the Stevenson family had been discussing whether shark meat was edible or not, and all but Joe expressed a desire to try it. He emphatically stated that "nothing could induce him to eat it, and that he would rather die of starvation first."

While cutting out the jaws of the shark, which Fanny wanted as a souvenir, Murray suddenly conceived of a scheme to pay Joe back for the incident involving the paintings. It was Murray's week to be in the galley, and he had just cut several shark steaks for the Polynesians when Lloyd came to the galley and asked if shark meat could be disguised so that it could not be identified. Murray responded in the affirmative, and seeing his opportunity to get back at Joe, ground up the shark meat, seasoned it well, and at dinner delivered a platter of what he identified as "curried minced beef with rice." Everyone enjoyed the dish, including Joe who took two large helpings. As everyone sat enjoying after-dinner coffee and cognac, Lloyd revealed the real ingredients in the entree. And while Louis and Fanny thought it a wonderful joke and had a good laugh, Strong went up on deck and vomited his entire meal. Joe never did forgive the young New Zealand cook.

November 13, 1889 was a very special day aboard the EQUA-
TOR. It was Robert Louis Stevenson's 39th birthday, and it represented a real high point in shipboard social life, just seven days
after the destructive white squall incident, which had threatened
the demise of both the famous author and the dauntless little
copra schooner.

The day dawned serene and sunny, and most of the day the
EQUATOR lay becalmed with sails almost motionless, making a
perfect backdrop for the birthday photo of the entire crew and
charter party. Lloyd posed everyone on the cabin roof just aft of
the main mast. Louis wore a blazer for the occasion, and Fanny
was dressed in a polka dot Mother Hubbard and a big straw hat.
Captain Reid posed just behind her wearing his tam o' shanter
and holding the little cabin boy Muggeree firmly by the ears.

Both Ah Fu and Murray combined their skills in preparing
the evening meal. Murray was charged with preparing the main
item of the birthday dinner—roast ham—which meant that he
had to execute Wiggins, the little pig which the EQUATOR had
kept aboard so long that it had almost become a pet. The bill of
fare also included haggis, canned green turtle soup, and the
Stevenson's last six bottles of champagne, which helped to make
up for deficiencies in the menu.

While a birthday cake and a raucous chorus of "Happy
Birthday" topped off the meal, the real highlight of the evening
was a song sung by its composers, Fanny and Lloyd, which had
several verses and a chorus which began:

I'll sing you a tale of a tropic sea,
On board the Old EQUATOR.
There never were passengers better than we,
On board the Old EQUATOR.

Captain Darling, where has your top-mast gone, I pray?
Captain Darling, where has your top-mast gone?

No one enjoyed the evening more than Captain Reid, in
spite of being teased about the top-mast, but he did demand that
he be allowed to be the final act of the evening which, of course,
consisted of his singing "Annie Laurie" the song he had repeatedly informed the passenger and crew was his "private property."

But the voyage to Samoa from then on was not much to sing about or celebrate. The lost fore top-mast did not present any great threat to the safety of the ship or its passengers, but the weather was foul. Writing to his friend Sidney Colvin when he was still 190 miles off Samoa, Stevenson described their situation as one involving "a prodigious heavy sea all the time, and the EQUATOR staggering and hovering like a swallow in a storm; and the cabin, a great square, crowded with wet human beings, and the rain avalanching on the deck, and the leaks dripping everywhere; Fanny, in the midst of fifteen males bearing up wonderfully." He added that she had confided that she was glad that Maggie was not on this voyage with all its hardships and discomfort. But then he added that she, strangely enough, told him that "I would do it all over again."

The island of Upolu was raised early on the morning of December 7, and Captain Reid shouted down the companionway, "Mr. Stevenson! Come up and see Samoa."

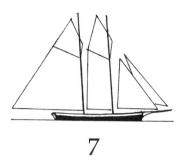

7
Samoa—Down Payment on a Dream

WHEN STEVENSON CAME on deck he found a typical South Sea morning—a bit of a chill and a wonderful fresh aroma in the sea air. A stream of golden sunlight gilded the seaway as the sun rose dead ahead. A light tradewind moved the EQUATOR comfortably along on a close reach at six knots and Louis leaned against the starboard rail and contemplated the landscape he had looked forward to seeing ever since he left San Francisco nearly two years earlier. Somewhat unlike other high volcanic islands the author had visited in French Polynesia, the two large islands of Western Samoa, Savai'i and Upolu, consisted of a chain of green-clad mountains rising in gentle slopes from coastal agricultural lands behind seaside villages. Crashing seas rolled over fringe reefs and washed snow-white beaches. As they passed waking villages, columns of smoke could be observed rising from early morning cooking fires. Here and there were coconut plantations with their orderly pattern of palms, and as they sailed past Savai'i, Louis could see where lava flows had run down through bush land into the sea.

Stevenson had come to accept more and more that his health had forever exiled him to this warm and tropical world, and he was particularly interested in Samoa as a permanent home. Disappointed with the fact that most of the Polynesian peoples he had encountered thus far in the Pacific had abandoned much of their traditional culture, including their house styles, RLS was fascinated by the appearance of the villages they were sailing past. There was not a European-style house in sight, only houses with beehive shaped roofs supported by a circle of house posts, but the center of each village had an English-style chapel with a steeple rising above the palms and breadfruit trees. He was pleased by what he saw and desperately wanted to believe what others had said Samoa's climate would do for his health. Yes, Samoa definitely had possibilities as a permanent home. The Sydney-to-San Francisco steamships stopped every two weeks, and there was a reliable scheduled mail service between both Sydney and Hawaii. He could maintain regular contact with his New York and London publishers, and there was even a telegraph link with Europe and America through Auckland, New Zealand.

By mid morning the EQUATOR had reached the mouth of Apia Harbor on the island of Upolu. Apia was the seat of government and the main commercial center. As Stevenson eagerly examined the port of Apia his eye followed the sweep of the shoreline from Mulinu'u Point on the west to Matautu Point on the east. The harbor was not a particularly protected one, and there was white water boiling over coral fringe reefs along the entire beach. There was no dock where ships could tie up, and they had to anchor and be unloaded with lighters or whaleboats.

Two features of the Samoan port caught Stevenson's eye. One was the jagged, rusting wreckage of the German warship ADLER on the reef to the west, along with the wrecks of the American ships, TRENTON and VANDALIA, to the south—evidence of the hurricane of the previous March. The other feature was a small mountain, Mount Vaea, which rose prominently just behind the town to the south. Why it had particularly caught his attention he did not know.

No sooner had the EQUATOR dropped anchor than it was surrounded by a swarm of outrigger canoes, each propelled by handsome brown-skinned people with lean, well-developed bodies and skin glistening with coconut oil. They weren't selling or trading; they were just curious about the newly arrived vessel and its passengers.

The Stevenson party was just as curious as they studied the town. Along the harbor's edge ran Beach Road, fringed with palms and crowded with European-style buildings—two storied ones with metal roofs and verandahs. In the very center of town, on the bank of the Mulivai River, a large cathedral and mission school fronted on the beach. To the west of the river was German Town, as the flags flying over public buildings testified. To the east of the river were the American and British sections, also with appropriate flags. To the far west was a flat promontory known as

Mulinu'u. It consisted mostly of a row of coconut palms backed against a mangrove swamp. A single village out near the point was traditionally known as the "seat of kings." At the extreme east, Apia ended at the Vaisagana River, but just beyond, the village of Matautu completed the curve of the harbor crescent.

At the time of the Stevensons' arrival the Samoan political situation was in a state of great turmoil, as the author was well aware, having followed the situation with great interest in the Honolulu newspapers and in discussions with King Kalakaua. During their charter passage aboard the EQUATOR Louis had also learned much about Samoan politics from Captain Reid and from Murray MacCallum, who had worked in Apia as a copra trader for nearly two years before sailing aboard the EQUATOR. In fact Murray was in Apia when the hurricane sent the six warships onto the reef.

Before the coming of the white men (called *papalagis* or cloud bursters by the Samoans) there had been several rival houses of nobility—those of Malietoa, Mataafa, Tamasese and others. Armed conflicts had often taken place as the supporters of potential monarchs vied for supremacy. This situation became highly intensified with the arrival of the Germans, the British and the Americans who wanted land, special royal favors, or just the profits from arms sales.

In 1884 a political crisis developed in Western Samoa. The German residents, numbering slightly over 300, unable to manipulate the Samoan King Malietoa Laupepa to their advantage, filed false claims concerning political corruption and mismanagement and, backed by a harbor full of their warships, removed the king from office and sent him into exile in the Marshall Islands. The Germans then installed their puppet, King Tamasese, but the Samoan people refused to accept him as their sovereign and 4,000 young men volunteered as warriors to support their choice of ruler, High Chief Mataafa. An eventual clash between Tamasese's supporters and those of Mataafa resulted in a Mataafa victory, and the warriors marched through the streets of Apia displaying the severed heads of the vanquished. When a company of German marines was dispatched to disarm the Mataafa warriors, they too were defeated with a loss of 40 lives. The German authorities then accused the ninety British and forty American residents of giving aid to the rebels and they declared martial law over all of Western Samoa. Warships were immediately sent by Great Britain and the United States, and on March 15, 1889 three German and four Allied warships were anchored in Apia Harbor, each waiting for the other side to start something. Although not a shot was fired, what happened on the following day took the life of 146 sailors, two-thirds of them German. A hurricane with winds over 100 miles an hour struck Apia sending three German and three American men-of-war onto the reef with only the British ship CALLIOPE managing to escape, albeit with heavy damage.

Entertaining the possibility that the hurricane was God's judgment on errant nations, the Three Powers came together in April and with the Treaty of Berlin established a tripartite regime in the islands. A commission was created to investigate land claims, and eliminate arms and liquor sales to islanders. Malietoa Laupepa was brought back from exile and reinstated as king, with a German and a Swede serving as royal advisors. Mataafa, however, was by far the people's choice, and he and his backers withdrew to the village of Malie, and there he established himself as rebel king. The European advisors to Malietoa Laupepa were hopelessly inadequate in their advisory positions. When Stevenson arrived on December 7, 1889, Samoa was a political powder keg ready to explode.

But on this bright morning it looked good to Stevenson. While waiting for Fanny and Lloyd to go ashore with him for an inspection of what might be his future permanent home, the author wrote to a friend in England, "Samoa, Apia at least, is far less beautiful than the Marquesas or Tahiti: a more gentle scene, gentler acclivities, a tamer face of nature; and this much aided, for the wanderer by the great German plantations with their countless regular avenues of palms."

And Samoa—at least the Reverend W. E. Clarke of the London Missionary Society—had a first impression of the Stevenson clan. The missionary was strolling along Beach Road when he encountered a rather unusual trio of strangers. Several years later the cleric would record in writing his initial perception of the new arrivals:

> It was still early in the morning when a little trading schooner scarcely more than 30 tons dropped anchor in the calm safety

of the bay. A boat was lowered and three passengers were rowed ashore. They were Europeans, two men and a woman. I watched as they strolled along Beach Road with its line of stores and saloons. Both the men were barefooted. My first thought was that probably they were wandering players en route to New Zealand, compelled by their poverty to take the cheap conveyance of a trading vessel. Imagine my surprise when the next day I learned that the stranger in shabby flannels was Robert Louis Stevenson, the author of *Treasure Island*, that the woman was his wife and the younger man his stepson.

That next day Reverend Clarke would contact Louis at the Tivoli Hotel and invite the family to tea at his house. That meeting began a deep and abiding friendship that would last the rest of Stevenson's lifetime. In fact Clarke would one day conduct Louis's funeral service.

As the family walked along Beach Road that first morning they were surprised to see how developed the community appeared. They saw well-stocked general stores, a post office, restaurants, a large Victorian hotel, a massive white Catholic Church with a school overlooking the harbor, and dozens of saloons. There were German, British and American consulates, a court house, a bank, and Methodist, Seventh Day Adventist, Mormon and London Missionary Society churches and schools. And there were well-established neighborhoods of frame houses with white picket fences to house the 400-plus European inhabitants. But in true RLS fashion, the author was less interested in the Europeans and their enterprises than he was in the Samoans. When Captain Reid asked him shortly after their arrival what he thought of the Samoan people, and how they compared to other Polynesians he had known, Louis stated,

"I am not specially attracted by the people, but they are courteous; the women very attractive, and dress lovely; the men purposeful, well set up, tall, lean and dignified. They are easy, and pleasure loving; the gayest, though by far from either the most capable or the most beautiful of Polynesians."

However, the longer Louis remained in Apia the more he came to respect the Samoans and the less enthusiastic he became in regard to the white population. In his journal and in letters to friends in the British Isles these are a few of his impressions of Apia and his fellow Europeans:

> There are three Consuls—British, German and American—at loggerheads with each other, three different sects of missionaries in a condition of unhealable ill feeling, an assortment of merchants of all degrees of respectability and a full complement of grog addicted sailors and beachcombers spilling out of the score of grog shops along Apia's main street. . . . Although Apia has been given the name "Hell of the Pacific" I don't find it much worse than a hundred towns I could name.

On December 9, the day before the EQUATOR departed Apia, RLS invited the officers and crew of the schooner to a farewell dinner and appreciation party at the Tivoli Hotel on Beach Road. The menu was extraordinary, considering the distance to gourmet food sources. Lloyd typed up copies which were placed at each setting. It read

MENU
Appetiser "Strong" Punch
Oyster Soup, à la Josephus
Cambridge Sausage, Mashed Potatoes
Chicken Fricassee, French Beans
Salade Marinée
Roast Suckling Pig, Truffled Dressing, Sweet Peas

DESSERT
Cakes, Pie and Fruit

WINES
St. Emilion Claret, Chateau Rabart Sauterne
Montaldo Sherry, Champagne
Schlitz Milwaukee Beer

The dinner was followed by a series of toasts and verbal bouquets for the captain and crew delivered somewhat self consciously by Louis. He closed by stating that he had never enjoyed a voyage as much as the one they had just completed nor had he ever found a company more pleasant. He then turned the floor over to Lloyd who announced that the Stevenson family had added several more verses to their old EQUATOR song which they first introduced at Louis's birthday celebration. He invited everyone to join in on the chorus. At this point Lloyd produced his banjo from under the table and the Stevensons jumped to their feet and began their performance.

VERSE I'll sing you a tale of a tropical sea
   On board the old EQUATOR.
   There never were passengers better than we
   On board the old EQUATOR.
CHORUS Captain, darling where has your top-mast gone I pray?
   Captain, darling where has your top-mast gone?
VERSE Of chequers the captain did blow and boast,
   On board the old EQUATOR.
   The passengers did him as brown as a roast,
   On board the old EQUATOR.
CHORUS (Repeated)
VERSE In Santa Pedro was our delight
   On board the old EQUATOR.
   When the bobbery struck us along in the night,
   On board the old EQUATOR.
CHORUS (Repeated)
VERSE The captain he ran from a fifteen hand,
   On board the old EQUATOR.
   I'll be damned if that old-topsail will stand,
   On board the old EQUATOR.
CHORUS (Repeated)
VERSE The sail was the rotteness't ever was bent,
   On board the old EQUATOR.
   But blamed if it wasn't the stick that went,
   On board the old EQUATOR.
CHORUS (Repeated)
VERSE The captain he turned to the mate
   On board the old EQUATOR.
   I guess you are learning some sailor craft,
   On board the old EQUATOR.
CHORUS (Repeated)
VERSE There's one thing you know at the least and the last,
   On board the old EQUATOR.
   You know how to lose a fore-mast,
   On board the old EQUATOR.
CHORUS (Repeated)

The evening ended with a great deal of hugging and hand-shaking and even the most dispassionate of men wiped away a tear or two as they bid each other goodbye. When Murray, who had become something of a favorite with Louis, offered his hand in a parting handshake, the author quietly said, "Remember, Murray; there is always a sunny side, if you look for it. And another thing, don't worry. It does not matter much, what you accomplish. The only thing that really matters is that you tried."

The next day when the winds and tide were right the Stevensons watched as the EQUATOR weighed anchor, spread her sails and glided out toward the open sea. Louis and Fanny stood on Beach Road watching until their cherished little schooner disappeared from view. Then Louis turned to Fanny and asked, "Well, where do we go from here?" And she replied, "Maybe we don't go anywhere. Maybe this is where we belong."

Shortly after the Stevensons had arrived in Apia, Joe Strong made contact with Harry J. Moors, an American entrepreneur from Michigan whom Joe had met when he accompanied King Kalakaua to Samoa on a diplomatic mission in January 1887. Upon learning that the Stevenson family was in Apia staying at the Tivoli Harry Moors invited the family to move to his house until they could find something to rent for the duration of their stay in Samoa. Moors was in the import/export business, a banker, an importer of native labor from Melanesia, a leader of the English-speaking business community and an outspoken member of the anti-German political faction. Even after they had found a small cottage to rent, Moors insisted that Louis should use his upper balcony where it was cool and quiet and an ideal location for writing. Moors was a very intelligent, even intellectual man, and he and Louis became very close friends although Fanny never much cared for the man and Moors thought Fanny a domineering and nagging wife.

Shortly after settling into their small cottage Ah Fu approached Louis and informed him that a letter had been forwarded to him from Hawaii from which he had written home to China telling relatives of his existence and making inquiries concerning the welfare of his mother. The letter, which he had just received, informed him that he had inherited land, houses and livestock in China and his relatives urgently needed him to return. While Ah

The Stevensons at Vailima with housestaff. *Beineke Rare Book and Manuscript Library, Yale University*

HMS KATOOMBA crew at a Vailima party. *The Writers' Museum, Edinburgh*

Samoan warriors marching in Apia. *Drawing by Otto H. Bacher from a photograph, Scribner's Magazine*

Rebel King Mataafa. *Augustin Kramer from Die Samoa-Inseln (1902)*

Portrait of Robert Louis Stevenson shortly before his death. *The Writers' Museum, Edinburgh*

Robert Louis Stevenson lying in state at Vailima. *The Writers' Museum, Edinburgh*

The schooner CASCO as sealer.
San Francisco Maritime National Historical Park

The schooner EQUATOR as tugboat in Seattle. *Joe Williamson marine collection, Puget Sound Maritime Historical Society*

Fu was enjoying his position as head cook and house man for the Stevensons, and hoped to continue in that role, he felt that it was his duty to return to China to visit his mother and adjudicate the property distribution. Apparently a younger brother was holding the property pending Ah Fu's return and was treating the family members badly.

Ah Fu told Louis that he wanted to go home for a brief visit and "lick um my bludder" and teach him his proper duty and respect for his mother and his siblings. "Just one trip and I come back. I settle it damn quick and be back Samoa again."

Louis and Fanny were heavy hearted over the prospect of losing Ah Fu even for a short time, but RLS cooperated in every way imaginable to make Ah Fu's mission possible. He calculated the amount of the man's accumulated wages plus a farewell gift of 50 pounds, secured gold pieces for that sum and had Fanny sew them into a leather belt which Ah Fu would wear around his waist under his clothing.

When the day of his departure arrived, Ah Fu appeared before the Stevensons in a new suit of clothes with his baggage neatly stacked by the door. He anxiously revealed the plan he had worked out for the reunion with his mother. He said he knew where she lived and he would dress himself in the rags of a beggar and knock on her door and ask for food. He said he would ask her for "just a little lice." Since she was a very kind lady he knew she would bring him food. At this point he said he would tell her he was her long lost son. And he was certain she would tell him that she was a poor widow woman but would gladly share everything she had with her boy who had made her heart glad at his return. Then Ah Fu would take off his belt and give her all of his gold coins which could let her live in comfort the rest of her life.

Louis, Fanny and Lloyd accompanied their Chinese friend down to the landing where he would board the ship's tender which would take him out to the steamer. RLS gave him a packet of self-addressed envelopes to write them if he ran into trouble on his journey. He also gave him a letter to show to British authorities in any port where he might run into trouble and need help or advice. As Ah Fu stepped down into the tender and placed his gear on the thwart beside him he gave the Stevensons a brave smile and shouted, "I promise come back and work for you all my life." Those were the last words his foster family would ever hear from him. Although Louis made numerous inquiries through the British consular service in the Orient, their beloved Ah Fu had vanished forever leaving the Stevensons with a belief that their faithful house servant and culinary expert surely had met with foul play.

Upon arriving back at their cottage Fanny urged Louis to find Samoan help to assist with cooking and other household chores which might be required if the family were to decide to settle in Samoa permanently.

The next member of the Stevenson extended family to sail away was Joe Strong, who was severely ill with a heart condition and needed the kind of medical attention available in Sydney. Since Belle and her son Austin were there, she could make sure that his medical needs were met. Fanny believed that the man was dying, probably from the effects of alcohol, and she told Louis that she thought it "no bad thing for himself and the world at large." Louis, of course, was now the sole support of Joe, Belle and Austin. Joe, however, recovered his health in Sydney and would live to make the Stevensons' life miserable later in Samoa.

Early in January Stevenson was invited by Senior Tutor Reverend James Edward Newell to visit Malua College, the London Missionary Society's training school for prospective Samoan pastors. When Newell was about to introduce the author to his students he realized that the peculiarities of the Samoan language would have forced him to tell the students that his name was *Setevinisoni*, so he presented him to the students as *Tusitala* which was derived from the Samoan word *tusi*, (to tell or to write) and *tala*, (tales). Thus Stevenson became "Teller of tales."

After a few weeks in Apia, the Stevensons had pretty much made up their minds that this would be their permanent home. There was not only good communication with the Western world but the climate had proved to be ideal as far as Louis's health was concerned. In a January letter to Sydney Colvin Fanny revealed that in the six weeks they had been in Apia RLS had experienced no cough, no hemorrhaging, no fever and no night sweats. Not only could he spend long hours writing without exhaustion, but it was not unusual for him to spend entire days in the saddle exploring the island in spite of occasional tropical showers which drenched him to the skin.

While Stevenson had originally planned to remain in Samoa

only long enough to acquire data for a book on the recent political history in Samoa, the longer he stayed the better it suited him. Upon arrival Louis was somewhat unimpressed by Samoa, Samoans and the European population, but the longer he stayed the more the Samoan scene appealed to him. And most importantly it was a place where RLS was convinced that he had old "Bluidy Jack" on the run. Therefore, it was not surprising to Fanny when one evening in their little rented cottage Louis revealed that he had hoped to go back to England or at least somewhere near so that he could enjoy old friends again, but that he had realistically decided that he could not survive in climates other than those he had enjoyed in the South Seas. He maintained that he would like to see "seven or eight people in England and a couple in the States, but aside from that I really prefer Samoa." And having said that he looked hopefully at Fanny and she smiled and said, "We'll make it work Louis, I know we can make it work."

Early the next day Stevenson stopped by Moors' office on Beach Road and asked his friend if he would help him acquire land where they might settle permanently. The problem was that there was a new law which forbade Samoans selling land to Europeans, but Moors knew of a property owned by a European, Thomas Trood, that he had heard was for sale. The real estate consisted of 314 1/2 acres of partially cleared land some 800 feet above sea level and 3 miles inland from Apia. The price, to which Louis happily agreed, was $1500—half down and half in six months. The land, which was partially covered with forest and scrub vegetation, was located between two streams which flowed down from Mount Vaea which lay just to the west. Since RLS could not find the appropriate number of streams of water on his newly purchased estate he was puzzled by its name—*Vailima*—which he incorrectly translated "five waters." Actually he found out later that the name derived from an ancient Samoan legend about a maiden who saved the life of her elderly father by bringing him water from a *Vailima* stream in her cupped hands. *Vailima* should have been translated "water in the hands" since *lima* is also the word for "hand."

In January 1890, an article in the *Samoan Times* reported: "We feel proud that after examining many places in the South Seas, Mr. Stevenson selected as his future home Samoa. He will be an immense acquisition to Samoa."

While Harry Moors arranged for his Samoan and Melanesian laborers to do the major clearing of the *Vailima* acreage, Louis, for the first time in his life, found strength to take part in a bit of heavy labor himself. He proudly wrote to his friend Sidney Colvin:

"This is a hard and interesting and beautiful life we live now. Our place is embowered in forest, which is our strangling enemy, and which we combat with axes and dollars. Nothing is so interesting as weeding, clearing and path making. To come down covered with mud and drenched with sweat and rain after some hours in the bush, change, rub down and take a chair on the verandah, is to taste a quiet conscience."

On January 29, while the land the Stevensons had purchased above Apia was being cleared by Moor's labor crew, Louis had an opportunity to accompany Reverend W. E. Clarke on a *malaga* (a journey of official or ceremonial nature) to Fagaloa, a small village a dozen miles up the coast. Clark was on mission business and Louis appreciated the opportunity to learn as much as possible about the lifestyle of the people in the outlying villages.

Starting before dawn, they traveled by whaleboat in the deep lagoon-like water just inside the protecting fringe reef. As their boat moved quietly along, with only the click of the oarlocks of a dozen oarsmen, they watched sleeping villages stir to life. Now and then they would encounter a lone fisherman jiggling a handline over the side of his outrigger canoe. The whaleboat proceeded past Vailele and on to Falefa where the reef ended and the coast was exposed to the open sea. Here they sighted a fleet of bonito boats heading offshore looking for circling gulls which would reveal the location of schools of bonito. Once past Falefa the ocean grew angry and the boat, running dangerously close to sheer cliffs that rose out of the sea, was buffeted by the surging white water of the backwash of the surf. At last they rounded a long spit of rockbound shoreline and entered Fagaloa's relatively peaceful bay. As they approached the beach they heard the high-pitched voices of children shouting *"Palagi! Palagi! Ua sau le va'a* (white men!, white men! the boat is coming)." and soon the visitors saw villagers—mostly women and small children—streaming down to the beach to watch the whaleboat come through the surf. As they shot the gap through the coral fringe reef, the man with the sweep oar shouted rowing cadence to the oarsman while Reverend Clarke shouted *Malo foeuli!* (Good steering!) *Malo le fa'a malosi* (Good strong rowing!). And then the bow of the whaleboat went aground on the beach sand and the two men slipped over the side and waded ashore.

By now the sun had cleared the tops of the coconut trees and the village workday was well in progress. A column of young people came up the beach carrying baskets of mature coconuts on wooden yokes on their shoulders and left the baskets in front of a *fale* (house) on the beach. There young men and chiefs were busy husking and splitting open the nuts and removing the meat for what would be copra.

Shouldering their own gear, Clarke and Stevenson headed up the path which meandered for several hundred yards through Fagaloa's jumble of guest and sleeping houses, resembling giant mushrooms rising out of the well-kept lawns. As they passed elderly women sitting in front of their *fales* weeding, cheerful *talofas* were exchanged as well as inquiries into one's good health, *"malolo."*

The arrival of Reverend Clarke had been greatly anticipated, for Samoans were avid churchgoers, almost fanatical in their commitment to the London Missionary Society. Introduced by John Williams just 60 years earlier, the London Missionary Society theology had produced enthusiastic congregations compulsively dedicated to church-building and with a fierce loyalty to their clergy—both European and Samoan. Stevenson and the Reverend were escorted to the guest house of the Paramount Chief with whom they would stay. After they had been given time to rest and enjoy the refreshing liquid of a green coconut, they were summoned to the *malae* (village ceremonial grounds) where a *kava* ceremony of welcome was about to take place.

After a flowery and flattering official greeting the village Talking Chief announced that the *kava* ceremony should begin. Within the circle of chiefs and the visitors the village ceremonial maiden, the *taupou,* sat behind a large wooden four-legged *kava* bowl mixing the ceremonial beverage, with young men called *taule'le'a* seated on either side of her. They would carry the coconut shell cups of the liquid to those whose names were called by the Talking Chief. As guest of honor, Reverend Clarke was awarded first *kava*. Then the Talking Chief sent a young man to ask Clarke what name should be announced for his companion. The young man returned with the answer and the orator chief called out *"Tusitala*, receive your *kava* cup." Stevenson now officially had a ceremonial name that would be recognized and honored by all Samoans for a hundred years or more.

While Louis was gone on his *malaga*, Fanny began taking over the responsibilities of homemaking in their little rented cottage and hired a Samoan housegirl and a handyman to aid her in adjusting to her new environment. In a way she was assessing her ability to relate to a new variety of Polynesians in what Fanny perceived to be a very different cultural environment than they had experienced before. The experiment was not without trauma, but while she was less understanding than Louis would have been, she saw hope for the future. Something of her ambivalence is reflected in her letter to Fanny Sitwell in which she wrote, "The Samoan people are picturesque, but I do not like them. I do not trust them. My time must be so arranged as not to clash with them. . . . A great part of the housework I shall have to do myself, and most of the cooking." Stating that she thought Marquesans and Tahitians more amicable than Samoans, she added, "I am assured I shall like the natives very much when I really know them. Perhaps I may, but I have my doubts."

Satisfied that the clearing of Vailima land and the construction of a small temporary house on the property was well underway the Stevensons boarded the steamer S.S. LÜBECK for Sydney, Australia on February 3, 1890. It had been over seven months since they had seen Belle and Austin in Hawaii, and Fanny was especially anxious to learn how her daughter and grandson had fared during the interval. She was also minimally interested in the state of Joe Strong's health. Louis was very enthusiastic about boarding a steamer for England after a short stay in Sydney, as there were friends he wanted to see and affairs to be put in order before returning to Apia for the rest of his days.

As they steamed out of Apia Stevenson's attention was once again drawn to Mount Vaea which now had special significance for him, since it marked the location of his soon to be constructed permanent residence in the South Seas.

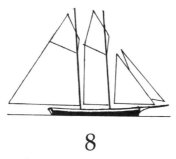

8
The JANET NICOLL—
The Jumping Jenny Adventure

WHEN THE STEVENSONS' ship docked in Sydney, they sent Lloyd to the bank where Louis had established an account for Belle so that he could locate her and bring her to their hotel. They took a brougham cab to the Victoria Hotel which was reputed to be the best hotel in Sydney. When they arrived, several bellhops unloaded a motley collection of gear which included several worse-for-wear leather traveling bags, two bulging pandanus baskets, a roll of tapa cloths (gifts for friends in England), a typewriter, a banjo, a guitar, and a beat-up steamer trunk filled with Stevenson's manuscripts and books. When piled in the middle of the lobby it was a horrid site to behold, at least that is what the desk clerk thought as its owners, looking more like beachcombers than affluent world travelers, approached the registration desk.

Stevenson addressed the clerk cordially:

"Good morning young man. I am Robert Louis Stevenson from Bournemouth, England. My family and I would like you to accommodate us with a suite of rooms in your very fine establishment, and I would prefer them on the first floor."

The clerk looked somewhat troubled by the request but pushed the register forward for Louis to sign. The young man, obviously unaware of who the author was, looked disinterestedly at the signature and called a bellhop to remove the Stevensons from his lobby. They were taken, not to a suite on the first floor, but to a very small room on the fourth. Stevenson took one look in the room and angrily returned to the lobby. Louis burst out of the elevator just as Lloyd and Belle had arrived, and it was clear to them that something was decidedly wrong. Before Belle could inquire what the problem was Stevenson growled, "We are obviously not good enough for their grand hotel. We are going elsewhere."

When Belle suggested that they go to the Oxford Hotel, which she said she had found to be very nice, the family immediately started moving their unacceptable luggage out onto the sidewalk where they hailed a cab. When they reached the Oxford they were treated with every courtesy and moved into a suite with large, attractive rooms. The people at the Oxford Hotel, fortunately, knew exactly who Stevenson was. His book, *The Strange Case of Dr. Jekyll and Mr. Hyde,* had been a bestseller in Australia, and the day after the family's arrival the author's visit was front page news. After reading the paper the manager and desk clerk of the Victoria Hotel came over, apologized and begged the Stevensons to return to their hotel, but Louis refused their offer, telling them they could accommodate him by having his mail, which would be addressed to the Victoria, sent over to him.

Once settled in at the Oxford, Fanny and Louis were anxious to hear how things had gone for Belle and Austin since they left them in Hawaii, and they in turned filled her in concerning their Gilbert Archipelago experiences.

Clearly, things had not been pleasant for Belle and Austin. They had comfortable accommodations on the s.s. MARIPOSA, but early in the trip to Sydney the weather was bad and Austin was quite ill with seasickness. However, Belle soon met a "very nice man" named Frank Johnson who helped entertain Austin by playing checkers, and with whom she enjoyed many pleasant hours of conversation. He said that he was worried about her traveling alone and asked her where she kept her money. When she said in a tin box in her cabin he insisted that she take it to the purser and have him lock it in the safe. Upon arrival in Sydney, Johnson suggested that instead of looking for a boarding house where Belle and Austin were expected to take up residence, she should stay at the Oxford Hotel for a few days and he would take Austin and her sightseeing. The three of them had a wonderful time dining out and seeing the sights in Sydney for two days, but then Frank did not contact them again. Belle was perplexed until she saw his picture in the paper with a story which informed her that he was not Mr. Frank Johnson at all, but a well-known English criminal who had just been arrested and sent to Melbourne for imprisonment.

With her pleasant alliance obviously terminated, Belle decided that she must start putting her affairs in order, and she began looking for long-term housing for her and her boy. Before leaving Hawaii Louis had told Belle that he was having a local bank send a letter of credit to a particular bank in Sydney where she was to go each week to obtain living expenses. Upon arriving at that bank Belle was told that they knew nothing of any such account in her name, and like the Victoria Hotel desk clerk, the bank officer said that he had never heard of Robert Louis Stevenson. From there Belle went for help to the American consulate where an officer told her only that he had "no funds to support destitute Americans." As Belle stomped out of his office she bravely informed him, "This consulate is American soil. If I can't find a place to go, I'll bring my child and stay right here." His only reply was a timid statement that he was a bachelor and there were no accommodations for ladies.

After paying her hotel bill for the week, Belle had but two pounds left and therefore began looking at cheap rooming houses, all of which seemed to be in poor neighborhoods with smelly hallways, dark gas-lit rooms and intimidating landladies. After a depressing day looking at unacceptable lodgings she finally found Miss Leaney's Theatrical Boarding House where a large clean room with board was available for her and Austin for one pound ten shillings a week. She paid for a week in advance and then settled down to try and figure out what she would do in the weeks to come.

Suddenly it dawned on her that she remembered King Kalakaua saying that he had a chargé d'affaires in Sydney to handle diplomatic matters. She found out that his name was Abraham Hoffnung, and that he was a well-known banker and business man. She went to his bank, sent in her card, and was warmly welcomed. After she related her problem, Hoffnung told her she was right to come to him and that she should not worry. He said, "Consider me your banker and draw on me for all you need." He then offered her a handful of bills, but she took only enough for her next week's board and room.

A couple of weeks later the American steamship ALAMEDA arrived from Honolulu and Belle went down to the ship to see her good friend Purser Smith and tell him her troubles. When she finished her sad story he looked at his watch and said, "It's

Saturday and the bank closes at noon. You have just time to reach it." Belle told him that she had been treated so badly she would never return there, but Purser Smith said that he knew exactly what had happened. The bank clerk in Honolulu had allowed the letter of credit to miss the boat and the ALAMEDA was the next one out. He said that the mail had gone ashore several hours ago and she should return to the bank immediately. When she arrived at the bank her account had been established and her funds for the month were handed to her. After paying back Mr. Hoffnung she told Miss Leaney about her problem, and the landlady assured her that she would have taken care of them until the Stevensons arrived anyway.

Belle had not seen much of Joe after he recovered from his health problems, for he had found lodging elsewhere in town; however, he still apparently expected to be supported by RLS.

Several days after the family's arrival in Sydney Louis happened to run across a letter in a church publication, the Sydney *Presbyterian*, written by the Reverend D. Hyde of Honolulu to the Reverend H. B. Gage, describing Father Damien of Molokai. In response to a query about who Damien was, Hyde had written, "The simple truth is, he was a coarse, dirty man, headstrong and bigoted. He was not sent to Molokai, but went there without orders; did not stay at the leper settlement (before he became one himself). . . . He was not a pure man in his relations with women, and the leprosy of which he died should be attributed to his vices and carelessness."

The letter had actually not been for publication, having been printed by Gage by mistake, but Louis was so incensed that he published an *Open Letter*, dated February 1890, that was clearly libelous, but not without first obtaining permission from his family, since he believed that Hyde would very likely sue. After Stevenson read the final draft to his family he turned to Fanny with a look on his face which seemed to ask the question whether or not he should put his family in jeopardy by having it published. With great emotion in her voice she cried, "Print it! Print it!" The letter was widely circulated to international political and religious leaders and finally published by Charles Scribner's Sons, the royalties being sent to the Molokai lepers. Quoting particular lines from Hyde's letter Stevenson wrote,

Damien was *coarse*. It is very possible. You make us sorry for the lepers who had only a coarse peasant for their friend and father. But you who were so refined, why were you not there, to cheer them with the lights of culture?

Damien was *dirty*. He was. Think of the poor lepers annoyed by this dirty comrade! But the clean Dr. Hyde was at his food in a fine house.

Damien was *headstrong*. I believe you are right again; and I thank God for his strong head and heart.

Damien was *bigoted*. I am not fond of bigots myself, because they are not fond of me. But what is meant by bigotry, that we should regard it as a blemish in a priest? Damien believed his own religion with the simplicity of a peasant or a child; as I would, I could suppose that you do.

Damien was *not sent to Molokai, but went there without orders.* Is this a misreading? or do you really mean the words for blame? I have heard Christ, in the pulpits of our Church, held up for imitation on the ground that His sacrifice was voluntary. Does Dr. Hyde think otherwise?

Damien *was not a pure man in his relations with women.* How do you know that? Is this the nature of the conversation in that house (of Hyde) on Beretania Street—racy details of the misconduct of the poor peasant priest, toiling under the cliffs of Molokai?

While Dr. Hyde was undoubtedly embarrassed and angry over Stevenson's reply, he did not sue, but merely passed the letter off as that of "a bohemian crank."

During her stay in Sydney, Belle met a Dr. Ross and his wife, who often invited her to dinner. When Louis caught a cold in Sydney's temperate climate, Fanny became very alarmed, and Belle called Dr. Ross, who made a professional call and suggested that the author should move into the Union Club, of which Ross was a member. He claimed that it would be quiet and comfortable and a place where Stevenson would not be available to visitors. Hoping Louis's health could be improved by a complete rest, Fanny insisted that he move to the club, and she moved in with Belle and Austin at Miss Leaney's boarding house. RLS found the Union Club, its members and its personnel much to his liking, and put his time to good use writing in bed. In spite of Stevenson's ill health, which he considered temporary, the Stevensons continued to make plans for their trip to England. Suddenly the weather grew colder as it does in the early autumn month of March in Sydney and Louis suffered a relapse. Now Dr. Ross said that it was imperative that he return to the South Seas as quickly as possible.

Stevenson's relapse could not have come at a worse time, as there was a union seaman's strike in Sydney. All along the waterfront ships sat idle, and it appeared that nothing was leaving for the South Sea islands. But Fanny, who was naturally inclined not to take no for an answer, went to all the steamship offices as well as to island trading establishments in a frantic search for some kind of transportation to take her Louis to a more beneficial climate.

At the office of one of the Pacific trading companies she was told that she might talk to someone over at the JANET NICOLL, a steam/topsail schooner that was owned by Mr. George W. Nicoll of Sydney but presently was being chartered by the Henderson-Macfarlane Trading Company of Auckland. Apparently Mr. H. W. Henderson was aboard, and it was rumored that they would be leaving on an extended trading trip through the Cook, Tokelau and Gilbert Islands in a matter of days. Since the ship was manned by an all black crew from the Solomons and the New Hebrides who were not union seamen, there was a good chance that this was the one ship available for transport to the tropical isles.

Fanny found the ship tied up at the wharf, went aboard and asked to see Mr. Henderson. She was taken to a stateroom that also served as his shipboard office where she was cordially received. She introduced herself as the wife of the Scottish author Robert Louis Stevenson, whom she described as seriously ill and in danger of dying if he could not return to the South Sea islands immediately. She told Henderson about their cruises on the CASCO and the EQUATOR and how it had improved Louis's health, and that she knew a few weeks aboard the JANET NICOLL could return him to good health once more.

Mr. Henderson, a middle-age fatherly type of gentleman said that he sympathized with her but that there was just no way he could help. Not only was he involved in a serious labor problem with pressure from striking white sailors demanding that he not leave port, but his black crew of Melanesians were very superstitious and believed that women passengers were bad luck and therefore they might refuse to sail if she were aboard. And while Fanny pleaded with him, the final answer was a definite "no," although he expressed his sorrow at having to turn her down.

Fanny left the ship and went directly to Dr. Ross and told him of her predicament, and he in turn went down to the waterfront and found the JANET NICOLL and Mr. Henderson. After confirming the seriousness of Stevenson's illness and his own personal belief that a tropical cruise would save his life, Henderson finally agreed to take the family, but only under the strictest secrecy—no newspaper stories or large farewell parties. The passengers had to be ready to leave within 36 hours and not tell anyone outside the family. While the ship had accommodations for 16 passengers, there would be no others except an island trader named "Tin Jack" Buckland who would be returning to the island of Tapituea in the Gilberts, where he operated a trading station for Mr. Henderson.

Dr. Ross returned to Fanny with the good news and then went to the Union Club where Louis was in bed. Both welcomed the news and Fanny and Lloyd began a frenzied preparation for the voyage. The vessel's itinerary was a strict secret and so they packed personal belongings and gifts for island people much as they had for their CASCO and EQUATOR cruises. But compared to these earlier vessels, travel aboard the JANET NICOLL would seem like being on a luxury liner with its 184-foot length, its 772-ton displacement, and its dining saloon, good-sized cabins, and two bathrooms for passenger use. All Fanny was told when she bought their steamer tickets for the voyage was that it would extend for "two to five months," but there was no information as to what islands would be called at. She did know, however, that the usual territory of the trading vessel was Tonga, Fiji and Samoa and sometimes other island groups if they had passengers or sufficient cargo to make it profitable.

On April 11, 1890, the day of the ship's departure, it was cold with a light drizzle. The JANET NICOLL had left the dock the day before and was anchored out in the harbor just in case there might be some trouble from striking seamen over her departure. When the Stevensons reached the wharf where the ship has been moored, a lifeboat awaited them. Louis was placed on a board laid fore and aft on the thwarts and covered with blankets until he resembled a mummy. Fanny and Lloyd sat on either side of him and Belle, Joe Strong and Austin huddled together under an umbrella in the stern.

As the lifeboat drew near the ship their attention was drawn to a slender, well-dressed young man, who they later learned was Tin Jack (Mr. Jack), standing at the top of the accommodation ladder in white flannels with a flower in the buttonhole of his navy blazer. Appearing to be somewhat inebriated and therefore unsteady on his feet, he playfully waved his hat and shouted at a passing navy gig filled with shorebound sailors. Suddenly he lost his balance, emitted a loud expletive, and fell headlong into the water. As the lifeboat crew fished him out of the water he affected a very graceful bow and climbed arrogantly up the gangway with a look on his face which seemed to say, "And for my next dive . . ."

At that moment a brawny black crewmember came down the gangway, picked up Stevenson and his cocoon of blankets and carried him up the steps. The high bulwarks on the JANET NICOLL made it somewhat difficult to get RLS aboard, but Ben Hird, the ship's supercargo (the person responsible for trade transactions and cargo management), was on deck doing his best to direct the activity. He too had had a bit too much to drink that morning, as his red face appeared to be a perfect match for his red hair.

Belle, Joe and Austin came aboard briefly to examine the accommodations and then were respectfully asked to depart, as Captain Henry was anxious to be underway. After final goodbyes were waved from the lifeboat on its way ashore, Belle could not help but think that she might never see Louis again considering the state of his health. She had been ambivalent in regard to her feelings for Louis, often jealous of the attention he received from Fanny, but she knew the two were meant for each other and so she wished the union well. She really thought, however, that Fanny and Louis had hit rock bottom, leaving for who knows how many weeks on a grimy old black cargo ship, crewed by a bunch of drunken white men and menacing-looking Melanesian deck- and engine-room hands. Much to her surprise, however, when she received her first mail from her mother, posted in Auckland, Fanny had said that they were having a "wonderful time." She wrote, "Think of two bathrooms and only one passenger besides ourselves, a nice wide deck to walk on, steam to run away from squalls with, and no flopping about in calms." But in reality the ship was a grimy work vessel, painted black with coal dust and cinders everywhere. An hour after leaving Sydney, Stevenson had decided that the JANET NICOLL was "the worse roller I have ever been aboard of." Even the crew called her the "Jumping Jenny." But at this critical time anything would have been acceptable to the Stevensons, except, perhaps, Dr. Hyde's missionary vessel. In the weeks ahead RLS would again return to health and happiness in the South Seas that he loved and which took such good care of him physically.

Crossing the Tasman Sea from Sydney to Auckland was pretty grim for Stevenson. It was a week of heavy weather, and since he was quite ill, he was confined to his cabin with all the ports dogged shut, and for the first few days his nourishment consisted solely of eggnog.

While Louis rapidly adjusted to his new seagoing experience in spite of the foul weather, and Fanny remained less than happy to be at sea again, as was her usual proclivity, the two of them found their South Sea voyage on this third ship, the JANET NICOLL, a somewhat different experience than they had encountered on either of the smaller sailing vessels. To begin with, they were aboard a ship with 49 crewmembers—nine white and forty black. Apprehensive about what she originally considered "sinister-looking black boys," she soon discovered them to be "friendly, gentle creatures, fond of singing hymns" and extremely efficient and cheerful workers.

The ship provided excellent accommodations, and the Stevensons ate with the owner, Mr. Henderson, Captain Henry and Chief Engineer Stoddard in a large, airy saloon located amidships on the main deck. The food served was excellent, and even the seamen told Stevenson that it was the best food they had ever eaten in their lives. Staterooms were large and well ventilated, and there was ample room on deck for walking or lounging in deck chairs under awnings rigged over the bridge area and aft of the smokestack.

While the JANET NICOLL was generally described as a topsail schoooner, she actually had two 90-horsepower steam engines with screw propellers, which gave her a cruising speed of about eight knots. In the late 1800s it was not unusual to find most steam ships also carrying sail, and the JANET NICOLL carried fore and aft gaff rigged sails on her mainmast aft, and fore and aft gaff rigged and square topsails on her foremast. Although it did little to improve the speed generated by her steam engines except when the wind was dead astern, carrying sail did normally help to reduce the ship's rolling, which, incidentally, was a real problem with "Jumping Jenny."

The ship's two large lifeboats were hung from davits on either side of the bridge, and each had oars and an auxiliary mast and lugsail. When the wind was from the right direction even these sails were set to give the vessel a little extra push.

By the end of the seven-day passage to Auckland the sea air had proven beneficial enough to Louis's health that the Stevensons dined at the Star Hotel with Ben Hird, the ship's supercargo, and Tin Jack, the island trader returning to his station. Louis and Fanny took a room at the hotel and arranged to meet Lloyd and his cabin mate Tin Jack the following morning for shopping.

After purchasing gifts the next day for the Hawaiian missionary Maka and his wife, from whom they rented their house in Butaritari in the Gilberts (on the possible chance that the JANET NICOLL might be calling there), Fanny returned to the hotel and Tin Jack and Lloyd sought out a chemist shop where Jack could buy fireworks to "entertain his native retainers." Tin Jack was a great practical joker and when he returned from annual leave in Sydney or Auckland, (which always consisted of extended binges), he invariably brought back funny hats, horns and mechanical toys to amuse, amaze and frighten the people of Tapituea, where his trading station was located. According to Fanny's journal Tin Jack's purchases this trip were:

> Besides the fireworks, which included ten pounds of "calcium fire," Tin Jack also purchased cartridges, grease paints, a false nose, and a wig. Lloyd was a little doubtful about the calcium fire and questioned the man at the chemist shop rather closely, particularly as to its inflammability, explaining that it was to be carried on board ship. The man declared that it was perfectly "safe," said he, "as a packet of sugar, adding that fire from a match would not be sufficient to ignite it."

Fanny and Louis returned to the ship in the afternoon and RLS took to his bunk, exhausted after a day of sightseeing. In the afternoon Tin Jack's fireworks were delivered aboard along with other parcels, none of which had information concerning their contents. Since Tin Jack and Lloyd were sharing a cabin, Lloyd put the packages holding fireworks, cartridges and a pistol of Louis's, which Tin Jack had taken ashore to be repaired, on his bunk until his cabin mate could come below and sort them out. The JANET NICOLL's mooring lines were taken in and she began making her way out of Auckland harbor about 8 p.m. on April 19. It was a clear evening and the passengers enjoyed watching the bright city lights making twinkling reflections on the smooth water of the harbor. When they were just about abreast of Auckland Light, Louis decided to turn in, dead tired after an exhausting day. Tin Jack Buckland and Lloyd had moved into Mr. Henderson's cabin where they were drinking coffee and discussing economic and political issues with him, and Fanny was enjoying a late evening snack in the saloon. Suddenly, without warning, there was a deafening explosion in the cabin of Tin Jack and Lloyd followed by red, green, and blue streaks of rockets hurtling along the deck, arching high in the sky and ricocheting through the saloon. Obviously, the fireworks had been ignited by the supposedly foolproof calcium fire that was now producing gorgeous flames and a terrible chemical odor. Everyone had, of course, been caught by surprise and it took the captain to personally organize the fire fighting effort. He wrapped himself in blankets and crawled into the blazing stateroom with a fire hose and began dousing the inferno, while Lloyd stood outside the door worrying that at any moment the cartridges which had come aboard with the fireworks would begin exploding. But the ship might have had worse problems than this, for all at once it was noticed that there was no helmsman at the wheel. When the rockets began bouncing down the deck and careening off the ship's superstructure, the man had abandoned his post. Fortunately, one of the mates had rushed to the bridge when the excitement began and had managed to put the ship back on course.

Meanwhile, with most of the fire out in Lloyd and Tin Jack's cabin, the captain ordered the crew to throw anything overboard which was burning or smoldering. This included suitcases, books, linen and steamer trunks. Fortunately, Fanny had arrived to investigate the disaster scene just as two crewmen were dragging out one of Louis's trunks which was being stored in the young men's cabin. As they were about to throw the trunk overboard, Fanny recognized it as the trunk in which Stevenson kept his partially completed manuscripts and research notes and she rushed forward to save it from oblivion.

When everything was relatively back to normal aboard the ship, Lloyd found that most of his clothing was destroyed or thrown overboard and a large selection of photographs from their South Sea travels were ruined. The Stevensons had discovered that the JANET NICOLL would call at Apia within about 10 days so Lloyd's clothing losses could be taken care of there, but dozens of valuable photos were gone forever.

In discussing the fire later, Captain Henry (who incidentally had respiratory problems for nearly a week after the event) maintained that if the wind had been blowing from a different direction, or if the cartridges had exploded, the ship might have been lost. He had very complimentary words for his black crewmembers who had "worked swiftly and obediently." Then he made a statement that made Fanny and Lloyd look at each other quizzically but remain silent. Captain Henry had said how lucky it was that he had a man at the wheel whom he could trust. Of course the man had left the wheel and the ship would have been in serious trouble if not for the mate's sudden action. When colored fire and white vapor were pouring out of the JANET NICOLL's portholes a steamer was passing very closely as it entered the narrow harbor channel. Had the explosion occurred an hour or so later when Louis and Tin Jack might be asleep they could have been seriously burned or suffocated.

The trading ship passed the small islands of Curtis and Sunday. Sunday Island had once been inhabited by an American family who remained in residence until the island's volcano threatened to erupt. While others had tried to settle there recently, few were able to accept the threat of the active volcano or the hordes of rats that were said to infest the place.

On April 26, after several days of gale and continuous rain, the JANET NICOLL's anchor was put down in the bay off the village of Alofi on the island of Niue, or what was sometimes referred to as Savage Island. This oval-shaped island, measuring 13 miles north and south by 9 miles east and west, has an upthrust coral plateau rising some 220 feet above the sea and encircled by a narrow terrace 90 feet above the water. With fertile but not plentiful soil, the inhabitants managed to export copra, bananas, cotton, breadfruit and *bêche-de-mer*. Discovered by Captain Cook in

1774, the island was thought to have been settled by migrants from Samoa and Tonga. They were governed by a king, four chiefs and four subchiefs.

Since the first Christian missionaries had not established themselves on the island until 1861, there were still a number of followers of traditional religion, and a number of *tapu* still remained in force—such as women not being permitted to leave the island or even to go aboard a visiting ship. The island had one day a year which was called "a day of judgment." On that day everyone had to gather in their village, and one by one confess their sins to an elected jury and whipper, made up of both Christians and indigenous believers. The jury and the whipper also set the judgments even on themselves—whipping or an equivalent fine, and the next day everyone would start with a clean record.

Here on Niue Fanny added to her island artifacts which would one day grace Vailima walls. She was given what were known as "peace sticks." The sticks were made of black ironwood about three feet long and shaped like spears, and were ornamented with coconut fiber sennit and yellow bird feathers much like those used in the cloaks of Hawaiian royalty. They traditionally had been used in tribal combat situations by women who stood by on the sidelines and would rush out between the combatants waving these "peace sticks" when they thought a battle had lasted long enough and the affair would end.

Before leaving Niue, Tin Jack, not dissuaded by his fireworks debacle, decided to try out his comic disguise of wig, whiskers and false nose on the local population. When he appeared thus disguised, the Niueans were "at first much alarmed and some of the women frightened to the point of tears."

The JANET NICOLL steamed past Ta'u, Ofu and Olosega, commonly known as the Manu'a Group of Eastern Samoa, before dawn on April 30, ran up the coast of Tutuila in mid-morning, and by dusk was safely anchored in Apia Harbor. Fanny's perception of Upolu was quite different from what it had been on her initial visit aboard the EQUATOR. Now she was coming home and in her diary she lovingly described her island:

> We ran along Upolu for a couple of hours, the scenery enchanting; abrupt mountains, not so high as in Tahiti or Hawaii,

nor so strangely awful as the Marquesan highlands, but with a great beauty of outline and colour, the thick jungle looking from the deck of the ship like soft green moss. Through the glass I could see a high, narrow waterfall drop into the sea.

Rounding Matautu point they could see the topmasts of ships anchored in the harbor and beyond them the string of white frame buildings that fronted on Beach Road. At this point Fanny noticed Mount Vaea and called, "Oh, Louis, look! there is our place." A signal flag was sent aloft requesting a pilot and in a matter of a very few minutes a pilot boat was headed their way. The pilot came aboard and guided them to an anchorage just off the landing dock and the JANET NICOLL soon was gently tugging at her anchor chain. It was too late to try to eat ashore, but as soon as the evening meal was over the Stevensons were in a lifeboat on their way to town. It seemed like being home again as they walked down Beach Road shaking hands with European friends and offering friendly *talofas* to the Samoans. They stopped by the livery stable and ordered horses to be brought down to the boat landing the following morning so they could visit their island sanctuary, Vailima, to see what progress had been made in the construction of a cottage and the clearing of the land.

It was very early the next morning when Louis trained his binoculars on the boat landing and announced that their riding horses had arrived. They all threw a few gift items for friends and their camera (which fortunately had not burned in Auckland) in a knapsack and they were on their way. Since Stevenson had often rented horses during their previous visit to Apia, he was looking forward to a very pleasant and rewarding day. He was not disappointed. The horses were good, the weather was pleasant, and he was on his way to his own South Sea island estate which lay at the foot of Mount Vaea. When Louis, Fanny and Lloyd reached Vailima, they found the road had been widened and improved, and a crew of Melanesian laborers, who were employed by Harry Moors, were hard at work cutting and burning trees and bush. In the middle of a well-cleared area was a cottage for temporary housing until the manor could be built. When they stood on the balcony of their little house, the Stevensons could see the JANET NICOLL lying at anchor and far beyond that was the horizon with the noonday sun beating down and turning the deep blue of the ocean to shimmering silver as it met the sky.

Two hundred miles north of Samoa was the Tokelau Island group where the JANET NICOLL was scheduled to stop at Swains Island, also known as Olosega, or Quiros Island. The island was privately owned by Eli Hutchinson Jennings, Jr., whom Fanny referred to in her journal as "King Jennings." The island had been acquired by the present owner's father in 1856 when he was living in Apia. He had been much involved in Samoa's inter-tribal warfare and had contracted to build a vessel of war for the Samoan government. The ship he built, however, was propelled by paddle wheels operated by men turning a crank. While this curious man-of-war was armed to the teeth with every form of armament imaginable, the Samoan government considered the means of propulsion inadequate and refused to honor their contract.

Jennings was so angry that he moved his Samoan wife and a group of Samoans to Swains, an island which he had bought from an English sea captain by the name of Turnbull. Once on the island Jennings began fashioning his own little fiefdom. The island was completely surrounded by reef until Jennings blasted a boat passage. Then he built two schooners using local woods and sold them to a German exporting company in Apia. Eli Sr. and his Samoan workers established a very profitable copra enterprise and built beautiful houses, a church and a school house and then imported a pastor and a school teacher. This is the community that the Stevensons found on Swains Island in 1890, although the tiny dynasty was now run by Eli Hutchinson Jennings, Jr., who had been sent to the United States for his education. Evidence of his national allegiance was noted by the fact that he flew the stars and stripes from his flagpole, albeit with a white dove superimposed on the blue field. It seems that in Swains Island mythology, a white dove flying over the island portended sickness, so in order to appease the bird it was superimposed on the stars.

Jennings had an extremely large amount of copra to be transferred to the ship, but the job was made considerably easier by the fact that, although the height of the island was only 20 feet above the ocean, the copra shed and a railway had been so situated as to provide a gentle incline down to the landing dock. Loaded wooden carts filled with bags of copra could be easily pushed down the tracks and even returned empty with little effort. The village, the roads, the acres planted in coconuts and subsistence foods were well kept, and Fanny was much impressed by the fancy horse and carriage tied up in front of the house of King Jennings.

The JANET NICOLL next stopped at Pukapuka, the only inhabited island of the Danger Island cluster in the Northern Cook Islands. When they arrived on May 4 they found a culture which had been considerably changed by mission activity since the 1860s. The people were wearing European-style clothing—trousers for men and "coverings," i.e., Mother Hubbard-style dresses, for women—living in European-type houses, and they had turned their backs on old-time beliefs and customs. It was even a sin for these islanders to talk about pre-Christian religious practices.

The island was governed by a king who allowed no one to gather more nuts than needed for bare subsistence without his permission. Consequently, very little copra was produced. On this island the nuts were dried in the shell to prevent cockroaches from consuming the meat. The copra was therefore white and of excellent quality, but so little was produced that it was not profitable to keep a trader on the island. They did, however, export a considerable amount of pearl shell, which meant that trading schooners would make periodic calls at the island.

The JANET NICOLL was the first steamship the islanders had ever seen, and when her anchor was put down offshore, dozens of canoes were launched and began paddling out. When the canoes were close to the ship, the skipper blew the steam whistle which not only frightened the men in the canoes but also the people lining the beach. In time, however, the paddlers gingerly approached the ship and came aboard. While the ship did not stay very long, Stevenson's anthropological interests were very much awakened by the Pukapukans. Their culture appeared to be somewhat related to that of the Samoans, but even before the advent of missionaries they had never practiced tattooing, nor had arched houses or brother and sister *tapus*. The principal gods of the Samoan pantheon—Tagaloa, Tane, Ru and Rogo—were unknown; however, their fishing techniques were much like the Samoans' and their wet land taro cultivation methods without irrigation were the same. But they did not manufacture bark cloth (tapa) although they had strong affiliations with western island people such as Samoa and Tonga who did. Their language, however, appeared to be influenced by those of island people both to the east and west of them.

After having received very little cargo from Pukapuka, the ship departed with one last intimidating blast from the ship's whistle and headed for Manihiki to the east. The atoll was sighted two days later, and the Stevensons went ashore by landing on the beach, since there was no boat passage through the reef. The island consisted of about 1,250 acres of land and had an excellent lagoon from which the people acquired pearl shell and *tridacna*, the shells of the giant clam. Like Pukapuka, Manihiki culture had been greatly affected by missionaries. Their first actual contact with the western world came in 1821, when the London Missionary Society ship JOHN WILLIAMS arrived and dropped off two teachers. By 1852, the majority of the inhabitants had been converted and were cooperatively collaborating in the destruction of *marae* (traditional sacred ceremonial sites) and the rejection of traditional gods and priests. House and clothing styles were altered by the introduction of western materials and new codes of morality.

The JANET NICOLL had arrived at the time of the annual jubilee, when for one week no laws were enforced, allowing riotous celebration without fear of consequences. The people were even allowed to sing and dance in the old heathen manner.

There was one half-caste trader on the island, and three white men: a former produce merchant, a deserter from the marines and a young Englishman who had been shipwrecked on a nearby island. Since the regular diet of Manihikians was almost entirely coconuts, these men, who lived off the generosity of the islanders, disliked eating only "coconut steak" but seemed physically none the worse for that diet. In fact, the three "beachcombers," as Fanny labeled them, were well dressed and quite good-looking. All were quite content to remain on the island and, in regard to their monotonous diet, stated, "We have no right to complain; they give us what they have." They did say they felt deprived without tobacco, which they had not had for months.

The island trader's Polynesian wife took Fanny under her wing and invited her to her house, where Fanny immediately became an object of attention of children who filled the open doors and windows in an attempt to view the odd-colored lady. The trader's wife explained, "Manihikians have said that the first sight of white people is dreadful, as they look like corpses walking."

Lloyd, who had managed to rescue both cameras in the Auckland fire, spent much of his time photographing the important and the colorful people of the island such as the English beachcomber, the island judge and the king, who appeared for his photo in a pair of white duck trousers and a black velveteen coat underneath a black cloth poncho with gold fringe. Around his neck was suspended a tinsel star and on his head was a crown of red and white pandanus leaves.

On the day that the JANET NICOLL was departing for Penrhyn the shipwrecked English beachcomber said that he was anxious to get off the island because he was very sick of eating nothing but coconut. But when offered a chance to work his way home on the ship, Fanny recalled that "he asked anxiously if it were a 'soft job,' refusing any other." Before leaving Manihiki Louis gave him a tin of tobacco, but he got very little of it, as his hosts expected their share, and the young man wound up with the makings of a single cigarette.

Penrhyn Island, often called Tongareva, is the largest of the Northern Cook atolls with approximately three square miles of land and a 40-mile reef that encircles a very nice lagoon. While the island was sighted at 5 p.m., Captain Henry decided to lay off, as the island had a very dangerous passage through the reef. It was late in the day, and the weather was squally. The following morning Captain Henry proved the wisdom of his decision, at least to Louis who was at his usual observation point on the wing of the bridge, and saw that the passage was scarcely wider than the ship itself. Later Fanny would describe their arrival into the Penrhyn lagoon in her journal:

> Our route, until we dropped anchor, was studded with "horses' heads" as thick as raisins in a pudding. There would be a rock just awash on either side of us, a rock in front almost touching our bows, and a rock we had successfully passed just behind us. We were all greatly excited and filled with admiration for the beautiful way Captain Henry managed his ship. . . . The native pilot was on the masthead nearly mad with anxiety. It was the first he had had to do with a steamer and he was convinced that the JANET was on the point of destruction every moment.

Once anchored, there was a bustle of activity aboard the JANET NICOLL—getting out their boxes to hold the pearl shell and making new ones. They expected a substantial cargo, and considering the number of canoes laden with shell paddling out, they would not be disappointed. Soon there was a considerable crush of pearling boats waiting to discharge their cargo of mother-of-pearl, and Fanny was charmed by the gay chromatic scene which had developed on the water below her. With the facility of an Impressionist artist she recorded the brilliant color of the spectacle in her journal:

"The colours are enchanting: the opaline sea, the reds and blues of the men's clothing, running from the brightest to the darkest shades, the yellow boats wreathed with greenery, the lovely browns of the native skin, with the brilliant sun and the luminous shadows."

In the afternoon Fanny and Louis went ashore on one of these island boats, landing near the white trader's house. As they viewed the house from the water, they had been puzzled by what appeared to be a strange statue on the trader's verandah. When they drew closer they saw that it was a figurehead of what had been a timber vessel that had been wrecked on the reef. It was a magnificent work of art, and Stevenson was so impressed by this extraordinary piece of carving and its existence on this desert isle that he later included the figurehead in the violent climax of his novel *Ebb Tide*. When it first appears in the novel and is viewed by the three beachcombers plotting homicide, Stevenson gives a masterful description:

"A woman of exorbitant stature and as white as snow was to be seen beckoning with uplifted arm. The second glance identified her as a piece of naval sculpture, the figure-head of a ship that had long hovered and plunged into so many running billows, and was now brought ashore to be the ensign and presiding genius of that empty town." That empty town would soon see murder, not of the island squire but rather of the degenerate intruder and with the figurehead as backdrop.

When a timber ship broke up on the reef and the figurehead was brought ashore the people were frightened by the "white" lady, and naughty children were still threatened with being handed over to her.

Unlike most island populations the Stevensons had encountered, the Penrhynians apparently were somewhat ambivalent about their commitment to Christianity. They had a huge European-style church big enough to hold twice the population of the island, but the Penrhyn churchgoers had a reputation of suddenly turning on their pastors and telling them to leave immediately since they were "tired of being missionary." Although the island had a strict curfew which had crewmembers, and particularly Tin Jack, running from the police on several occasions, they also had an annual "week of jubilee" when the whole island was on a gigantic spree, and at this time Penrhyn was reputed to be "not a pleasant, or hardly a safe, abiding-place."

It was also here that the Stevensons encountered a series of most bizarre incidents associated with death and dying. There was the case of an island man who was paralyzed on one side of his body and had convulsions with spasmodic contractions on the other side. In response to this development his family immediately began constructing a coffin. When the supercargo, Mr. Hird, called upon the family he looked at the coffin and said "But the man is not dead." The family reply was, "Oh yes, he is dead enough; it is the third time he has done this, so we are going to bury him." Even appeals by Hird to the native missionary were of no avail and the man was buried and, of course, did indeed soon die.

A second incident involved a Penrhyn "wake watcher," a man who was assigned the duty of watching over a corpse on the night prior to burial. The man fell asleep but was awakened by a loud noise, only to find the "corpse" sitting up in his coffin. But the frightened wake watcher maintained that "I was equal to him; I ran at him and knocked him down, and now he is decently quiet again." The man's blow had once and for all rendered the so-called corpse lifeless.

When it was nearly time for the JANET NICOLL to move on to other atolls the self-styled comedian Tin Jack apparently thought things a bit boring and went below, put on his wig, beard and false nose, and appeared on deck as a "devil" to what instantly became a terrified group of young women who had swum out to see this strange ship that belched smoke. Two of the girls immediately leaped overboard while others sought comfort with Fanny, who tried to explain that this horrible creature was only a misguided post-adolescent named Tin Jack and not a "devil," which was the local term for all evil spirits.

After a profitable two-day stay at Penrhyn, the JANET NICOLL weighed anchor at 5 o'clock on May 11 and negotiated what was, for the passengers as well as the native pilot, a disquieting passage out of the lagoon. The ship returned to Manihiki, stopping only long enough to land passengers and lumber and pick up a man, woman and boy for Suwarrow, a nearly uninhabited island in the Cooks where it was believed that only six persons were presently in residence, and their passengers would swell the population to nine. However Mr. Hird, the supercargo, was not sure that this would be the case as he had recently had a dream wherein the white trader in Suwarrow was lying dead and was ready for burial. He said that the dream was so realistic it was more like a vision than a dream and that he had noted the time it had occurred and written down the hour, the date and the details.

When the ship arrived in Suwarrow on May 13 it was discovered that Mr. Hird's dream was indeed prophetic. The island trader had died of a liver ailment at exactly the time and on the date of Hird's dream.

On this remote, lonely atoll Mr. Henderson had more interests than just trading. He had planted coconuts in much of the area several years before, but the trees were not bearing and the sheep and goats he had introduced to the island had not survived. The island appeared a bare and lonely place although flowering trees provided a touch of brilliant color here and there. At one time Suwarrow had supported a vibrant, thriving community, but now Fanny commented that it appeared "very like the desert stronghold of a pirate." There was a well-built pier, a cluster of houses (almost all now empty), and beacons to guide ships into the lagoon. Some of the houses seemed to have offices and many contained collections of marine gear, undoubtedly salvaged from shipwrecks. The town looked as if someone expected the return of its residents to once again attend the church, work the land with the rusting tools in a large toolshed, and drink the water stored in a cistern in the ground which was fed by rain water caught on galvanized iron roofs. Feeling that "stirring events have happened here and that its history should be wild and romantic," Fanny finished her journal account of

Suwarrow with "We departed from the most romantic island in the world, regretting that to us its history must always remain a mystery unsolved."

After leaving Suwarrow Mr. Henderson had the ship return to Pukapuka where, due to the people's involvement in time-consuming church activities during this season, very little copra was brought aboard. In spite of the islanders' earlier promises to make it worth his while, his return was not rewarded. Henderson consequently ordered the islanders off his ship, sternly said, "No copra, no tobacco," and sailed off for Nassau Island. Here the surf was high and the landing bad, and although they could not safely bring out some forty boxes of copra, Henderson had supercargo Hird give everyone whatever trade items they wanted on credit.

The JANET NICOLL returned to the Tokelaus, stopping at various islands in the group for additional copra between May 19 and 23, once more visiting the Jennings family and including in their itinerary Atafu, the smallest atoll in the group. There was nothing extraordinary about the island but the people were unique, and upon leaving, the Stevensons declared it "the island of flatterers." What else could they do when the people who knew very little English told Louis, "You good papalagi," and Fanny, "You good woman," and Lloyd "You handsome man?"

Their next port of call was Funafuti, the capital of the Ellice Islands, an archipelago of nine atolls with a total land area of only 11 square miles. Lying just south of the Gilbert Islands the Ellice Islands are inhabited by a Polynesian people who differ considerably from their northern neighbors both physically and linguistically. They are taller, lighter skinned and speak a dialect closely resembling Samoan or Tongan. Like people on most atolls they cultivate coconuts, pandanus, a few bananas, and taro, grown in artificial pits. At the time of the Stevensons' visit there were no more than about 150 people living on Funafuti, and this could be explained to a great extent by the activities of slavers. Just four years earlier two American ships flying Peruvian flags arrived at the island, distributed gifts, and suggested that as many as wanted to could go to Peru to be educated. Even the island king, being anxious to have as many of his subjects as possible participate in the opportunity, blew his horn, thereby issuing a royal summons. The ships carried away hundreds of his subjects never to be seen again. Fanny was not surprised when some of the JANET NICOLL's officers told her that the people of Funafuti had a reputation for being dishonest. If true, she thought, it certainly was a character trait learned from white role models.

It was here that Louis began his serious study of marine geology and biology, which he pursued on a number of islands. After breaking off a piece of outer reef with numerous blows of a hammer, he was surprised to find it contained a multitude of tube-dwelling worms hanging like "a dreadful thick fringe." They greatly resembled earthworms in size and color, and in fact, they undoubtedly were polychaete worms, of the phylum Annelida, which also includes earthworms and are quite common inhabitants of coral reefs throughout the South Pacific.

The JANET NICOLL departed Funafuti early on the morning of May 28, arriving after dark at the island of Niutao. When Fanny came on deck the following morning she commented that this was "the only one of the Ellices I have as yet seen that gave me such an unpleasant impression that I shall not be disappointed if I cannot go ashore." To a certain extent this was because there was no real landing area on the island and the surf was dangerously high. Here they found another ship anchored, and surprisingly enough, it was painted white and greatly resembled the EQUATOR. Stevenson's reaction to seeing this close facsimile of their former charter vessel was, according to Fanny's journal, "that every time he looks at her he expects to see ourselves." In the afternoon there was considerable activity associated with the other ship, as they brought out and took aboard nearly 180 people for an excursion around the Ellice Islands, for which they received 25 tons of copra in payment.

The following day was Sunday, normally a day of rest for the Melanesian crew, but Henderson was afraid of a change in the weather and asked the men to work as a matter of necessity. Much to the Stevensons' surprise, the crew consented and cheerfully set to work. Tin Jack rode ashore in the first boat and set off with his own hammer to see if he could replicate the experience Louis had had. In a small enclosed lagoon he also broke off samples of coral rock and found they contained the same kind of pallid earthworm creatures that Louis had found, but he also found worms which greatly resembled centipedes. He caught the last boat carrying out cargo for the day, and when back on board, he found that most of the Melanesian crew had already gathered on the afterdeck and were about to hold a Sunday religious service which he discovered would include singing Scottish hymn melodies with their own Melanesian words.

Henderson was right about the change in weather. When the JANET NICOLL arrived in Nanumea several days later, the surf was so high that the first whaleboat containing a Henderson company trader, an independent trader and a missionary and his wife, capsized, turning end over end, and the independent trader was nearly drowned. Before the day was over many canoes carrying copra were broken to pieces, and the steamer's own boats had many narrow escapes. Great waves would swamp a boat, followed by crewmembers popping up around the boat and then hauling it ashore. Aboard the ship those who were not in the boat details served as a cheering section for the crews.

On June 9, the ship raised Arorae, the first of what would be many Gilbert Islands ports of call. Still fascinated by his discovery of coral reef worms, and wanting to collect more samples, Louis went ashore with his hammer. It was a scorching hot day and as hard as he worked he found the coral rock impossible to break. Rather than risk his own delicate health, Stevenson turned to a young Gilbertese watching him and offered him a stick of tobacco if he would do the job for him. The young man took the hammer and struck just one hard but unsuccessful blow. "Too much work," he said, and handed back the hammer.

Arorae had suffered greatly from slavery. In 1871 three slave ships arrived looking for "recruits." The king, fearing for his life, offered the slavers all of his people except the very young and the very old. Supposedly, the recruits would be brought back from South America after a period of indentured service, but few ever survived the ordeal.

On June 13 the JANET NICOLL arrived at Naukanau atoll, where the Stevensons would meet a most extraordinary man, trader Tom Day, described by Fanny as the "flower of the Pacific." Fifty years old, Tom was well-built with the looks of an actor and with an affinity for drink and revelry. In fact, he claimed that "Tom Day" wasn't his real name and "Tom Drunk" might be more appropriate. "You see," he said, "some time ago I went to the expense of a shilling to have my real name changed, since I had deserted from the navy three times and I was afraid they might catch up with me." Tin Jack was fascinated with Tom's representation of himself as a most desperate type of ruffian, and invited him to go back to Sydney with him for a holiday. Tom rejected the offer stating, "I couldn't leave my old woman behind. The fact is that I've got another wife there, and besides I got into a bit of trouble there and I'd better keep away."

Stevenson had heard about his Sydney troubles and wondered if the bizarre story which had been circulated throughout the islands was really true.

"You are the Tom Day who had a native's head cut off, I believe. I'd like you to tell me the truth of that story; these kinds of tales have a habit of getting very distorted as they are told and retold."

With very little hesitation Tom Day described the following situation. It seems that on Marakei Island in the Gilberts an islander shot at him with a pistol without provocation, grazing his ear and the side of his head. Livid with anger, Tom rushed home, got his rifle and returned to the scene of the shooting only to find that the man had disappeared. Since there was a well-established rule that native folks must not shoot white folks, Tom Day urged other islanders who had witnessed the shooting to bring the man back to be tried for his criminal act. The men said, however, that the shooter was a chief and had many men to protect him. Then trader Day said that one man came over to him and whispered "Better we kill him." In response, Tom had said "If you do, fetch me the head." At that point Stevenson asked, "Why in the world would you want his head? Wouldn't killing the man be enough? "Oh no," said Tom, "If I had not asked to see the head they'd just have gone and killed some poor inoffensive fellow and I'd never have known the difference." That night the men brought the head of the guilty man and Tom verified that it was the right man and then threw the head out into the darkness where by chance it hit his wife, who fainted and had to be revived by his throwing three pails of water in her face.

In conclusion, Tom Day indignantly stated, "They wanted to make trouble about it in Sydney—they said I had killed a man. I never killed no man; I only told them to fetch his head so I could be sure it was him."

*   *   *

On June 15 the Stevensons awoke to find they were lying off Tapituea, the island where Tin Jack was serving as the trader for Mr. Henderson's company. He had packed all his gear the day before and was anxious to get it ashore safely along with a pig which was tied up on the deck. It was a very sad day for everyone, as Tin Jack, with all his pranks, had become almost a member of the family. Fanny said she thought his island was dreary looking and the landing dangerous, and Captain Henry agreed, stating it would be impossible with this sea to land Tin Jack and all his provisions and gear. The ship departed for Nanouti, a nearby island where Tin Jack had a partner with the somewhat unusual name of "Billy Jones Cousin." Billy Jones Cousin came aboard and Tin Jack worked out an arrangement with Cousin to handle affairs for him ashore while he remained with the ship until it returned from the Marshall Islands in about three weeks. The Stevensons were glad his trip was extended, for they found him great company. He was handsome, well read, full of fun and mischief, and from a well-to-do family who kept him well-supplied with money for his annual vacation binge in Sydney.

After setting sail for King Tem Binoka's dominion in the Central Gilberts, Lloyd, Louis and Fanny lingered a while on deck reveling in a gorgeous golden sunset. After dinner they returned to marvel at the blue-fire brilliance of the evening star, which resembled a diamond in the twilight sky. After all these months at sea they never grew tired of these extraterrestrial displays.

Shortly after the three had returned to their staterooms Ben Hird came running down the deck shouting "Osbourne! Osbourne! We are just passing the EQUATOR!" and Lloyd who had just fallen asleep, leaped out of bed and began running up and down the deck scanning the horizon and shouting, "Where is she? I don't see her!"

It was a cruel joke Ben Hird had played on the young man so eager to see Captain Reid's schooner again. They were merely crossing that imaginary line that separates the southern from the northern latitudes. Lloyd took the prank well and even forgave the supercargo when he was reminded by him that their next port of call would be Abemama, where the Stevensons would have a reunion with their old friend King Tem Binoka.

However, when the JANET NICOLL entered the Abemama lagoon the next morning and anchored just off the king's royal residence, there was no sign of life. A boat was lowered and Mr. Henderson, Louis and Tin Jack went ashore to learn why the royal barge had not already set out from the shoreline below the palace.

They returned to the ship with the news that the king was visiting the island of Kuria, and when the steamer reached Kuria, a boat came out informing them that the king had been ill and was recovering from the measles. The king indeed must have been feeling bad, because his boat also brought Henderson an insulting letter in a white man's hand but signed by Tem Binoka. Mr. Henderson, as might be expected, was furious and showed the letter to Stevenson, who suggested that he be present when Henderson and the king would meet.

Henderson, the whole Stevenson family and Tin Jack went ashore and took gifts for the king. Louis would present him with a Turkish tobacco pipe; Lloyd, a filled cartridge belt with sheathed daggers; and Fanny, a copy of the flag she had designed for the king. As their boat ran along the beach in front of the houses where the king's wives were sitting, shouts of "Pani!" "Pani!" (Fanny! Fanny!) drifted across the water.

The king, looking older and thinner, met them on the beach with an air of nonchalance which would have left one to expect that he had just seen them yesterday. But he was delighted with his gifts, and when Fanny, Lloyd and Tin Jack last saw Louis, Mr. Henderson and the king seated in the king's residence, he was happily smoking his *chibouk* with his cartridge belt hung over his shoulder.

Leaving the men to work out their problems emanating from the king's insulting letter to Mr. Henderson, Fanny, her son and Jack walked through the large huts constituting the harem until they found the king's mother and sat down beside her, where they received enthusiastic expressions of welcome and friendship.

As the three of them walked through the series of houses, Fanny noted that in each of them she found a "devil box" like one they had bought from a medicine man (dog-star) when they were in Abemama several months before. One house contained a large circular piece of "devil work" surrounded by a ring of white shells. These boxes holding charms and talismans were undoubtedly there in response to the measles epidemic that had swept the islands. Fortunately, Tin Jack was fluent in the local

Gilbertese and was able to serve as translator for the king's mother and Fanny, who learned that many had suffered greatly from the measles but fortunately only four people had died. Children seemed to have light cases of the disease but the elderly were very ill, and the king was at one time very close to death. The first question of the king's mother to Fanny was about Stevenson's health, and when the answer was that he was doing well, she said that they must still have their "devil box," which she assumed was responsible.

By the time Fanny returned to the royal residence the Tem Binoka-Henderson misunderstanding had been settled. The discord had been traced to a white man (probably a competitor) whom the king would not identify. When Louis suggested that an apology might be in order, it was handsomely made and accepted, and the king was invited to come on board the JANET NICOLL.

When the Stevensons and Mr. Henderson had been preparing to go ashore to meet the king earlier, Henderson advised Fanny to wait until later to present Tem Binoka with her gift—the royal ensign which she had designed. Now Henderson sent a message out to the ship for Ben Hird to send up the king's flag when Tem Binoka, Henderson and the Stevensons would approach in the royal gig. The king, steering his gig himself, brought the party out to the JANET NICOLL, and as they drew near the ship Henderson shouted "Hird, elevate the royal bunting." Up it went, much to the satisfaction of the monarch. The party boarded the ship by way of the accommodation ladder, the king not having his own rope boarding ladder for this ship, and all went down to the cabin where "champagne was opened." Then Louis and Fanny were left alone with the king. Tem Binoka seized Stevenson by one arm and Fanny by the other and pulled them close, kissing them and crying for joy. He told the couple that every day he searched the horizon with his long glass, watching for their return. He said he had often walked over to "Equator Town," had stood and said, "I too much sorry. I want see you."

It was soon time for the JANET NICOLL to leave, and emotional goodbyes were exchanged. The king's flag was hauled down and given to him, and he left the ship very depressed, although he was informed that they would return in approximately two weeks, after a sweep through the Marshall Islands.

As final preparations were being made for departure, the

steward came over to Louis and Fanny, who were still in the cabin relaxing over a cool drink, and told them that someone at the porthole wanted to speak to them. They looked up and there, looking in was Uncle Parker. As they talked through the open porthole, Uncle Parker informed them that there had been further trouble with the reprobate cook that Tem Binoka had provided for them in "Equator Town" and consequently the king had shot him.

After a brief call at Marakei, the JANET NICOLL steamed north past Butaritari, the last of the Gilberts, and then proceeded northwest toward Jaluit with all sails set, even those in the lifeboats.

Arriving on July 19 at Jaluit, the German seat of government for the Marshalls, the Stevensons were anxious to pay their respects to the commissioner, whose house could be seen from the harbor. It was painted terra-cotta red and looked very attractive sitting within a grove of frangipani, hibiscus and shower trees. Although it was a hot and humid day, the Stevensons dressed in their finest—which meant for Louis, his best trousers, yellow silk socks, soiled white canvas shoes and a white linen coat he borrowed from the trade room. The coat could not be buttoned so he held it together with his gold watch and chain. Fanny donned her usual long *holaku* dress which she concealed completely with a full-length lace cloak, and on her head she wore a black turban with a spotted veil. Her stockings were red, and easily seen through the many coral cuts in her canvas shoes. She had no gloves, but put on all the rings she owned. Strangely enough, the pair's appearance caused a great sensation aboard ship with comments like "most respectable" and "reflecting great credit on the ship."

The commissioner received them warmly, offering them a glass of wine and an invitation to lunch later. While sipping their wine and exchanging polite conversation, they were joined by Captain Brandeis, a slender colorless man about 45 years old, who had played a major role in Germany's struggle for power in Samoa. Brandeis, a former Bavarian artillery officer who had served with distinction in war, had resigned his commission and traveled the world involved in a variety of adventurous enterprises. He went to Samoa as a clerk for a German firm, but in reality was primarily involved in training military forces for the rebel king Tamasese with whom the Germans wanted to replace King Malietoa Laupepa. With the help of Brandeis the Germans filed false claims concerning Malietoa's misdeeds. With Apia Harbor filled with their warships, they removed Malietoa Laupepa from office, exiled him to Jaluit and installed their puppet king Tamasese with Brandeis as Premier. The year that followed was one of tyranny and oppression, and was marked by the rebellion of the forces of a third legal claimant to the throne, Mataafa, who by most accounts was the "people's choice."

At first Fanny feared that the meeting of Brandeis and Stevenson would be stormy, since Louis was very critical of Germany's heavy-handed involvement in Samoan politics and the fact that H. J. Moors had been the major political opponent of Brandeis. But RLS had long wished he could meet Brandeis, because he was collecting data on Samoan politics for a book to be called *A Footnote to History*. What actually happened at the meeting of the two men was carefully recorded in Fanny's journal. Describing Brandeis' appearance she began, "He was pale, and I thought he was prepared for an unpleasant meeting with Louis; that wore off quickly, and the two were soon deep in conversation. . . . Louis is fascinated by the captain and I do not wonder; but his eye is too nervous, and his nose is not to be depended upon—a weak and emotional nose. A man, I should say, capable of the most heroic deeds . . . a born adventurer, but never a successful one."

The JANET NICOLL's next stop would be Majuro, where they would be loading copra and other cargo for several days before returning once more to Jaluit. After learning of their itinerary, the commissioner showed Louis the Marshall Island navigation chart which he had in his collection. He said that there was but one old man who knew how to make these traditional charts, and when the ship returned to Jaluit, he would like to present RLS with one as a gift. The charts, called *rebbelib*, were constructed of a framework of the ribs of coconut palms tied together with coconut fiber (sennit) with islands represented on the frame by cowrie shells. The chart was designed not only to show relative positions of islands but to represent wave and swell phenomena.

The Stevensons were much taken with Majuro, calling it "a pearl of atolls." The entrance to the lagoon was dotted with enchanting small islets, all very green and soft, and the lagoon water was clear and, according to Fanny, green as a chrysoprase gem. Here Henderson offered them the use of a house on the island's windward side. It had but a single room, but it was a pleasant alternative to sleeping in stuffy staterooms. They did not take as much copra aboard here as they had anticipated, because these islanders had also suffered a measles epidemic. In fact, while they were there the king, old Jebberk, lay close to death and was *tapu* to white people.

Since the ship was not scheduled to return to Jaluit until the end of July, Fanny unpacked her paints and headed out looking for interesting models. To her good fortune she found an attractive and charming island girl by the name of "Topsy," the wife of a handsome white trader. The young woman dressed beautifully in cotton prints, colored handkerchiefs, and rows of tasteful necklaces. Her hair, smoothly drawn back over her head, was ornamented with two bands of colorful beads. On one arm she exhibited the tattoo "Majuro" and on the other the word "Topsy." Fanny learned that she was a castaway from another island, the sole survivor of an over-turned canoe. She knew a number of English words but was as innocent of the outside world as a little child. Someone mentioned something about her heart and she seriously said that she had no heart, that she was solid meat all the way through. Perhaps the most interesting thing about this beguiling little charmer was that her constant companion was a little organ grinder's monkey, a rather rare sight in the South Sea islands.

On the ship's return to Jaluit, RLS went to see the commissioner, as the official had requested. As promised, Louis was given a Marshall Island navigation chart and he, the commissioner and Captain Brandeis immediately set to work trying to identify the islands represented on the chart by cowrie shells with those on a European map. After considerable time and effort they had to admit that they had failed, but Stevenson was assured that the maker of the chart (presently off island) would be consulted and a complete key to the islands on the chart would be sent to Louis in Samoa.

The JANET NICOLL left that same day for Namorik where the only event worth noting was that Stevenson went ashore and returned aboard with the news that he had just met a "wicked old man" who would make a wonderful character in a South Sea novel. Interestingly enough, that character did appear as the odious and loathsome Captain Randall in his book *Beach of Falesa*, which would be published in 1892.

The following day they were at Ebon, where they anchored in the boat passage into the lagoon just opposite the wreck of the American schooner HAZELTINE, which they had first discovered while aboard the EQUATOR. Then, during a two-day passage to Abaiang, Louis became ill and was confined to bed much to the distress of everyone, since good health had marked his JANET NICOLL voyage up until then.

Now it was on to Tarawa, where the ship stayed only briefly as there was no copra. They called at Ananuka on July 3, where Tem Binoka and his people, who had moved from nearby Kuria Island, were taken aboard as passengers for Abemama. One of the first men of the king's party to come aboard was a pleasant-looking young fellow who, like all the rest, stopped to shake hands with Fanny. When he asked about Louis and learned that he was ill, he immediately requested that he be taken to see him. Obviously a medicine man, he stood beside Stevenson's bed asking about his symptoms and encouraging him in a very professional manner. When they returned to the deck, Fanny felt a tap on the shoulder and turned to find the king smiling and holding out both hands to her. When told that Louis was ill, he was very concerned and inquired as to the severity of his illness. Fanny said that she believed it was just a cold but that anything of that nature could be very serious to a man of Stevenson's physical condition.

Mr. Henderson personally supervised the loading of the king's people and their possessions. This was a sizable job, and boat after boat arrived with people and an extraordinary variety of valuables. One boat brought out 25 large zinc pails, while the next several boats brought sewing machines, music boxes, camphor-wood chests, rolls of mats and large baskets, and packages of taro pudding, every sort of nut, and giant taro pounded up with pandanus syrup and coconut milk which had been baked underground. The last thing to come aboard was the king's royal gig which was hoisted aboard for the trip back to Abemama. When the JANET NICOLL weighed anchor at 8 p.m., there were 200 deck passengers—mostly the king's wives, body-guards and retainers plus a considerable number of babies and dogs. Each and every woman had her devil box beside her, guaranteeing a safe voyage. When the people rolled out their sleeping mats on the deck, there was barely room to walk around. The harem occupied the after deck and a *tapu* was placed around them. But the ship's crew put on a good show for these ladies, exhibiting their great strength in raising the lifeboats in the davits. The women of lower rank on the forward deck were not *tapu* and had a delightful evening as the crewmembers sang and danced for them far into the night. The very old ladies—the king's mother (who was extremely drunk on gin), and the king's aunt, plus one or two relatives—spent the night on the captain's bridge.

It was a very friendly night for all, and all the Abemama people showed great affection for the Stevensons, who they re-membered had spent several weeks among them at "Equator Town." They were approached by their old friend Snipe, who was one of the slave girls serving them at that time.

In the morning they landed the king's court first and then proceeded to clear the decks of people and belongings, which took most of the morning and afternoon. In the evening Louis felt well enough to participate in a farewell dinner that had the appearance of a gala party, as there were champagne toasts, and speeches. Then they went ashore for a display of fireworks, cour-tesy of Tin Jack, which was followed by a display of distress flares and signal rockets from the JANET NICOLL.

The next day was Sunday and the king came out and had breakfast with the Stevensons in the saloon, while out on deck the Melanesian crew lay in a row under the awning reading the Bible while one of them played hymns on an accordion. When goodbyes were exchanged, Tem Binoka seemed less depressed, as he said he knew he would see them again. As he left the ship he presented Fanny with a very valuable fine mat.

It was an overnight trip to Nanouti, where Tin Jack would leave them. Immediately after anchoring offshore the Stevensons vis-ited the island with their friend, who wanted Lloyd to take his picture at his new trading station. As parting gifts Henderson gave Tin Jack two black pigs and a handsome sleeping mat. Fanny presented him with several bottles of medication carefully labeled and with instructions for use, a pillow and an extra pillow case. It actually took two days to get Tin Jack's things ashore and take on the island's copra, as the tide was low. The last view they had of him was the boat taking him to the edge of the reef where they could see him being carried over it on an islander's back. There were about 50 bags of copra to come aboard and these were packed out across the reef to the ship's boats on the backs of locals or the ship's crew.

As the ship departed the island in the evening, they blew the steam whistle in farewell, burned a blue light, and set off the rockets. Jack responded with one from the shore. One of the rockets set off by the captain on the bridge boomeranged and hit the bridge, where it sputtered and threw sparks and fire everywhere, and considering their past experience at Auckland, put a real scare into everyone.

Very much concerned with Stevenson's lingering ailment, and recalling an earlier remedy which returned him to health in Tautira, Fanny begged a fish from one of the deckhands and collected some coconut meat, a pinch of cayenne pepper, a lemon and some sea water to make *miti* sauce and she gave her husband a dish of raw fish for his dinner. He relished it and made her promise to make more in the future.

Although Louis's health was improving and he was able to write, the last two weeks of the trip seemed to pass slowly. After several months at sea in this part of the Pacific, one atoll began to look much like another and they had seen many of these before while on the EQUATOR.

While at the island of Beru in the Southern Gilberts it was discovered that the ship's coal supply was very low, and Stevenson thought there might be a change in routing to where fuel might be available—to Suva, Fiji perhaps.

At Arorae, the southernmost island in the Gilberts, one of the boats steered by supercargo Ben Hird disappeared in the surf, and Mr. Henderson immediately went to his assistance. When she capsized, a forward section in the boat was stove in. No one was hurt, and only the chief engineer was inconvenienced. He had to wait on shore so long to get another boat back that he did not make it back in time for dinner.

The ship arrived at Nankomea, the most northerly atoll in the Ellice Island group on July 18, and left that night under sealed orders steering south-southwest. Eight days later they sighted Erromango, a mountainous island in the New Hebrides where the foremost London Missionary Society evangelist, John Williams, was killed by natives in 1839. This was the Stevensons' first Melanesian island.

At this point Captain Henry had become seriously ill with a stomach disorder, and there was much concern for him. Louis's health, on the other hand, had greatly improved and he was hard at work on a novel as well as his book on the Samoan wars and politics.

After reaching Mare Island of the Loyalty group, which lay some 45 miles from Nouméa, Stevenson suddenly decided that he had had enough of "Jumping Jenny" and that he would make a brief stopover in Nouméa, New Caledonia, where he claimed he wanted to be exposed to Melanesian culture, and where he wanted to visit the French penal colony. It is possible that several months of shipboard togetherness with Fanny and Lloyd was beginning to pall on RLS, especially with Fanny's controlling behavior in regard to his health. The Stevenson marriage was not always blissful, and at this point in time they were having heated arguments concerning *Footnote to History,* which Fanny very much objected to, feeling that it was not the kind of writing Louis did well, and therefore was a waste of his valuable time and talent.

As much as Fanny would have liked to have stayed by Stevenson's side in Nouméa, she also was anxious to join Belle and her family, who had received little word from them since leaving Apia. Besides, she now wanted to reach Sydney with its civilization and its many comforts and conveniences.

As the ship drew near Nouméa, the Stevensons, particularly Fanny, laid out their best going ashore apparel and went on deck to observe the arrival at their final port of call. They approached Nouméa through a series of lovely bays studded with small islands, some with hills and some looking very much like atolls with low strips of beach fringed with palm trees. Given their earlier concern about a dwindling coal supply, the Stevensons expected that they would tie up at a fuel dock, but this, strangely enough, was not the case. Apparently the officers now believed that they could make Sydney with their present holdings.

Whatever the reason for Louis deciding to jump ship, he certainly made the right decision, for the JANET NICOLL had nothing but trouble all the way to Sydney. Shortly after leaving Nouméa, the ship got caught in a terrible storm with waves that washed over half way up the masts, the coal supply was exhausted, the crew was unable to utilize the sails to gain an advantage, and for two days and nights could not establish a position because of overcast skies. The passengers and crew were neither able to lie down nor sit without constantly having to hold on to anything that would not give way.

Captain Henry was so seriously ill with gastric fever that Henderson and the other officers had to assume his responsibilities, and by the time they managed to reach port in Sydney, both Fanny and Lloyd were so exhausted it took days for them to recover. Louis, on the other hand, had a fast and smooth passage to Sydney where he once again moved into the Union Club with its comfort and privacy, and where he would stay until it was time to return to Apia. On this occasion the Stevensons managed to arrive so quietly that none of the newspapers even knew they were there. Lloyd and Fanny both took rooms at Miss Leaney's Theatrical Boarding House, and after many serious discussions between Fanny and Louis out at the Union Club concerning their property in England and their future home in Samoa, it was decided that they should sell Skerryvore, the family home in Bournemouth, England, and use the proceeds for the construction of the Vailima house. It was also decided that Lloyd should return to England and make arrangements for shipping the Skerryvore furniture to Samoa. On his return he would bring Aunt Maggie with him, and it was more or less taken for granted that they would be joined by the rest of the family in Samoa when the new house at Vailima was finished.

Belle definitely did not want to do this, but every time she expressed a negative attitude toward moving to Samoa she would be told, "You will love Samoa, Belle," or "How can you decide until you have seen the place?" While Fanny and Louis believed they should have Belle and Austin under their protection, Belle had never completely reconciled herself to her mother's divorce and second marriage and did not want to be dependent on Stevenson. However, Louis was very upset in regard to Joe Strong's alcoholic ways and financial dependency on him. Stevenson had recently learned that while they were on the JANET NICOLL, Joe had sold some of his paintings and spent the money entirely on himself. Even more exasperating was the discovery that money sent to Joe so that Belle might have a vacation never was given to his wife.

In Belle's own journal (later published) she described how her relationship was worked out with RLS:

> One day he asked me to go shopping with him for supplies to be sent to Vailima. Quite suddenly I burst out with all I had wanted to say for months. I begged him to let us stay in Sydney. I was very grateful for all he had done for us, but I hated being a burden on him. Besides it wasn't necessary; we could take care of ourselves. . . . "Building a new house and starting a plantation must be a heavy expense to you. Why should we add to it? You work so hard; you're not well." Here I began to cry.
>
> Then he gave me his side. It is the only time I ever knew him to be despondent in any way. He described the despair he felt when told he could not go back to London, to his home in Bournemouth; he would never see his native city Edinburgh again. Sentenced to exile for the rest of his life, what he wanted now was to make that exile bearable.
>
> "You and Lloyd are all the family I have, "he said. "I want a home and family, my family, round me." He told me, too, that Lloyd's great ambition had been to go to Oxford but he had given it up to stay with Louis and our mother in Samoa.
>
> We talked till late, going back over old scores, clearing up old misunderstandings. Though I admired Louis and respected him, there had always been a hidden antagonism between us. Perhaps because I had adored my father I was unconsciously critical of him. Even if he was the head of our family, I saw no reason why he should plan my life.
>
> But now all was changed. He talked with such kindness, such understanding, that every bit of resentment I had held toward him melted away, and I felt myself to be truly his loving daughter.

By August 1890 Stevenson had definitely decided that he would never again be able to return to his native land and at this time he wrote Henry James, "I must tell you plainly. . . . I do not think I shall come to England more than once, and then it'll be to die."

At the end of October Fanny and Louis were aboard the LÜBECK on their way to Samoa with the rest of the clan to follow as soon as Lloyd and Aunt Maggie would arrive from England, and when there would be adequate housing for everyone. In Samoa the Stevensons would occupy the somewhat rustic cottage which had been built for them by Harry Moors' workmen. From this "rough barrack," as RLS chose to call it, they would supervise the development of their plantation and lay plans for what would ultimately be referred to as the Flash House, or Marble Halls.

As the ship left Sydney Harbor Stevenson did not look back but concentrated his attention on the open sea, thinking only of what lay ahead. He was going "home" to Samoa, the only real home he could ever have now—one where he would establish a mansion on a hill, where he could live among a gentle, caring people, and where he could write without fever and hemorrhages threatening his life and his work.

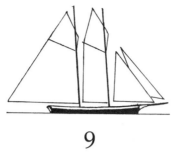

9
Vailima—Home is the Sailor, Home from the Sea

FOR THEIR FIRST six months at Vailima, Louis and Fanny lived alone with one servant, a German cook and handyman, in a two-story, four-room dwelling that Fanny decided to call "Pineapple Cottage," in preference to "the rough barrack." It was anything but elegant housing, but it would do until the land was cleared and a permanent house was built on a plateau some 200 yards higher up the hill. While Louis was able to do some writing—three chapters of a book he was co-authoring with Lloyd and eight chapters of the book *In the South Seas*—he and Fanny diligently applied themselves to the development of their plantation. In a short note to Sidney Colvin, Stevenson confessed "I went crazy over outdoor work, and had at last to confine myself to the house, or literature must have gone by the board."

While Louis enjoyed the work and was proud of his ability to do manual labor, Fanny was the real pioneer who seemed to thrive on the back-breaking toil. She worked from dawn to dusk establishing a cacao plantation (something rather unique in Samoa at that time), directing the planting of coconut trees as well as fruit trees, supervising the building of a carriage house, pig pens and chicken coops, maintaining a huge vegetable garden, and even seeking out a spring on Mount Vaea and bringing the water down to the house site in pipes. Every day brought a new creative enterprise into fruition. One of her more successful was the still in which she produced an excellent perfume from *ylang ylang* blossoms. And if all this were not enough, she used several evenings to write a short story titled *Anne* for *Scribner's Magazine* for which she received $200.

It was during this period that the Stevensons received a surprise visit from Henry Adams, the cultural and intellectual pessimist and self-labeled "proper Bostonian," and artist John La-Farge, neither of whom had ever met the author. According to Adams' account of the meeting, he found the Stevensons in a "clearing dotted with burned stumps, living in a shanty as squalid as a railroad laborer's hut." He described Louis as "a man so thin and emaciated that he looked like a bundle of sticks in a bag, wearing dirty striped cotton pajamas, the baggy legs of which were tucked into heavy woolen stockings—one brown, the other purple." As for Fanny, Adams described her as "grubby, dark and wild as a Mexican half-breed or an Apache squaw and wearing a missionary nightgown."

Not expecting company of any kind, the Stevensons had nothing to offer them except tea and ship's biscuit. But the visitors, apparently concerned for their health and well-being, politely excused themselves, stating they had pressing business in Apia and disappeared down the muddy path leading to town.

Prior to their return to Apia in the fall of 1890, the Stevensons had consulted an architect in Sydney. After drawing some preliminary sketches, his estimation of the cost of the Vailima building was $20,000, an unheard-of price for a home at that time, and a bit too much for the author whose income was unpredictable. While retaining the general style of the building, Louis and Fanny had local European carpenters in Apia begin construction on something considerably smaller than what the Sydney architect had proposed. The resulting house contained 3,000 square feet of living space and looked much like two adjacent wooden blocks, equal in size and two stories high. Spacious verandahs, twelve feet deep, skirted the front and side of the house. The first phase of construction involved three rooms downstairs and two large rooms upstairs for sleeping. A second phase of construction created additional bedrooms, a library upstairs, and a great hall on the first floor. The exterior of the house was painted peacock blue, and the corrugated iron roof was a bright red. When the construction was completed the cost of the house was close to $7,500.

In January 1891, Louis left Fanny in charge of Vailima and sailed for Sydney to meet his mother and Lloyd, who would stop over there with Belle on their way to Apia. Because of a broken propeller shaft in the Fiji islands, the LÜBECK arrived four days late and was replaced by another ship for Apia. As might have been expected, the author fell seriously ill while in Sydney and suffered delirium for two days before being brought on board a "wonderful wreck." However, during the week's voyage to Samoa he was "a good deal picked up, but yet not quite a Samson." What troubled him most was the fact that "it is vastly annoying that I cannot go even to Sydney without an attack."

While Vailima looked good to Lloyd, Maggie's first glance at her new home convinced her that it was definitely not quite livable yet, and she reboarded the inter-island steamer and returned to Sydney, where she would stay with Belle until the main house would be completed.

In March 1891, the American consul, Harold Sewall, invited Louis and Lloyd on a three-week *malaga* to Tutuila in eastern Samoa, which the author enthusiastically accepted, having heard Pago Pago described as "this beautiful land-locked loch of Pago Pago."

Much like his initial emotional experience at encountering a mountainous South Sea island, Stevenson was deeply moved by the serenity of the harbor of Pago Pago, and fortunately he left a record in his journal of that inspiring experience.

The island at its highest point is nearly severed in two by the long-elbowed harbour, about half a mile in width, cased everywhere in abrupt mountain sides. The tongue of water sleeps in perfect quiet, and laps around its continent with the flapping wavelets of a lake. The wind passes overhead; day and night over-head the scroll of trade wind clouds is unrolled across the sky, now in vast sculptured masses, now in a thin drift of debris, singular shapes of things, protracted and deformed beasts and trees and heads and torsos of old marbles, changing, fainting, and vanishing even as they flee. Below, meanwhile, the harbour lies unshaken and laps idly on its margin; its colour is green like a forest pool, bright in the shallows, dark in the midst with the reflected sides of woody mountains. At times a flicker of silver breaks the uniformity, miniature whitecaps flashing and disappearing on the sombre ground; to see it, you might think the wind was treading on and toeing the flat water, but not so—the harbour lies unshaken, and the flickering is that of fishes. Right in the wind's eye, and right athwart the dawn, a conspicuous mountain stands, designed like an old fort or castle, with naked cliffy sides and a green head.

The "old castle" mountain was of course Mount Pioa, or "rainmaker mountain," whose 1,886 foot summit turned the tradewinds to clouds and clouds to rain, drenching the fertile hillsides of what was once a volcanic crater. So it was that when the night came on, Pioa's rain began to beat down on the corrugated roof of their harborside guesthouse and nearly obliterated the sound of the bell from the Catholic Mission across the bay. But it was a pleasant diversion from the sound of the rats which infested the shores and houses and frolicked on the metal roofs.

Sewall planned a round-the-island *malaga* by whaleboat to visit all the villages of Tutuila, including those not accessible by road, and there were also plans to visit the islands of Manu'a by trading schooner, but this could not be arranged. Stevenson would not again have an opportunity to visit Manu'a until 1894 when a British warship would take him there as a guest. The Manu'a islands were culturally the most traditional of all Samoan regions. They were normally ruled by their own monarch, the Tuimanu'a (King of Manu'a), but at this time their sovereign was a queen, described by Stevenson as a "21 year old part-Samoan girl, Makalita, who sits all day in a pink gown, in a little white European house with about a quarter of an acre of roses in front of it." Shortly following Stevenson's visit the young Queen of Manu'a died in a tragic fire and was buried where her roses had bloomed.

The trip around the island of Tutuila by whaleboat was delightful, with Tusitala reveling in this "coast of classical landscapes, cliffy promontories, long sandy coves divided by semi-independent islets, and the far-withdrawing sides of the mountain, rich with every shape and shade of verdure." The crew of eight half-nude oarsmen sang as they went and never seemed to tire, not even when they had to return to Apia. Fortunately the weather cooperated, for the 23-hour, 65-mile open boat passage from Pago Pago to Apia could have been a dangerous voyage even for a small schooner. Arriving well after dark they all proceeded to the American consul's house where a bottle of Burgundy had been promised. After breaking open the wine storeroom, the keys to which the consul had lost, they all relaxed over a friendly glass and then Stevenson fell into bed exhausted. He did, however, manage an early departure and horseback ride up to Vailima the following morning. Fortunately the journey and exposure did not prove debilitating to Louis, and he was able to write a friend, "It is like a fairy-story that I should have recovered liberty and strength, and should go round again with my fellow-men, boating, riding, bathing, toiling hard with a wood-knife in the forest."

Louis and Fanny moved out of Pineapple Cottage and into the villa in March 1891, but they were still pretty much camping out since their furniture had not yet arrived from Scotland and England. Maggie returned early in March, but in many ways did not feel comfortable at Vailima and decided that she would once again return to Sydney and wait until affairs at the Samoan residence were in better order. She returned on May 15 and expressed the opinion that the house looked very nice indeed, although they still did not have their European furniture.

Maggie brought her own personal maid, Mary Carter, from Sydney. She took excellent care of her mistress, but when anyone else in the house requested something of her, the maid's firm response was "That is not my department." Maggie likewise had some definite ideas on how things should be at Vailima. Normally the Stevensons did not say grace before meals, and Maggie, a devout Christian, stated that "she would not be left to pray with only servants." They thereby established a tradition which resulted in Louis composing a collection of devotions, one of which was offered before each meal.

Apparently it was Fanny's opinion that her mother-in-law was not particularly happy with her life at Vailima, and in her diary she wrote, "I see again she dislikes the life here which we find so enchanting and is disappointed and soured that she is not able to persuade us to throw it all up and go to the colonies. We have given the colonies a fair trial and they mean death to Louis, whereas this is life and reasonable health."

Villa Vailima afforded a marvelous vista of some fifty miles of blue Pacific, and Louis loved to stand on the upper verandah and watch the ships sail in and out of the harbor. On quiet nights he could hear the crashing of the surf on the coral shore. The Stevensons house was by far the most elegant in Samoa. It dominated the countryside like a castle, and Samoans, when wanting to express a superlative would say, "Like the house of Tusitala."

Joe Strong, Belle, and Austin arrived in Samoa the latter part of March with three cats and a cockatoo named Cocky, whose total vocabulary consisted of the word "mama." They were given the Pineapple Cottage, which by this time was quite livable. The furniture for the main house (several tons of it) arrived from Scotland and England on July 1, 1891.

When everything was moved in and sorted out, the first floor had a formal dining and sitting room which was called the "tapa room." It contained one of only two fireplaces in Samoa. The other was right above it on the second floor in the library. Neither hearth was ever used, however, because the builders were unfamiliar with proper chimney construction, and every time they tried to light a fire the room filled with smoke. The room received its name from the fact that the walls were completely covered with barkcloth (tapa) tapestries and artifacts from various South Sea cultures. The main floor also contained a kitchen with cast iron wood-burning stoves, and a great hall measuring 35 by 50 feet paneled in California redwood and with a polished hardwood floor which could accommodate as many as 100 dancers. A piano sat in one corner covered with a giant tea cozy to protect it from the humidity. A stairway leading to the second floor was flanked by two golden Burmese Buddhas.

The second floor contained Fanny's bedroom, which was also paneled in natural redwood and had a secret hideaway in the wall to be used in the event that Samoan warfare might reach Vailima. Maggie's room was the largest of the bedrooms and it was furnished with her personal belongings from Edinburgh. Her verandah afforded a wonderful view of the grounds and of the sea.

Louis's room was actually the library; it contained his bed, a desk and his writing table. Here the author often wrote in bed starting as early as 6 a.m. The library walls were lined with bookcases, and the books were varnished and specially treated to withstand the climate and insects. Samoan mats and oriental rugs covered the floor, and Piranesi engravings and a brace of Colt six guns adorned the walls.

From the very beginning Fanny insisted that the second

floor should also include a medicine room. While she maintained that it was a necessity for Louis, she was somewhat of a hypochondriac herself. The room was equipped with a hospital bed, bed pans, a medicine chest, scales and other apothecary instruments. Here Fanny practiced a good deal of folk medicine, and she maintained that "Dr. Fanny" was prepared for any medical crisis which might develop with Stevenson or anyone else in the family. Other bedrooms on the second floor served as guest rooms and later as the bedrooms of Austin and Belle.

In front of the house was a lawn with a croquet area and a tennis court. Everywhere there were floral hedges of tube-roses, jasmine, gardenia and hibiscus. Flowering trees, purposely saved during the land clearing, filled the air with their fragrance. The house gardens were a paradise of fruit trees bearing mangos, oranges, limes, lemons, pears, breadfruit, bananas and papaya.

A grassy paddock stretched for about a quarter of a mile to a stable which quartered the Stevensons' riding horses, including RLS's Samoan-bred mount, Jack, and the team which they used to draw their carriage on trips into Apia. East, west and south of the clearing the land was covered with heavy bush, and here and there were lofty trees, affording a resting place for the flying foxes, the large fruit-eating bats which took to the air at dusk. A short distance from the house was a stream that cascaded into a bathing pool—a favorite spot for the family after a warm and humid day.

While the Stevensons were living in Pineapple Cottage and in the early days in the villa, some of the household help were Europeans, but ultimately the staff became completely Samoan. It was predominantly male and varied in number from 13 to 21, and it was a carefully selected group chosen for good looks, polished manners, obedience, loyalty and physical strength. Everyone had his or her work outlined in advance, and several even had typewritten lists of duties. Breaches of discipline were punished by fines. Tusitala's house people were, however, treated more like family than servants. They were especially pleased when the Stevensons entertained, for then they could display their efficiency and knowledge of social graces. These were also the occasions when they were allowed to wear their dress uniforms—Royal Stuart tartan plaid lavalavas. Throughout all of Samoa the staff was known as *tama ona* (children of the rich man), or as the Scots would say "Mac Richies." *Ona* was actually short for *miliona* (millionaire).

When interviewed by W. H. Triggs, a staff member of the *Christchurch Press*, concerning his life in Samoa, Louis described his relationship with his Samoan staff :

> It may surprise you to learn that I pay lower wages than any-body in Samoa and it is my boast that I get better served; visi-tors have frequently said Vailima in the only place where you can see Samoans run. People always tell you that Samoans will not work, or even if they do, never stay with you beyond a few months. Such seems to be the general experience; it is not mine. The reason of this is neither high wages nor indulgent treatment. Samoans rather enjoy discipline; they like however to be used like gentlefolk. They like to be used with scrupulous justice—they like a service of which they can be proud.

Part of Stevenson's success may be attributed to the fact that he understood the nature of the Samoan social system, some-times referred to as the *"matai* system." The head of every ex-tended family was a *matai* with chief's rank who made all family decisions and for whom all family members worked. Louis played the role of the household *matai* and demanded the same loyalty and industry as would be expected from a Samoan coun-terpart.

While not always happy at Vailima, RLS was probably hap-pier there than he would have been anywhere in the world, and the tropical climate continued to allow him the kind of health he had coveted all his life. Steamships arriving every two weeks brought ice and fresh oysters from San Francisco and casks of Bordeaux wine from France. There was a good baker and butcher in Apia, and the staff bought fresh fish on the beach. Their own chickens supplied them with eggs, their streams pro-vided eels and fresh-water prawns, and Louis shot wild pigeons from his backyard. All of this was prepared with great dedica-tion by Talolo, their Samoan cook, who, after instruction in Eu-ropean cooking, stayed with the Stevensons for four years, leaving only once for a short period when called to the front with a six-shooter and beheading knife to fight with the forces of the rebel king Mataafa.

The only money that Stevenson had ever earned came from his writing, and write he did in Samoa. From his first effort, *The Bottle Imp*, which was written while Villa Vailima was being constructed, until the near completion of *Weir of Hermiston* in 1894, Louis worked diligently at his craft. He produced seven hundred thousand words for publication in his four years in Samoa. He wrote a series of books about the South Seas ranging from non-fiction accounts such as *In the South Seas, Footnote to History* and *Letters from Samoa,* to fictional works ranging from *Island Nights Entertainments, The Beach of Falesa* and works co-authored with Lloyd Osbourne—*The Wrecker* and *Ebb Tide.* He wrote the story of his own kin, *An Engineer's Family* and a travel account titled *Across the Plains.* It was at Vailima that he penned his three most important Scottish novels, *Catriona, St.Ives* and *Weir of Hermiston,* a book left unfinished at his death.

More and more, Tusitala linked literary production with lairdship. If he wanted to keep Vailima, he had to keep up production. It was during this time that Louis described his character to his friend Sir James Barrie: "In the past, eccentric. In the present, industrious, respectable and contented." Now Tusitala had a great estate to maintain and many mouths to feed, some with very elegant tastes.

Life was rarely dull at Vailima, at least in the evening. Dinner was at six and the family ate well—served by their house staff on expensive European china and exquisite crystal. Louis prefaced each dinner with a Vailima prayer, often more poetic than pious, which he had written specially for these evening occasions in order to please his mother. After dinner there was always a game of cards, a literary reading, good conversation or music. If there were any guests in the house able to play the piano or sing, the family would not take no for an answer. RLS often joined in with his flageolet, and he sometimes provided the less musical among them with penny whistles to do the same. Sometimes each of the family members merely went off by themselves to read books from the extensive Stevenson library.

Everyone was welcome at Vailima—Samoan chiefs, Apia business and professional men, missionaries, Europeans just stopping over in Apia, and sometimes even whole crews of visiting warships such as the KATOOMBA whose crew Tusitala described as "the nicest set of officers and men conceivable."

The Stevenson journal for September 12, 1893 reads:

> Yesterday was perhaps the brightest in the annals of Vailima. I got leave from Captain Bickford to have the band of the KATOOMBA come up, and they came, fourteen of 'em, with drum, fife, cymbals and bugles, blue jackets, white caps and smiling faces. Coming up the mountain they had collected a following of children and we had a picking of Samoan ladies to receive them. Chicken, ham, cake and fruits were served out with coffee and lemonade and rounds of claret flavored with rum and limes. They played to us, they danced, they sang, they tumbled. Our boys came in the end of the verandah and gave them a dance.

The Vailima household was, according to Stevenson biographer Gavan Daws, "a tangle of apron strings and other attachments around Stevenson which made for perpetual pulling and tugging rather than any easy equilibrium. Here was Stevenson's widowed mother living with her only child in the same house with his wife. Margaret Stevenson was a mere ten years older than Fanny, who was ten years older than Robert Louis. Fanny's daughter Belle was less than ten years younger than Stevenson, and attractive along her mother's lines."

Then there was Lloyd, who was in his early twenties when they occupied Villa Vailima. He greatly admired Stevenson and thought himself enough of a quality writer to attempt to co-author two books with Tusitala. While Lloyd served as a bookkeeper, general manager and overseer in charge of the outside people at Vailima, he never really held any other job, and his subsistence throughout his entire life time was derived almost entirely from the Robert Louis Stevenson estate.

Joe Strong, the irresponsible and alcoholic husband of Belle, who supposedly assisted Lloyd with estate management, seemed to have a strong aversion to any kind of labor, and was caught in the act of robbing the Vailima wine cellar and storeroom with a duplicate key. Not only was he found sleeping with the Vailima house maid Fa'auma, but for several months he had been cohabiting with a Samoan "wife" in Apia who had been his mistress when he was in Samoa with King Kalakaua in 1889.

Since the residents of Apia were very much aware of Joe's double life, Belle had no difficulty getting a divorce and having Louis awarded guardianship of her son Austin.

After the divorce, Joe went around Apia circulating rumors about the moral character of his ex-wife. Fanny was glad to have him out of the house as she could not stand the sight of him. To begin with, he never wore anything but a brightly flowered lavalava for trousers, a red bandanna knotted around his shirt collar, a visor cap and a cockatoo on his shoulder, which made him look like something out of Louis's novel, *Treasure Island.* Stevenson's response to the man's countenance and character was that he cut him out of all the family photographs.

Austin was 11 years old at the time of the divorce, and up to that time his education had been entirely at home. Louis would give him a daily history lesson, and he had begun teaching him French, but the boy's education actually derived from the whole Stevenson household. When Joe continued to stay in Apia after the divorce, Louis was concerned about what the man's influence might be on the boy, and he made arrangements for Austin to attend the preparatory school in Palo Alto, California, and board with Nellie Sanchez, Fanny's recently widowed sister.

It had also been discovered that Lloyd had succumbed to the erotic pleasures of the romantic South Seas by taking a Samoan lover whom Louis suggested that he marry, but Fanny demanded an end to the affair.

Fanny had what were called nervous breakdowns twice during her residence at Vailima, once when Belle was divorcing Joe Strong, and then again in 1893 when she became very seriously ill with violent personality swings. During this period Tusitala recorded: "She made every talk an argument, then a quarrel; till I fled her and lived in a kind of isolation in my room."

For several months Fanny exhibited psychotic behavior such as catalepsy, hallucinations, and violent outbursts which local doctors felt incapable of dealing with. At one point Fanny threatened to run away, and from time to time family members had to restrain her for as much as two hours for fear that she might harm herself. By April 1893, Fanny was on the road to recovery, however. Dr. Funk had diagnosed her problem as Brights

Disease, a kidney disorder plus high blood pressure, and had prescribed appropriate medication. Whether her psychotic state should be attributed to a physical or behavioral cause will forever remain a debatable question.

It was also during this year, Stevenson's fourth in Samoa, that the political situation in the islands reached a critical point. The Samoan people would not recognize Malietoa Laupepa, the chief the Germans had brought back from exile and reinstated as king, and refused to pay taxes to the government of Malietoa. The majority remained loyal to the rebel king, Mataafa. To ease tensions the European powers decided to keep Malietoa in power but to give Mataafa a high executive office similar to that of a prime minister. Malietoa refused to accept this arrangement and the country was plunged into war. Skirmishes even took place in the streets of Apia.

Mataafa's warriors came and camped one night on the grounds of Vailima. They stood around fires at the edge of the woods, rifles in hand, alert to any threatening sound. Pencil sketches by Belle record the event. They show warriors displaying a severed head and another group carrying the headless body of an enemy in a manner generally used for carrying pigs.

For the first time in his life, Louis, a man whose books so often described armed conflicts, was actually in the middle of a real live war. He was tempted to get involved in the fighting himself, and there were those who believed that he was functioning as Mataafa's military strategist, but instead he chose to play the role of war correspondent. On one occasion he reported: "In the rally of their arms, it is at least pretty; and I have one pleasant picture of a war-party marching out—the men armed and boastful, their heads bound with the red handkerchief, their faces blackened—and two girls marching in their midst under European parasols."

Visits to the Apia hospital gave Louis another view of war—one that was depressing and disgusting. What disturbed Tusitala even more was the mismanagement of the whole political situation which had brought on the armed conflict in the first place. Stevenson maintained that "idiots were in charge," and he was determined to do something about it. He let it be known at the Foreign Office in London that on the subject of Samoan native politics he was very knowledgeable, and he suggested that he himself replace the British consul since he could not stand to see others function in that role so badly. His hostile letters to the *London Times* (eight in number) and his ongoing campaign to rid Samoa of incompetent officials brought a local attempt to get Stevenson deported, but nothing ever came of it, nor were Louis's efforts in any way successful in improving the political situation.

Tusitala was a great admirer of Mataafa, describing him in *Footnote to History* as "the nearest thing to a hero in my history and really a fine fellow; plenty sense, and the most dignified, quiet, gentle manners." Mataafa was in his sixties, a tall and powerful person, with white hair and mustache. Stevenson thought Mataafa had the air of a Catholic bishop. Mataafa had taken a vow of chastity "to live," he said, "as our Lord lived on this earth." He had, in fact, never married.

Mataafa's headquarters were in the village of Malie, five miles west of Apia. Malie was described as prosperous and peaceful. There were no fortifications, and although it was believed that from 100 to 500 fighting men were readily available, there normally was no show of arms. On one occasion when Louis, Fanny and Belle visited Malie they found much to their surprise not armed pickets, but a cricket match in full swing on the village green.

Although Mataafa was only a rebel king, he played a dominant role in the political affairs of Samoa. Village envoys brought him gifts and were feasted in return. A score of talking chiefs were always in attendance, and his administration as well as his own deportment displayed a sense of tranquillity, order and traditional dignity.

The Samoans, Tusitala discovered, had their own unique form of warfare which seemed strange indeed to the Europeans. Battles often took place only in prescribed places and during daytime hours when the combatants would return to the battlefield after a good night's sleep in their own village. Combatants were often accompanied by their wives who helped them carry their weapons, drinking water and lunch baskets. The most frightful feature of Samoan warfare was the severing of heads, which were then displayed on poles as trophies of victory.

After the first few skirmishes between the rebel Mataafa

forces and those of the government-backed Malietoa Laupepa, the fortunes of war began to turn in favor of the king's troops. At a decisive battle near the village of Vaitele to the west of Apia the loyalist forces were victorious, routing the rebels and taking a dozen or more heads, including that of Mataafa's nephew and the nephew's wife, a *taupou*, or ceremonial maiden, from the island of Savai'i. It appeared that Samoan warfare had taken a shameful turn, for women, and particularly women with ceremonial rank, had always been immune to such atrocities.

Surrounded by Malietoa Laupepa forces at Vaitele, Mataafa's forces were routed. He burned all the houses in his village, Malie, except his own, which was dangerously close to the church, and he and his warriors escaped by war canoe to the island of Savai'i, where he expected to find military support. After a long and drawn out council meeting with the high chiefs of that island Mataafa found that one faction was definitely against him and another was neutral. Consequently, Mataafa and his forces withdrew to the tiny island of Manono, which lies between Savai'i and Upolu. As the Mataafa warriors were settling in and preparing to defend against the loyalists, the British man-of-war KATOOMBA arrived in Apia with orders to support the Malietoa Laupepa forces. Two German battleships lying at anchor in the harbor now had what they were hoping for, British political support, and the three ships sailed to Manono where Captain Bickford of the KATOOMBA issued an ultimatum that if Mataafa did not surrender within three hours they would bombard the island and he would land his marines.

Confronted with impossible odds, Mataafa and his top lieutenants surrendered, were returned to Apia, and then exiled to Jaluit in the German-administered Marshall Islands, where they would be held until 1898. Lesser ranking chiefs, including the father of Stevenson's cook Talolo, who supported the Mataafa cause, were imprisoned in Apia in quarters quite unsuitable to their rank. Shortly after the chiefs' incarceration, the whole Stevenson clan drove openly in a rented carriage to visit the chiefs and make them presents of tobacco and kava.

The following month the chiefs reciprocated with a feast in the jail courtyard. Great amounts of food and handicrafts, provided by their families, were presented to Tusitala and his family. It has also been documented that at this time Louis was talking to a circumnavigating yachtsman, Hungarian Count Festetics de Tolna, about the possibility of their sailing his yacht to Jaluit and spiriting Mataafa away.

When Talolo's father fell ill, Louis had Dr. Funk, the local general practitioner, go to the jail to attend to him. By the fall of 1894 the restrained and friendly intervention of Stevenson brought about the release of the imprisoned chiefs. The freed men spent one whole Sunday drinking kava and discussing how they might repay their benefactor. Finally the men agreed among themselves to construct a road connecting Vailima with the public highway. They announced that the work was to be their gift to Tusitala.

The task was a difficult one since they determined that the road should be 30 feet wide—requiring trees to be felled and boulders removed. When the road was completed, Tusitala suggested it be named Road of the Grateful Hearts, but the chiefs said "No; it should be called *Alo Loto Alofa*—Road of the Loving Heart." The completion of the project was celebrated with a feast given at Vailima, and a signboard was erected at the entrance of the road. It read: "We bear in mind the surpassing kindness of Mr. R. L. Stevenson and his loving care during our tribulations while in prison. We have therefore prepared a type of gift that will endure without decay forever—the road we have constructed." This was followed by a list of names of the several chiefs involved. Before the year was out these same chiefs would open another path at Vailima—one to the top of Mount Vaea.

In a speech of dedication following a kava ceremony Louis addressed his Samoan friends:

> When I saw you working on that road my heart grew warm; not with gratitude only, but with hope. It seemed to me that I read the promise of something good for Samoa. There is but one way to defend Samoa. It is to make roads, and gardens, and care for your trees, and sell their produce wisely, and in one word to occupy and use your country. If you do not, others will.

It had long been a common practice for Stevenson to read completed chapters of his books to his family for their reactions, and one evening in 1894 he anxiously assembled the clan and began to read the first three chapters of *Weir of Hermiston*, a book he thought highly of. When the author finished the reading, he noted that Lloyd had made no notes concerning possible revisions, as was his usual practice. Nor did Lloyd or anyone else make any comments at all. Lloyd merely said "Good night, Louis," and started across the grounds to his cottage. Agitated, and with his voice trembling with emotion, Louis shouted after him, "My God, you shall not go like that, without a note, a comment or the courtesy of a lie."

When Lloyd explained that he had been struck dumb by the beauty of the book and that it was truly a masterpiece, Louis burst into tears and Lloyd followed suit. And then they sat on the verandah and talked far into the night.

No doubt RLS communicated his belief that he was not a man of any unusual talent but that success had come because of his remarkable industry, and that if he had any genius it was for work. Perhaps he also shared his belief that his life was nearly done. Often lately he had talked about his past as though he were reviewing it. In recent weeks Lloyd had often observed Stevenson gazing up at the verdant dome of Mount Vaea. Several times Louis had expressed his wish to be laid to rest at its summit, but in spite of this urging Lloyd had never been able to bring himself to have the boys clear a path to the top. In fact, Louis was the only one in the family who had ever climbed to the top of the mountain.

On the evening of December 2, 1894, Tusitala was in excellent spirits and suggested that they should all play games.

"We are getting horribly dull up here." he said. "Everyone sticks around a lamp with a book, and it is about as gay as a Presbyterian mission for seamen."

He suggested that each in turn should enter the room and, using any accessories they could find, portray in pantomime one of their friends or acquaintances for the others to guess. Before long the family was roaring with laughter. Louis excelled at the game and said that it had been his most amusing evening at Vailima—it would also be his last.

On December 3, Tusitala worked steadily on the *Weir of Hermiston*. Never before had a book come so easily. Belle observed that Louis had very few preliminary notes yet he never faltered in his dictation. He said, "Belle, I see it all so clearly. The story unfolds itself before me to the least detail—there is nothing left in doubt. I never felt so before in anything I ever wrote. It will be my best work."

Stevenson finished dictating to Belle in time for lunch and then, satisfied with his progress for the day, rode into town to mail some letters. Upon his return he took a swim and then went to help Fanny in the kitchen. Fanny had been depressed for several days with a premonition of some impending disaster, and Louis played a game of cards with her to cheer her up. While they played he talked about the possibility of scheduling a lecture tour of the United States since his health had been so good in recent months. He said he was hungry and suggested a salad for dinner. Together they began its preparation and then RLS went to the wine cellar and returned with a bottle of Burgundy.

Suddenly he put his hands to his head and said, "Oh, what a pain! Do I look strange?" Fanny said "No" and helped him to a chair where he lost consciousness. She called out to Lloyd who had just returned to his cottage after a trip to town. Lloyd rode into Apia at once and returned with two doctors, one from a British warship and the other, Dr. Funk, the Stevenson family doctor. After examining the unconscious Stevenson, they shook their heads and said they believed he was dying of a cerebral hemorrhage, and there was nothing that medical science could do. With the family close beside him Tusitala died at 8 o'clock. As Dr. Funk left he, as head of the Public Health department, said, "You must bury him before three tomorrow."

Almost too stunned to act, the family nevertheless managed to wash the body and dress it in a soft white linen shirt and black trousers girded with a dark blue sash. A white tie, dark blue hose and patent leather shoes completed his attire.

The body was placed on the large banquet table in the great hall and was partially covered with the British Union Jack which normally flew over the house and had flown over the schooner CASCO. Chiefs from nearby villages had heard of the death and arrived with finemats which they laid over the body. They entered bowing, kissed him, said "Tofā Tusitala (goodbye, Tusitala)" and quietly went out. Candles were lit, and the Samoan staff begged the family to retire, allowing them to perform the all-night vigil. After announcing that they "wanted to make a church," the staff chanted prayers and hymns far into the night. Sosimo, Tusitala's houseboy, was inconsolable. He would not leave the body for a moment, and for days after the funeral he would place two glasses of fresh white flowers beside the author's vacant bed.

None of the family could sleep that night, but Lloyd was the most tortured of all. Why had he not had the path cut to the top of Mount Vaea as Louis had requested? The Samoans knew of Tusitala's desired grave site, however, and before six in the morning nearly 200 men arrived with axes, machetes and shovels to cut the path and dig the grave. Many of them were the Mataafa chiefs who had built the Road of the Loving Heart.

Lloyd made the climb to the top of Mount Vaea to select the grave site. The view he recalled was "incomparable; the rim of the sea, risen to the height of one's eyes, gave a sense of infinite vastness; and it was all so lonely, so wild, so incredibly beautiful, that one stood there awe stricken." Just below he could see the house and the grounds of Vailima.

Tusitala's mother, Margaret Stevenson, described the funeral in a letter to a relative:

> The ascent to the top of Vaea mountain was a very difficult matter, and many of the men found it more than they could manage. The coffin left half an hour before the invited guests, as the labour of climbing with it was so great; but there were many relays of loving Samoan hands ready to carry their dear Tusitala to his last home amongst them, and they took the utmost pains to bear him shoulder high, and as steadily and reverently as possible. Behind them came the few near and good friends that we had invited to be present; and when they reached the top of the mountain they found the coffin laid beside the grave, and covered with the flag that used to fly over us in those happy days upon the CASCO. As soon as it was lowered into place, and the wreaths and crosses thrown in till it was hidden from sight, our house-boys seized the spades from the "outside" boys who had dug the grave; no hands but theirs, who had been specially "Tusitala's family" should fill it in, and do the last service for him that was left to them. Mr. Clarke read portions of the Church of England burial service and also a prayer written by Louis himself, which he had read at family worship only the night before his death; and Mr. Newell gave an address in Samoan, so moving that all who understood Samoan wept, and also prayed in that language that Louis loved so well.

As the crowd of mourners left the grave, an old chief looked back and using chief's respect language said *"Tofā Tusitala, Tōfā Tusitala"* (Goodbye Tusitala, Sleep Tusitala). Following the Samoan custom of conspicuously marking the graves of men of high status, a large concrete marker was soon erected over the grave. A bronze plaque, which carried the epitaph Louis himself had penned, was provided by the Stevenson family. It read

> *Under the wide and starry sky,*
> *Dig the grave and let me lie.*
> *Glad did I live and gladly die,*
> *And laid me down with a will.*

> *This be the verse you grave for me;*
> *Here he lies where he longed to be;*
> *Home is the sailor, home from the sea,*
> *And the hunter home from the hill.*

The day of the funeral the chiefs of Upolu declared a *tapu* on Mount Vaea. From that time till now no one has been permitted to hunt the slopes for the birds whose cheerful songs had been so dear to Stevenson. And it is claimed that spirits still haunt the mountain and guard the grave. Tusitala's birthday, November 13, is celebrated annually by Samoan chiefs, who decorate the writer's tomb with flowers and sing the dirge performed at the grave over a hundred years ago. Vailima stands today much like it appeared in 1894, a shrine to the beloved Tusitala who for a few precious years lived among this island people and gained their respect because he demanded nothing of them except their friendship and their acceptance of him as a fellow artist, poet and compassionate human being.

Epilogue

"Bluidy Jack"

Most Stevenson biographers appear to accept the fact that Robert Louis Stevenson was tubercular. The author himself believed he had tuberculosis, and that had been the general diagnosis of doctors in Edinburgh, and at Dr. Karl Ruedi's clinic in Davos, Switzerland. In 1879, while camping out in the woods south of Monterey Stevenson collapsed, and for two days was in a stupor until found by some hunters and taken back to their ranch where for four days and nights they nursed him back to health. When he consulted a local physician, a Dr. Bamford, upon returning to San Francisco, he was diagnosed as having "galloping consumption." But at Saranac Lake, New York, during the winter of 1887–88, Dr. Edward Livingstone Trudeau had listened to his chest, and hearing nothing abnormal, declared Stevenson's tuberculosis to be in remission. There is, however, considerable evidence that the author did not have tuberculosis at all.

For over two years members of the Stevenson family traveled with him in confined schooner and steamship accommodations, yet no one else contracted the disease. In Samoa the chiefs, who came to know Stevenson well during his four-year residence, stated that through the many years of European contact their people had suffered greatly from tuberculosis. Therefore, they were well acquainted with the symptoms, and consequently, they were certain that Stevenson's ailment was not consumption. Having been touched by the tragedy of this disease in my own extended family I have spent considerable time researching this issue with pulmonary specialist Dr. Curtis Drevets of the Wichita Clinic in Wichita, Kansas. I compiled an extensive medical history of Stevenson's 44 years of intermittent health problems, and based on his extensive experience with pulmonary disorders, Dr. Drevets speculated on the nature of the famous author's poor health.

Stevenson's illness was obviously respiratory in nature, and apparently chronic. While the true nature of his problem could not have been accurately diagnosed and cured in the late 1800s, there is substantial evidence that he may have been afflicted with an ailment known today as bronchiectasis, which is an irreversible dilation of the bronchi. Today this disease is almost unheard of due to preventive immunization for whooping cough and the availability of antibiotics to treat cases that do occur, but in Stevenson's day there were no such drugs, and people suffering from this disease rarely lived much past their fortieth birthday. Stevenson died at age 44.

Over the years there has been some debate whether bronchiectasis can be a congenital or an acquired disease, but Louis could very well have contracted it either way, as it has been established that pulmonary weakness ran in his mother's family, having plagued both his grandfather and his mother. In addition, Stevenson's childhood was marked by almost constant ill health, particularly by such diseases as scarlet fever, bronchitis, and whooping cough, all of which can lead to the onset of bronchiectasis. Symptoms of the disease include chronic coughing, with expectoration of pus, periodic hemorrhage, fever, weakness and weight loss, all of which seemed to plague the author for some thirty years, particularly when he was in a temperate climate. Normally, bronchiectasis patients have been warned that cold air should be avoided and that warm and humid air is beneficial. Unfortunately, however, the illness is aggravated by smoking, and Stevenson and his wife were both chain smokers. Not only had the lifespan of bronchiectasis victims rarely exceeded four decades before the availability of antibiotics, but a common cause for their death was brain abscess which could rupture and cause rapid demise and would appear as a stroke. Robert Louis Stevenson's death was described by the two doctors in attendance as resulting from a cerebral hemorrhage, the overt appearance of which would be essentially the same as a stroke. Dr. Drevets' analysis also seems to support the Samoan chiefs' view that Stevenson did not have tuberculosis, because he maintains that bronchiectasis is not contagious and tuberculosis is, and none of RLS's associates contracted any form of respiratory disease regardless of how intimate and prolonged their contact with the author.

The Schooner CASCO

The CASCO was designed by Dr. Samuel Merritt, mayor of Oakland, and built at a cost of $35,000 by Mears and Havens Company of Oakland in 1879 as a pleasure yacht. Because of her great speed, she excelled in racing competitions in the Bay area but was also capable of ocean voyaging, as evidenced by Merritt's Pacific cruise to Hawaii and Tahiti in 1880, and by Stevenson's charter in 1888. Irritated by the considerable amount of erroneous information published concerning the CASCO, including that in Stevenson's official biography by Graham Balfour, Captain Bert Otis described the ship for the record to Arthur Johnstone, a Honolulu publisher:

> The boat was not a topsail schooner; she was a fore-and-aft schooner, built for cruising, and not for racing, and she was fitted in crimson plush, with panels in white and gold. As a vessel she was perfectly safe, and during her long cruise in the South Seas the water never came into the cockpit but once. This record by itself, when the bad weather encountered is considered, seems to be a very good record indeed from the seaman's point of view. Her sail-plan was wholly laid for a cruising yacht, and was fully suited to the conditions to be met in open seas. Now, did the CASCO fulfill her requirements? She certainly did, and she filled them well.

The literature is equally troublesome when it comes to documenting the dimensions of the CASCO. Since a variety of figures is to be found in print, we will again turn to Captain Otis for the proper measurements (it should be noted that the CASCO had two rigs—one for cruising and another for racing):

> The CASCO's hull length overall (LOA) was 94 feet; beam, 22 feet 5 inches; draught under fore-mast, 9 1/2 feet; draught aft, 12 feet. Mast, steps to cap: foremast, 76 feet; mainmast, 78 feet; topmast, 47 feet (less 13 feet for actual height above the deck). Bowsprit outboard, 35 feet; boom of jib, 41 feet; length of main boom, 69 feet; length of cruising boom, 59 feet; gaff, 46 feet; spinnaker boom, 51 feet. With the exception of a fisherman's staysail, all her canvas was in due proportion to her measurements; she was not over sparred nor was her sail plan excessive.

After Merritt's death in August 1890, the CASCO lay at anchor in the Bay until the spring of 1892, when she was sold to a man named George Collins and taken to Victoria, British Colombia, where she was outfitted for seal hunting. For four years the ship was very successful at this bloody and brutal business because of her great speed. But by 1896 seal hunting was becoming less profitable, and CASCO found herself left on mud flats near Victoria along with 11 other sealers. Fifteen years later an international treaty between the United States and Canada would ban pelagic seal hunting for 15 years.

As objectionable as this was, CASCO was next involved in an even more despicable enterprise—the smuggling of opium and Chinese immigrants. While illicit adventures on the high seas often get exaggerated as they are related in waterfront saloons, the following account involving the CASCO has been reported by several journalists. According to Portland, Oregon reporter Francis Dickie,

> When the smuggling of Chinese and opium was at its height, up and down the coast there were whisperings of the daring work of the smuggler CASCO. The revenue officers knew positively that she was laden with illicit Oriental cargo, and with Chinese immigrants; but she escaped them again and again, her old speed and lightness returning. Once, however, the wind failed her, and the revenue launch hauled alongside. Search for contraband was instituted; but not a Chinaman appeared, not a trace of opium. Fooled!—and they climbed sheepishly into their launch. Later it developed that while the revenue men were still far astern, the crew had weighted the sixty Chinamen and dumped them overboard along with the opium!

In 1912 CASCO was rescued from its odious activities by Captain August Arnet, who bought the ship for a mere $950, installed a small gasoline engine, and put her to work in the halibut fishing fleet based in Vancouver. When the fishing enterprise did not work out as expected, she was pulled from service and put in the care of Scoutmaster Louis V. Masters on Lulu Island and used as a training ship for British Columbia Sea Scouts, who maintained her in Bristol fashion.

In 1918 the ship was sold, this time to H. O. Wicks who returned her to San Francisco to be used in cod fishing for Northern Fisheries. The ship did make one Pacific island trading trip to Fiji that year under the command of Captain P. F. Troup. Troup had married Flora Collier of Tacoma on July 4, and 5 days later took his bride aboard for the trip to the islands. With Suva only a week away, Mrs. Troup was fishing over the side when a nine-foot shark swallowed her bait and the force of its struggle yanked her into the ocean. Seeing what happened, her husband seized a knife, leaped overboard, killed the shark and then kept his wife afloat until they could be picked up.

After taking a cargo of copra aboard in Fiji the ship started on what would be a 65-day voyage to San Francisco. After two weeks the ship's seams began to open up and two crewmembers were constantly required to man the pumps, day and night. Then a terrific gale descended upon them and all hands were needed to manage the sails, leaving the pumps idle. The bride, however, persuaded the cook to help her, and the two of them pumped for 12 hours straight while the gale raged. According to a *San Francisco Chronicle* account dated November 22, 1911 "When Captain E. E. Frazier, one of the San Francisco bar pilots, came on board . . . all hands were exhausted. Anchored off Meiggs Wharf, the old hull decided that the crew had worked enough, the seams seemed to close up and it was not necessary to pump any more. The cook said: 'The lads were becoming discouraged but Mrs. Troup and I kept them in rare good humor. I played the harmonica and the little girl sang. Then they all would join and forget they were tired and ready to quit'."

In 1919 CASCO departed on her final adventure. According to an *Oakland Tribune* story of June 2, four prospectors in 1915 had discovered an uncharted river of gold dust in Siberia from which they obtained $110,000. The secret location of the bonanza had been revealed to just one man, Leon McGurk, who ultimately established the Northern Mining and Trading Company. He solicited 30 investors to each put up $1,000 to finance an expedition aboard the CASCO to the gold site on the Kolyma River in Siberia, which emptied into the Bering Sea. McGurk assured the investors that their money was safe, for if the gold could not be located, the CASCO would remain in the arctic waters and engage in the fur trade. The CASCO, under the command of a former naval officer, C. L. Oliver, with a crew of experienced sailors left San Francisco with 29 passengers on June 8, 1919. The trip to Nome took 42 days, and then as they proceeded northwest across the Bering Strait they encountered strong winds and heavy seas with ice floes. The ship never got close to its Siberian destination. Strong headwinds and threatening ice slowed their progress and led to a decision to return to San Francisco for the winter.

The *Oakland Tribune* on September 24 carried the following story: "Six doughty sailors gnarled and weather-beaten as if they had just stepped from the pages of an adventure book climbed out of an open boat of skins at a dock in Nome last night . . . and related how they had come 60 miles through the ice flows to bring news of the CASCO's peril."

As she headed back toward Nome, CASCO had gone aground eight times. On King Island, 40 miles north of her destination, she had been permanently stranded and would have required aid to be pulled off. The men set up a signal station on a hill, but there was no help to be found in the area. The boom had hit the captain, breaking his jaw and knocking him overboard, and he had been taken to an Indian mission station seriously ill with pneumonia. That is where the six men borrowed an Indian canoe to go for help.

Those who remained on the ship set up a small shelter ashore and managed to get most of their stores off before they watched the CASCO be pounded to pieces on the rocks. Twenty-four miners and sailors were finally rescued by the Revenue Cutter BEAR, a famous ship which had worked the northern waters for many years and would take Admiral Byrd on his Antarctic Expedition in 1933–35. Leon McGurk, who organized the fiasco was said to have left the CASCO at some point "to hunt" and had returned to the States perhaps to work out another get-rich-quick scheme in a warmer climate.

Captain Bert Otis and Dr. Samuel Merritt

After the CASCO returned to Oakland in 1889, the ship's owner Dr. Merritt took a short cruise within the Bay area in July 1890. A month later, he died of uremic poisoning and diabetes, leaving $50,000 in a trust fund for the building of Oakland's Samuel Merritt Hospital, which was completed in January 1909. Captain Otis was not the skipper on Merritt's last cruise, for he married Alice Dyer in June 1890 in Portland, Oregon, just 19 months after the death of his first wife, Emma Duncan Otis. Bert and Alice had apparently known each other for some time and had common interests, for Alice had been aboard the CASCO on its first trip to Hawaii and Tahiti with Dr. Merritt back in 1880.

Strangely enough, Otis never again commanded a vessel or held any sort of maritime position. The Otises moved to Spokane, where Bert first tried his hand at selling real estate, but by 1894 he was working as property manager and collector of accounts-due for the Union Depot Company. After an unsuccessful attempt at gold prospecting in the Yukon in 1896, Otis returned to Spokane and worked at his receiver job until the outbreak of the Spanish-American War in the Philippines. He enlisted and was made an army captain in Company A of the Washington State volunteers. In February 1899, he was wounded in battle in the right cheek and ear, an injury which he described as "only a scratch." He was mustered out of the army nine months later and took a well-paying job as receiver at the San Francisco Central Railroad station.

The year 1900 found Otis and Alice in Honolulu, where Bert now became a partner in a drugstore and Alice began giving voice lessons in their home. After seven years, they decided that the climate did not agree with Alice, and returned to Oakland where Bert went to work with the Boca and Loyalton Railroad, a lumber line in the High Sierras. After three years at this job, which kept him away from home much of the time, Alice became seriously ill with breast cancer. Alice died July 17, 1911, and Otis resigned his railroad job, never again seeking regular employment. He did, however support himself with odd jobs for local railroads. At the age of 68 he was receiving a small veterans pension, and in 1937 his Veteran's Administration examination revealed signs of senile dementia. At this point he was brought back to his place of birth, Brunswick, Maine, by his nephew, Dr. George Cummings, and placed in a nursing home where he died on October 21, 1938 at age 78.

CASCO

Yacht built for Dr. Samuel Merritt

Oakland, California, 1878

MAINMAST 98.0 FT.
FOREMAST 96.0 FT.

CASCO

Registered Dimensions
LENGTH   80.0 FT.
BREADTH   22.5 FT.
DEPTH   8.2 FT.

LENGTH OVERALL 93.0 FT.

MIDSHIP SECTION

22.5

8.2

9.5'

80.0'
93.0'

12.0

FEET

CABIN ARRANGEMENT

Reconstruction by Raymond Aker
Palo Alto, California

Casco hull below deck accommodations and cruising rig

The Schooner EQUATOR

The EQUATOR was a Pacific island trading schooner built in 1888 by Matthew Turner of Benicia, California for K. C. Eldredge of San Francisco, who in turn sold her to the Wightman Brothers for duty as a copra trader in their Gilbert Islands trading enterprise. She displaced 72.21 tons and measured 78.5 feet in length, 22 feet in breadth and drew 8 feet of water. An extremely seaworthy vessel, the EQUATOR was one of the few sailing ships to survive a hurricane which struck the island of Upolu in the spring of 1889, destroying a number of German and American naval vessels. Between June and December 1889 the ship was under charter to the Stevensons, but continued to carry on her island trading in the Gilbert Islands.

After many successful Pacific island trading trips under Captain Dennis Reid, in 1897 the EQUATOR was sold to Hume Brothers and Hume. The company installed a steam engine but retained her masts and sent her north to Alaska to serve as a tender to their fishing fleet. In 1915, George E. Cary of the Puget Sound Tug and Barge Company bought her, and under charter to the U.S. Coast and Geodetic Survey she did wire drag work in Alaska. In the fall of 1917, her masts were cut off, and a 200-horsepower semi diesel was installed so that she could function as a log-tower and general duty tugboat. In 1923, the tug EQUATOR ran aground on the Quillayute River bar while towing a log crib to sea, and was abandoned. A storm with high seas pounded her for a week and washed her back over the bar into a lagoon. Her hull was filled with sand, but she was refloated and taken to Seattle for repairs, where the hull was found to have sustained little damage. Her semi-diesel engine was replaced by a 250-horsepower full diesel. From 1929 on, the EQUATOR worked as an extra boat, going on one occasion out 200 miles at sea to tow in a schooner. She remained in the Puget Sound Tug and Barge Company service doing tugboat work for arriving and departing ships until 1957, when her engine and machinery were removed and her hull was placed in a breakwater in Everett, Washington. In 1969 the ship was rescued by Dr. Eldon Schalka and the Everett Kiwanis Club and placed under a protective roof on the grounds of the Everett marina, where its weathered hull remains today waiting to be restored.

The EQUATOR **Crew**

In February 1891 upon leaving Butaritari, a small pig was lost overboard. Murray MacCallum, who was now full-time cook, leaped overboard to rescue it, but immediately saw the fin of a shark swimming toward him. Tatoma, the Hawaiian crewmember, also saw the imminent danger and dove off the roof of the deckhouse, and ripped open the belly of the shark with his knife.

This was the voyage in which the EQUATOR brought a boatload of Gilbert Islanders to Fanning Island as laborers in the guano beds of William Greig, the owner of the island. Greig had an excellent reputation for treating island labor well, and always made sure that his workers' journey home was paid, although it was said that many of his workers stayed on for several three-year contracts. In the early days most of Greig's labor came from Manihiki Island, and he had married a Manihikian woman of high rank. They had three sons and a daughter named Margaretha. During the brief time that the EQUATOR was at Fanning, Captain Reid met and fell madly in love with the young woman and proposed marriage, the result being that William Greig and his daughter decided to make connections with the mail steamer to go to San Francisco, where Reid and the young lady would be married.

Upon leaving Fanning island, the EQUATOR encountered an extended gale with hurricane force winds which required the captain to remain on watch for some 30 hours. At about 2 p.m. the storm appeared to abate somewhat, and Reid went below for some rest, while the mate took charge of the deck and put the boy La on the wheel. After two hours on the wheel the mate relieved him and told him to go forward and get a cup of hot coffee from the cook, since the boy appeared to be chilled through. While returning with the coffee a wave "like a small mountain" swept over the deck and washed the boy overboard. Hearing the call "man overboard" Captain Reid rushed on deck and took the wheel. Murray climbed aloft to keep an eye on the boy while Reid attempted to turn the vessel around, but within minutes La disappeared beneath the waves. The captain searched for nearly two hours before accepting the reality that the boy was lost. This was but the first of several EQUATOR tragedies.

On March 30, the schooner arrived in San Francisco after 53 days at sea, and three days after landing the captain came down with a cold which developed into pneumonia. Murray nursed him for a week and then became ill himself. After 10 days in bed Reid was on his feet again, but Anderson, the mate, had died of pneumonia the night before. Tatoma and little Muggeree were also both suffering from pneumonia, and in less than a week both of the boys were dead. A healthy Boston Tom had gone home to the east coast to visit his parents, and Charlie Selph, after a visit home, sailed again with Reid and was awarded a second mate rating. Murray MacCallum would not be aboard when they sailed, as he had decided to pursue other vocational interests. He received an official discharge and a warm handshake from Dennis Reid plus the captain's rendering of a modified version of an old sea chantey:

> *Leave her, Johnny leave her.*
> *For the captain, he's a brute,*
> *And the mate, he's a cuss,*
> *Yes, leave her, damn you, leave her*
> *But remember, you're leaving a home.*

Margaretha Greig and her father arrived on the next mail boat from Australia, and after she and Reid were married she accompanied him on his next trip to the islands, perhaps as Murray's replacement.

In Fanny Stevenson's preface to *The Wrecker,* she said that she had heard that Captain Dennis Reid was in jail in Suva for fraudulently selling a ship, but several people have checked the Fiji Archives and have found no such record. A Captain Fred Klebingat wrote a letter to librarian Barbara Bernhart of the San Francisco Maritime Museum, however, stating that he had heard that the Greig family had lost ownership of Fanning and Washington Islands, and that they blamed a man by the name of Reid for their loss.

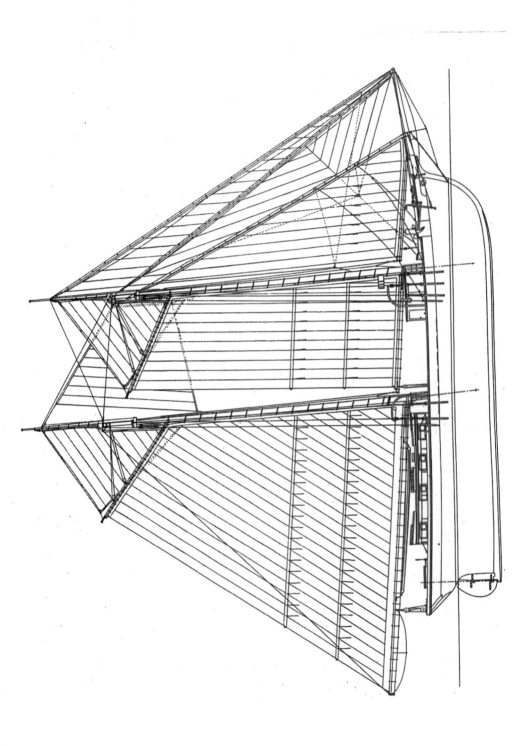

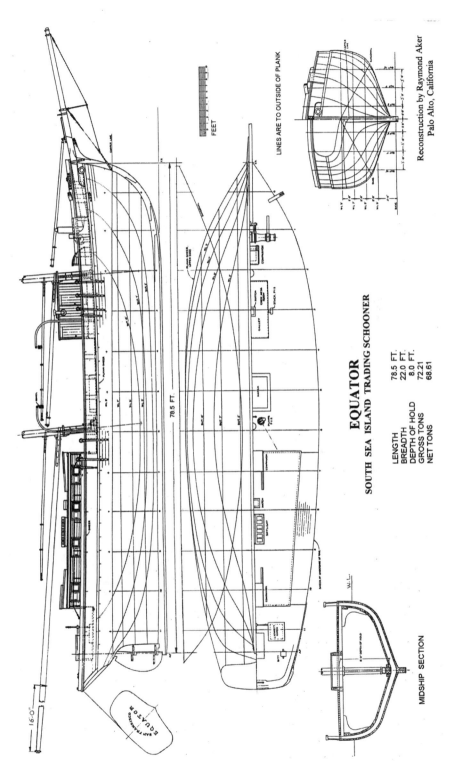

EQUATOR

SOUTH SEA ISLAND TRADING SCHOONER

LENGTH	78.5 FT.
BREADTH	22.0 FT.
DEPTH OF HOLD	8.0 FT.
GROSS TONS	72.21
NET TONS	68.61

EQUATOR hull lines and deck profile

LINES ARE TO OUTSIDE OF PLANK

Reconstruction by Raymond Aker
Palo Alto, California

MIDSHIP SECTION

78.5 FT.

16'-0"

FEET

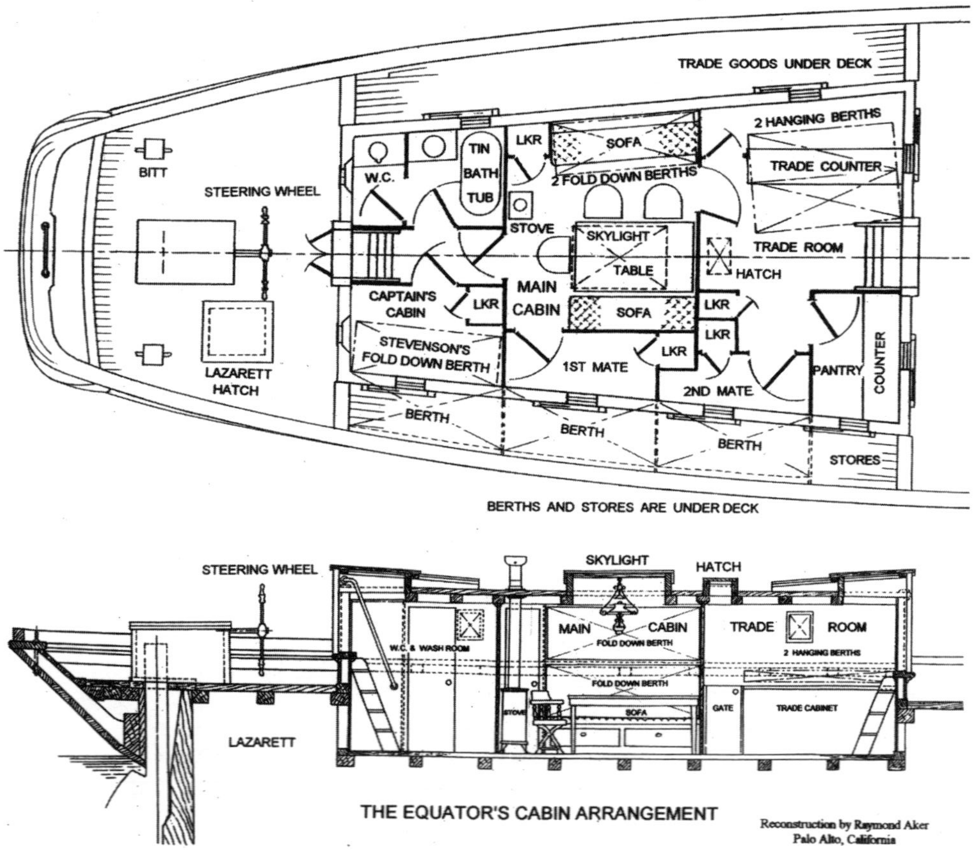
TRADE GOODS UNDER DECK
BITT
STEERING WHEEL
W.C.
TIN
BATH
TUB
LKR
SOFA
2 FOLD DOWN BERTHS
2 HANGING BERTHS
TRADE COUNTER
STOVE
SKYLIGHT
TABLE
TRADE ROOM
HATCH
CAPTAIN'S CABIN
LKR
MAIN CABIN
SOFA
LKR
LKR
LKR
STEVENSON'S FOLD DOWN BERTH
1ST MATE
2ND MATE
PANTRY
COUNTER
LAZARETT HATCH
BERTH
BERTH
BERTH
STORES
BERTHS AND STORES ARE UNDER DECK
STEERING WHEEL
SKYLIGHT
HATCH
MAIN
CABIN
FOLD DOWN BERTH
TRADE
ROOM
2 HANGING BERTHS
W.C. & WASH ROOM
FOLD DOWN BERTH
STOVE
SOFA
GATE
TRADE CABINET
LAZARETT
THE EQUATOR'S CABIN ARRANGEMENT
Reconstruction by Raymond Aker
Palo Alto, California

Cabin and trade room aboard the Equator. Also deck details—port and starboard (opposite page).

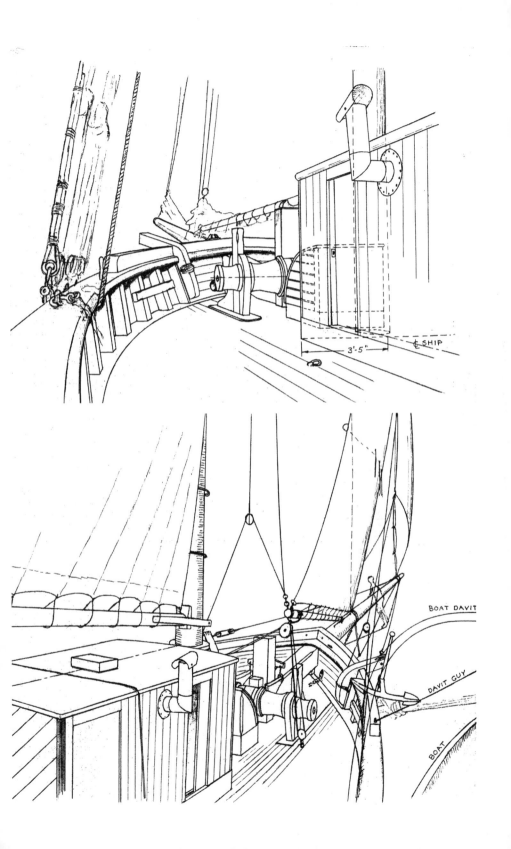

3'-5"   ℄ SHIP

BOAT DAVIT

DAVIT GUY

BOAT

The Topsail Schooner/Steamer JANET NICOLL

The JANET NICOLL was an iron topsail schooner/screw steamer of 779 gross tons. She was 184 feet long, 29.2 feet in breadth and drew 13.8 feet. In addition to fore-and-aft sails and square topsails set on the foremast, she was powered by two 2-cylinder 430-HP Palmers' Company steam engines giving her a cruising speed of about 8 knots. The ship was built at Palmers' Shipbuilding and Iron Company, Ltd. at Newcastle-on-Tyne in Britain in 1884 and delivered to Melbourne in a 60-day voyage by Captain Robert G. Hutton. She was owned by G. W. Nicoll, and her home port was registered as Sydney, Australia. The ship was primarily a freighter, but was designed to carry 16 saloon passengers and 10 in second class. The JANET NICOLL was purchased by Henderson and MacFarlane of Auckland in 1890, and it was at this time that she carried the Stevensons through Polynesia, Micronesia and Melanesia. Later that same year the JANET NICOLL was transferred to the Union Steamship Company in whose service she worked out of the port of Dunedin, New Zealand for 13 years. The details of the ship's history are sketchy after she was sold to Koe Guan and Company of Penang where she was in service until 1907. To a large extent this is because Penang registers were lost during the Japanese occupation, but we do know that the JANET NICOLL was transferred to Eastern Shipping Company Ltd. and worked out of Penang from 1907 to 1914 when she was wrecked at the southern end of Kopah Inlet, Thailand about 300 miles north of Penang, on November 5, 1914 on a passage from Penang to Moulmein.

The Janet Nicoll Crew

There is little in the way of information in the literature about the crew of the JANET NICOLL after the Stevenson family cruise, but in Fanny Stevenson's book, *Our Samoan Adventure*, she records that on December 13, 1890, Captain Henry, the former JANET NICOLL skipper and Mr. Hird, the supercargo, dropped by to visit them when their new ship, the S.S. ARCHER, was in port in Apia. And when the ARCHER called again on September 23, 1891, Mr. Hird and Tin Jack visited the Stevensons at Vailima.

    Tin Jack appparently had a fixed income from an inheritance which was not large enough to live on but gave him what has been described as "one wild burst of dissipation in Sydney" every year. His visit to the Stevensons probably took place en route to his Sydney holiday. While at his trading station in the Gilbert Islands some years later, news came to him that the trustee of his estate had absconded with all his funds, whereupon poor Jack put his revolver to his head and killed himself. When his corpse was discovered they found a copy of Stevenson's book The *Wrecker* beside him. Tin Jack was the inspiration for Louis's character Tommy Hadden in that book, and Jack proudly carried the volume with him wherever he went.

The Stevenson Family

When Stevenson's will was read, his estate in Britain, valued at £15,525 or roughly $76,000, went largely to Maggie but included a small legacy for Louis's family cousins and for Austin, and upon Maggie's death a considerable legacy would pass on to Belle. Fanny inherited Vailima and book royalties, plus a yearly pension of £60. Lloyd was also well taken care of by Louis, and at Maggie's death everything would go to the Osbournes.

Soon after Louis's death his mother returned to Scotland and lived with her sister until 1897, when she contracted fatal pneumonia. As she lay dying she rose up, and looking toward the foot of the bed said, "There is Louis! I must go." She then lost consciousness and passed away the following morning.

Austin Strong also left Vailima for New Zealand after Louis's funeral, where he attended Wellington College from 1894 to 1898 with Arthur Seed, whose father had recommended that Stevenson go to Samoa for his health when he was visiting in Scotland in 1875.

Fanny remained at Vailima until Maggie passed away, while Lloyd and Belle split their time between Samoa and San Francisco during this period. When Maggie died Fanny sold the estate to a retired German lumber merchant named Gustav Kuntz for the measly sum of £1,750. She did, however, keep an acre at the top of Mount Vaea where Louis's grave was located as well as the access road leading to the mountain. Fourteen years later

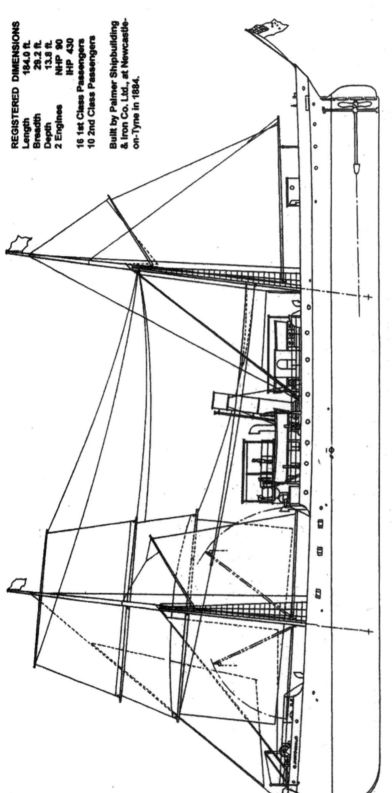

REGISTERED DIMENSIONS

Length	184.0 ft.
Breadth	29.2 ft.
Depth	13.8 ft.
2 Engines	NHP 90
	IHP 430

16 1st Class Passengers
10 2nd Class Passengers

Built by Palmer Shipbuilding & Iron Co. Ltd., at Newcastle-on-Tyne in 1884.

OUTBOARD PROFILE AND SAIL PLAN

JANET NICOLL profile and sail plan, boat deck plan and section.
Drawn by maritime historian and artist Raymond Aker

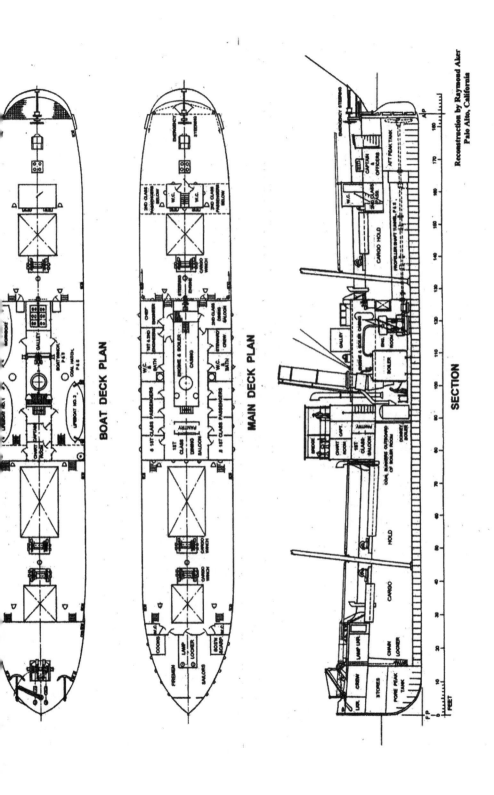

BOAT DECK PLAN

MAIN DECK PLAN

SECTION

Reconstruction by Raymond Aker
Palo Alto, California

the merchant would sell the property to the German government for £6,000.

Fanny and Lloyd visited Scotland and Britain in 1897 contacting many of Stevenson's friends, none of whom Fanny cared a great deal about. The very faithful Charles Baxter, who had handled all of the author's legal and business affairs, particularly those having to do with the building of the home at Vailima, was found to be struggling with severe money problems of his own. Fanny, however, turned her back on him, offering him little in the way of financial aid. Sidney Colvin fared little better. Louis had often said that he wanted Sidney to write his biography after his death, and he had recorded in his notes that Colvin should receive one-third of any royalty which might be derived from the publication; Fanny and Lloyd should receive the other two-thirds. Not liking those terms, and believing Colvin was too busy as curator to the British Museum to do a decent job as soon as they wanted it, Lloyd suggested that in lieu of the biography he could publish several volumes of Stevenson's letters for which he would be paid a lump sum. That sum turned out to be a paltry £100. The chore of writing Stevenson's official biography was given to Graham Balfour who the family knew could be counted on to produce a complimentary product which would meet with Fanny's approval.

In 1896 Lloyd met and married Katharine Durham, a Quaker from Springfield, Illinois, and when Fanny returned to San Francisco in 1899, Lloyd and Katharine shared her home. At first Fanny appeared to approve of the marriage, but after a while the two strong-willed, controlling women found it impossible to live together in the same household. Lloyd's wife was quite unprepared for the almost incestuous relationship which existed between Fanny and Lloyd. Whenever Lloyd needed comforting, consolation or advice it was to Fanny he went and not to his wife. The conflicts got so bad that Fanny demanded that Lloyd get rid of his wife, and Belle contributed to the problem by hinting to Lloyd that Katharine had been unfaithful on one occasion when he was on a business trip to New York. Katharine refused to give him a divorce, but he was able to obtain a legal separation, requiring him to pay $300 monthly support for her and the two children who had been born to the union. From the very beginning Lloyd had maintained that he didn't want children, because they were a "great expense." They were indeed now taking a good bite out of his bank account. With Maggie's death Fanny's income had increased dramatically. She visited Europe on two occasions and bought a large townhouse in San Francisco and a retreat in Santa Barbara. Fanny ultimately pressured Lloyd to secure a divorce regardless of what it might cost him. He did manage to do so, and several years later he remarried, but only after his wife-to-be promised to have no children.

While Fanny was busy having holidays in Europe and America, Lloyd managed to publish a number of light novels and short stories, some based on his love of fast motorcars. Belle wrote her autobiography, *This Life I've Loved*, and a novel, *The Girl from Home*, which was about Hawaii and the fast Royal Court crowd.

During the final ten years of Fanny's life, she had an intimate relationship with her secretary Edward (Ned) Salisbury Field, 40 years her junior. He traveled everywhere with her and was commonly believed to be her lover. In 1914, the year of Fanny's death in Santa Barbara from a stroke, Belle, 56, married Ned Field who was 35. Ned was a fairly successful playwright, and he and Austin, who had also gained recognition as a successful writer of plays, both had productions running on Broadway at the same time. Mr. Field didn't really have to write for a living, however, as oil had been discovered on land he owned, making him a millionaire.

After Fanny's death her ashes were taken back to Samoa for burial on Mount Vaea next to Louis by Belle and her new husband. The only one of the Stevensons' Vailima house staff present at the funeral service atop the mountain, Mitaele, was now a grey-haired father of nine children. Chief Sitione, Mrs. Lauli'i Willis and New Zealand Administrator Colonel Logan performed the funeral service. After the ceremony was over an old chief turned to Belle and said "Tusitala is happy now. His true love has come back to him."

At this time Western Samoa was being administered by the New Zealand Government under a League of Nations mandate. The islands had been seized from Germany by New Zealand troops during World War I without a shot being fired. Vailima was being used as a government house with a Union Jack flying from its flagpole. After Western Samoa received its independence from New Zealand in 1961, Vailima was used as a house for special political and ceremonial occasions and is today a museum, having been returned to what is believed to be its original condition by a non-profit preservation foundation.

Fanny's estate, worth £120,500 (approximately $589,000), was left to Belle with instructions that she pay Lloyd a $300 a month stipend for life, although he would also be the recipient of all of Stevenson's royalties. Belle died a millionaire in 1953 with Stevenson's money as well as Ned's, who had died in 1936.

With the Stevenson royalties which came to him after Fanny passed away, Lloyd was able to buy expensive sports cars and become known as a man about town at the most exclusive and expensive night spots in New York and Hollywood. He died in California in 1947 without ever knowing what it meant to earn a living.

BIBLIOGRAPHY

Allen, Gwenfread, *Hawaii's Iolani Palace and its Kings and Queens.* Honolulu: Aloha Graphics and Sales. 1978

Allen, Maryland, "South Sea Memories of R.L.S." *The Bookman* 43:591–603. 1916

American Boating staff "From Riches to Rags." *American Boating* November:19–20. 1974

Anderson, Charles Roberts, *Melville in the South Seas.* New York: Columbia University Press. 1939

Balfour, Graham, *The Life of Robert Louis Stevenson.* Vol. II. New York: Charles Scribner's Sons. 1901

Ballantine, R. M. *The Coral Island: A Tale of the Pacific Ocean.* New York: Viking Penguin. 1995

Barrow, I., *Art and Life in Polynesia.* Rutland, VT: Charles E. Tuttle Company. 1973

Bell, Gavin, *In Search of Tusitala.* London: Picador. 1994

Bell, Ian, *Dreams of Exile.* New York: Henry Holt and Company. 1992

Berman, Richard A. *Robert Louis Stevenson in Samoa: Home from the Sea.* Honolulu: Mutual Publishing Company. 1939

Bevan, Bryan, *Robert Louis Stevenson, Poet and Teller of Tales.* New York: St. Martins Press. 1993

Black, Margaret Moyes, *Robert Louis Stevenson.* London and Edinburgh: Oliphant, Anderson and Ferrier. 1979

Bok, Edward W. "The Playful Stevenson." *Scribner's Magazine* August:179–183. 1927

Brill, Barbara, *Robert Louis Stevenson.* Loughborough: Ladybird Books Ltd. 1975

Brown, George E. *A Book of R.L.S.* New York: Charles Scribner's Sons. 1919

Bryan, Edwin H. Jr. *American Polynesia, Coral Islands of the Central Pacific.* (Chapter 25 Swains Island) Honolulu: Tongg Publishing Company. 1941

Burgess, Gelett, "An Interview with Mrs. Robert Louis Stevenson." *The Bookman* 8:23–25. 1898

Butts, Dennis, *Robert Louis Stevenson.* New York: Henry Z. Walck. 1966

Calder, Jenni, *Island Landfalls, Reflections from the South Seas.* Edinburgh: Conongate Publishing Company. 1987

Caldwell, Elsie Noble, *Last Witness for Robert Louis Stevenson.* Norman: University of Oklahoma Press. 1960

Cameron, John, *John Cameron's Odyssey* (Transcribed by Andrew Farrell). New York: The Macmillan Company. 1928

Campbell, Robert D. "The Cruise of the Janet Nicoll." *New Zealand Marine News* 43(2): 92–99. 1994

Chester, Sharon, H. Baumgartner, D. Frechoso, & J. Oetzel, *The Marquesas Islands Mave Mai.* San Mateo, CA: Wandering Albatross. 1998

Churchill, William, "Stevenson in the South Sea." *McClure's Magazine* Feb.:278–285. 1895

Clarke, W. E. "Robert Louis Stevenson in Samoa." *The Yale Review* 10:275–296. 1920–21

Colvin, Sidney (Editor), *The Letters of Robert Louis Stevenson.* Vol.I 1868–1880, Vol.II 1880–1887, Vol.III 1887–1891, Vol.IV 1891–1894. New York: Charles Scribner's Sons. 1917

"More Letters of Mrs. Stevenson." *Scribner's Magazine* January–June: 408–420. 1924

Cunningham, Glenn, *Appointment in Paradise.* New York: A Hearthstone Book, Carlton Press Company. 1994

Cyclopedia of Samoa, Tonga, Tahiti, and the Cook Islands. Sydney, Australia: McCarron, Stewart and Company. 1907

Daiches, David, *Robert Louis Stevenson and His World.* London: Thames and Hudson. 1973

Daws, Gavan, *A Dream of Islands, Voyages of Self-Discovery in the South Seas.* (Robert Louis Stevenson, pp. 163–215). New York: W. W. Norton. 1980

Day, A. Grove, *Hawaii and Its People.* New York: Meredith Press. 1968

Adventurers of the Pacific. ("The Brothers Rorique, Pirates de Luxe," pp. 253–287). New York: Meredith Press. 1969

Travels in Hawaii: Robert Louis Stevenson. Honolulu: University of Hawaii Press. 1973

Dening, Greg (Editor), *The Marquesan Journal of Edward Robarts, 1797–1824.* Honolulu: University of Hawaii Press. 1974

Islands and Beaches: Discourse on a Silent Land: Marquesas 1774–1880. Chicago: The Dorsey Press. 1980

Dewar, J. Cumming, *Voyage of the Nyanza.* London & Edinburgh: William Blackwood and Sons. 1892

Dickie, Francis, "The Tragic End of Stevenson's Yacht Casco." *World Magazine* January:4. 1920

Duncan, John E., *The Sea Chain.* Scotia, NY: American Review. 1986

Eaton, Charlotte, *Stevenson at Manasquan.* Cedar Rapids, Iowa: The Torch Press. 1921

Edmond, Rod, *Representing the South Pacific.* (Chapter 6, "Taking up with Kanakas: RLS and the Pacific"). Cambridge: Cambridge University Press. 1997

Ellis, William, *Polynesian Researches.* London: Fisher, Son & Jackson. 1829

Ellison, Joseph W. *Tusitala of the South Seas.* New York: Hasting House. 1953

Ferdon, Edwin N. *Early Observations of Marquesan Culture, 1595–1813.* Tucson and London: University of Arizona Press. 1993

Field, Isobel, *This Life I've Loved.* New York: Longmans, Green & Company. 1937

"Stevenson did not Die from TB in Samoa." *Pacific Islands Monthly* July:63. 1951

Findlay, Alexander, *A Directory for the Navigation of the Pacific Ocean,* Part II. London: R. H. Laurie. 1851

Furnas, J. C. *Anatomy of Paradise.* New York: William Sloane Associates. 1948

Voyage to Windward. New York: William Sloane Associates. 1951

Gray, J.A.C. *Amerika Samoa.* Annapolis, MD.: United States Naval Institute.

Grimble, Arthur, *A Pattern of Islands.* London: Cox & Wyman, Ltd. 1952

Hambidge, Roger A. "Schooner Equator". Seaways, May/June:33–38. 1991

Hamilton, Clayton, *On the Trail of Stevenson.* Garden City, New York: Doubleday, Page & Company. 1915

Hammond, J. R. *A Robert Louis Stevenson Chronology.* New York: St. Martin's Press. 1997

Handbook of Western Samoa, Wellington, N.Z.: W.A.G. Skinner, Government Printer. 1925

Handy, E. S. Craighill, *The Native Culture in the Marquesas.* Bulletin #9. Honolulu: Bernice P. Bishop Museum. 1923

Handy, Willowdean C."The Marquesans: Fact versus Fiction." *Yale Review* 11:769–786. 1922

Forever the Land of Men. New York: Dodd, Mead & Company. 1965

Hartman, Howard, *The Seas Were Mine.* New York: Dodd, Mead & Company. 1935

Heinz, John, "The Janet Nicoll of the South Pacific," *Model Ship Builder* May/June (77): 44–48. 1992

Hennessy, James Pope, *Robert Louis Stevenson.* New York: Simon and Schuster. 1974

Herbert, T. Walter, Jr. *Marquesan Encounters: Melville and the Meaning of Civilization.* Cambridge: Harvard University Press. 1980

Hillier, Robert Irwin, *The South Seas Fiction of Robert Louis Stevenson.* New York: Peter Lang. 1989

Hinz, Earl R. *Landfalls of Paradise: The Guide to Pacific Islands.* Ventura, CA.: Western Marine Enterprises,Inc. 1980

Holmes, Lowell D. "Treasured Islands, Robert Louis Stevenson in the Pacific." *The World and I* January: 462–473. 1988

Hoyt, Edwin P. *The Typhoon That Stopped a War.* New York: David McKay Company. 1968

Jaffe, Harry J. and Sol Katz, "Current Ideas about Bronchiectasis," *American Family Physician* 7(1): 68–76. 1973

Knight, Alanna, *Robert Louis Stevenson Treasury.* New York: St. Martin's Press. 1985

Robert Louis Stevenson in the South Seas. New York: Paragon House. 1987

Kramer, Augustin, *Die Samoa-inseln,* Stuttgart: E. Schweizerbartsche, Verlagsbuchhandlung. 1902

La Farge, John, *Reminiscences of the South Seas.* Garden City, NY: Doubleday Page. 1912

An American Artist in the South Seas. London: Pacific Basin Books, KPI Limited. 1914

Lapierre, Alexandra, *Fanny Stevenson, A Romance of Destiny.* New York: Carroll & Graf Publishing Co. 1995

Lawson, McEwan, *On the Bat's Back.* London: Lutterworth. 1950

Linehan, Katherine, "Taking up with Kanakas: Stevenson's Complex Social Criticism in 'The Beach of Falesa.' *English Literature in Transition* 33(2): 407–422. 1990

Linton, Adelin and Charles Wagley, *Ralph Linton.* New York: Columbia University Press. 1971

Lucas, Edward V. *The Colvins and their Friends.* New York: Charles Scriber's Sons. 1928

Luce, John M. "Bronchiectasis." In *Textbook of Respiratory Medicine,* John F. Murray & Jay A. Nadel (Eds.) Chapter 45, pp.1107–1116. Philadelphia, W. B. Saunders Company. 1988

MacCallum, Thomson Murray, *Adrift in the South Seas.* Los Angeles: Wetzel Publishing Company. 1934

Mackay, Margaret, *The Violent Friend, The Story of Mrs. Robert Louis Stevenson.* Garden City, NY: Doubleday & Company. 1968

Mason, Leonard (Ed.), *Kiribati, A Changing Culture.* Suva, Fiji: Institute of Pacific Studies, University of the South Pacific. 1985

Masson, Rosaline (Ed.), *I Can Remember Robert Louis Stevenson.* New York: Frederick A. Stokes Company. 1922

Maude, H. E. "Baiteke and Binoka of Abemama: Arbiters of Change in the Gilbert Islands." In J. W. Davidson & Deryck Scarr (eds.) *Pacific Island Portraits.* Canberra: Australian National University Press. 1970

McClure, S. S. *My Autobiography.* New York: Frederick A. Stokes Company. 1914

McCurdy, H. W. *Marine History of the Pacific N.W.* (Gordon Newell, Ed.)

Casco, pp. 207, 299, 312 Seattle: Superior Publishing Company. 1966

McGaw, Sister Martha Mary, *Stevenson in Hawaii*. Honolulu: University of Hawaii Press. 1950

McLynn Frank, *Robert Louis Stevenson*. London: Hutchinson. 1993

Melville, Herman, *Typee: A Peep at Polynesian Life during a Four Months' Residence in a Valley of the Marquesas*. New York: Airmont Publishing Company. 1844

Menikoff, Barry, *Robert Louis Stevenson and the "The Beach of Falesaa."* Stanford, CA.: Stanford University Press. 1984

Morris, Aldyth, *Robert Louis Stevenson—Appointment on Molokai*. Honolulu: University of Hawaii Press. 1995

Moors, H. J. *With Stevenson in Samoa*. Boston: Small, Maynard & Company. 1910

Some Recollections of Early Samoa. Apia: Western Samoa Historical and Cultural Trust. 1986

Mrantz, Maxine, *R. L. Stevenson: Poet in Paradise*. Honolulu: Aloha Graphics and Sales. 1977

Osbourne, Lloyd, *An Intimate Portrait of RLS*. New York: Charles Scribners's Sons. 1924

Oliver, Douglas L. *Ancient Tahitian Society*. 3 Vols. Honolulu: University of Hawaii Press. 1974

Pears, Sir Edmund Radcliffe, "Some Recollections of Robert Louis Stevenson, with a visit to his friend Ori, at Tahiti." *Scribner's Magazine*. Jan.:3–18. 1923

Plotz, Helen (Ed.), *Poems of Robert Louis Stevenson*. New York: Thomas Y. Crowell Company. 1973

Proudfit, Isabel, "A Psychiatric Study of Robert Louis Stevenson." *The Psychoanalytic Review* 23(2):121–148. 1936

The Treasure Hunter. New York: J. Messner. 1939

Nakajima, Atsushi, *Light, Wind and Dreams*. Tokyo: Hokuseido Press. 1962

Newell, Gordon, *Pacific Tugboats*. Superior Publishing Co. Seattle, WA. 1957

Rankin, Nicholas, *Dead Man's Chest*. London & Boston: Faber and Faber. 1987

Rather, Lois, *Stevenson's Silver Ship*. Oakland, CA: The Rather Press. 1973

Rennie, Neil, *Far Fetched Facts, The Literature of Travel and the Idea of the South Seas*. Oxford, Clarendon Press. 1995

Rice, Edward, *Journey to Upolu, Robert Louis Stevenson Victorian Rebel*. New York: Dodd, Mead & Company. 1974

Rivenburgh, Eleanor, "Stevenson in Hawaii." *The Bookman*, September–February:113–124, 295–307, 452–461. 1917–1918

Robson, R. W. "Marquesas Islands." *Pacific Islands Handbook* pp. 116–122. New York: Macmillan Company. 1946

Sabatier, Ernest, *Astride the Equator*. Oxford: Oxford University Press. 1977

Salmon, Tati, "On Ari'i in Tahiti." *Journal of the Polynesian Society* 19:40–46. 1910

Sanchez, Nellie Van De Grift, *The Life of Mrs. R. L. Stevenson*. New York: Charles Scribner's Sons. 1921

San Francisco Chronicle, "Novelist's Old Ship Is In Port. Schooner Casco, in which Stevenson Cruised, Arrives Here," November 12, 1918
"Saga of the Yacht Casco—Blood, Opium and Disaster," February 10, 1953

Scarr, Deryck (Ed.), *More Pacific Islands Portraits*. Canberra: Australian National University. 1979

Scribner's Magazine staff, "A History of the Last Quarter Century: The Samoan Hurricane." *Scribner's Magazine* 19 (1):195–197. 1896

Smith, Janet Adam, *R. L. Stevenson*. London: Duckworth Great Lives Series. ND

Stern, G. B. *Robert Louis Stevenson, The Man Who Wrote Treasure Island*. New York: The Macmillan Company. 1954

Steuart, John A. *Robert Louis Stevenson, A Critical Biography*. Boston: Little, Brown, and Company. 1924

Stevenson, Margaret I. *From Saranac to the Marquesas and Beyond*. New York: Charles Scribner's Sons. 1903

Stevenson, Robert Louis, *Cruise of the Casco*. (MS journal) The Huntington Library, San Marino, California. 1888
"The House of Tembinoka." *Scribner's Magazine* 8:95–99. 1890
Island Nights' Entertainments. New York: Charles Scribner's Sons. 1892
The Beach of Falesa. New York: The Heritage Press (1956) Originally in *The Illustrated London News*, 2 July–6 August 1892.
In the South Seas. London: Chatto and Windus. 1900
Vailima Papers and *A Footnote to History*. New York: Charles Scribner's Sons. 1925

Stevenson, Robert Louis and Lloyd Osbourne, *The Ebb Tide*. London: Messrs. Heinemann. 1894
The Wrecker. New York; Charles Scribner's Sons. 1925

Stevenson, Mrs. R. L. *The Cruise of the Janet Nichol*. New York: Charles Scribner's Sons. 1914
"More Letters of Mrs R. L. Stevenson—Ocean Travels in the Pa-

cific." (Edited by Sir Sidney Colvin) Scribner's Magazine Jan.–June: 408–420. 1924

Stevenson, Mrs. R. L. and Robert Louis Stevenson, *Our Samoan Adventure*. New York: Harper and Brothers. 1955

Stoddard, Charles Warren, *Summer Cruising in the South Seas*. London: Chatto & Windus Publishers. 1873

South-Sea Idyls. Boston: James R. Osgood and Company. 1873

Exits and Entrances. Boston: Lothrop Publishing Co. 1903

Strong, Austin, "The Most Unforgettable Character I've Met." (Fanny Stevenson) *Reader's Digest* March: 33–37. 1946

Strong, Isobel, "Vailima Table-Talk," *Scribner's Magazine*, May:532–547, June:736–747, July:532–547. 1896

Strong, Isobel and Lloyd Osbourne, *Memories of Vailima*. Westminster: Archibald Constable and Company. 1903

Suggs, Robert, *The Island Civilizations of the Pacific*. New York: Mentor Book, The New American Library. 1960

The Hidden Worlds of Polynesia; The Chronicle of an Archaeological Expedition to Nuku Hiva in the Marquesas Islands. New York: Mentor Book, The New American Library. 1965

Swearingen, Robert G. *The Prose Writing of Robert Louis Stevenson: A Guide*. Hamden, CT.: Archon Books. 1980

Terry, R. C. (Ed.), *Robert Louis Stevenson: Interviews and Recollections*. Iowa City: University of Iowa Press. 1996

Thomas, Nicholas, *Marquesan Societies: Inequality and Political Transformation in Eastern Polynesia*. Oxford: Clarendon Press. 1990

Thomson, Rev. Robert, *The Marquesas Islands: Their Description and Early History*. (1980 edition has notes by Robert D. Craig) Laie, HI: Institute for Polynesian Studies, Brigham Young-Hawaii. 1841

Theroux, Joseph, "Some Misconceptions about RLS." *The Journal of Pacific History* 16 (2): 164–166. 1981

Thompson, Francis, *The Real Robert Louis Stevenson and other Critical Essays*. (Edited by Terence Connolly). New York: University Publishers, Inc. 1959

Triggs, W. H. "Stevenson's Life in Samoa." *The Bookman* 73:158–163. 1931

Webb, Nancy and Jean Francis, *The Hawaiian Islands: From Monarchy to Democracy*. New York: The Viking Press. 1956

Wood, Charles E. *Charlie's Charts of Polynesia* (The South Pacific, East of 165° W. Longitude). Surrey, BC: Charlie's Charts. 1983

INDEX

Other books of interest from Sheridan House

IN SHACKLETON'S WAKE
by Arved Fuchs
"It takes a touch of hubris to willingly set out to recreate one of history's most desperate and dangerous journey... But Arved Fuchs, a 47-year old German polar adventurer, couldn't resist."
Cruising World

SONG OF THE SIRENS
by Ernest K. Gann
"In this, his twelfth book, Gann does some of the best writing about the sea and the joys and perils of small ships that has been done in many years...This is a book to be read and then kept comfortably close at hand to be read again, simply for the sheer joy of reading."
Chicago Sun Times

WANDERER
by Sterling Hayden
"A superb piece of writing...Echoes from Poe and Melville to Steinbeck and Mailer. A work of fascination on every level."
New York Post

FLIRTING WITH MERMAIDS
THE UNPREDICTABLE LIFE OF A SAILBOAT DELIVERY SKIPPER
by John Kretschmer
"The book is filled with a myriad of sea stories—all eminently readable—as well as a salting of practical information about sailboats and the sea, all delivered with a wry and self-deprecating sense of humor." *Sailing*

SAILING TO HEMINGWAY'S CUBA
by Dave Schaefer
"Schaefer wasn't going to Cuba just to write another story. His mission was to broaden his cruising skills and seek out the heritage of his lifelong hero, Ernest Hemingway, for whom Cuba was both home and inspiration...entertaining and informative."
Coastal Cruising

America's Favorite Sailing Books
www.sheridanhouse.com

The Mariner's Library Fiction Classics Series

AN EYE OF THE FLEET
A NATHANIEL DRINKWATER NOVEL
by Richard Woodman
This is the first book in the acclaimed Nathaniel Drinkwater series. Action in Admiral Rodney's dramatic Moonlight Battle of 1780, when CYCLOPS' capture of the Santa Teresa plays a decisive part, is the start of Nathaniel Drinkwater's life at sea.

A BRIG OF WAR
A NATHANIEL DRINKWATER NOVEL
by Richard Woodman
Drinkwater's fight to bring a half-armed ship safely to the Cape of Good Hope is beset with personal enmity, the activity of the French and the violence of the sea.

WAGER
by Richard Woodman
Sailing his tea clipper, ERL KING, in 1869, Captain "Cracker Jack" Kemball races Captain Richards of the SEAWITCH from Shanghai to London. The wager: his daughter's hand in marriage.

ENDANGERED SPECIES
by Richard Woodman
Captain John Mackinnon and his ship, the MATTHEW FLINDERS, embark on their last voyage. Their journey to Hong Kong will prove to be anything but quiet. They encounter a typhoon, the rescue of a boatload of Vietnamese refugees, and mutiny.

THE DARKENING SEA
by Richard Woodman
From the clash of mighty battleships at Jutland in 1916 to the cold splendor the present day Arctic, *The Darkening Sea* traces the fortunes of the Martin family throughout nearly seventy years of British maritime history.

America's Favorite Sailing Books
www.sheridanhouse.com

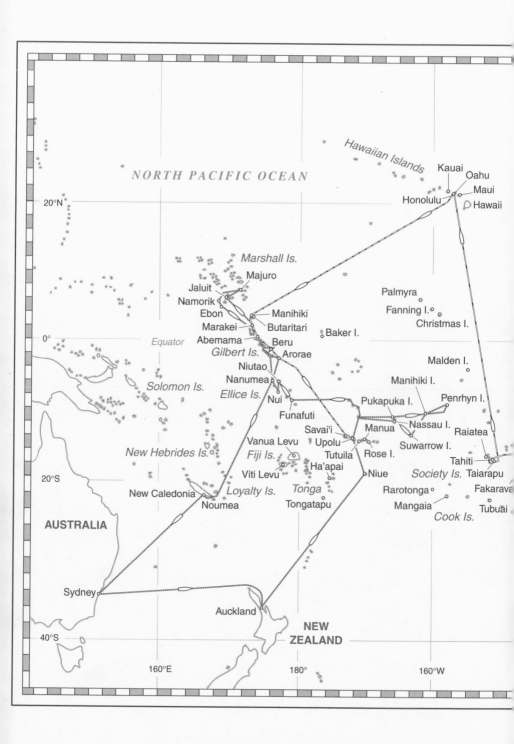